D0265596

'YOU KNOW THE FAIR RULE'

Second Edition

Strategies for making the hard job of
discipline and behaviour management
in school easier

BILL ROGERS

FINANCIAL TIMES
Prentice Hall
An imprint of Pearson Education

London · New York · San Francisco · Toronto · Sydney
Tokyo · Singapore · Hong Kong · Cape Town · Madrid
Paris · Milan · Munich · Amsterdam

PEARSON EDUCATION LIMITED

Head Office:
Edinburgh Gate
Harlow CM20 2JE
Tel: +44 (0)1279 623623
Fax: +44 (0)1279 431059

London Office:
128 Long Acre
London WC2E 9AN
Tel: +44 (0)20 7447 2000
Fax: +44 (0)20 7240 5771
Website: www.business-minds.com

First edition published in Australia in 1990 by The Australian Council for Educational Research Ltd
and in Great Britain in 1991 by Longman Industry and Public Service Management

This revised and expanded edition first published in Australia in 1998 by The Australian Council
for Educational Research Ltd, 19 Prospect Hill Road, Camberwell, Melbourne, Victoria 3124 and
in Great Britain in 1998 by Pitman Publishing (now Financial Times Prentice Hall). This British
edition is not for sale outside the UK.

ISBN 0 273 63277 9

British Library Cataloguing in Publication Data
A CIP catalogue record for this book can be obtained from the British Library

10 9

Line drawings by Kevin Burgemeestre
Typeset by Pantek Arts, Maidstone, Kent
Printed and bound in Great Britain by Bell & Bain Ltd, Glasgow

The Publishers' policy is to use paper manufactured from sustainable forests.

I wish to acknowledge the article 'A memorandum for your child' (Anon),
which I have adapted and used to illustrate self-esteem as a child might
see it. In the section on rights, rules and responsibilities (Chapter 4 and
Appendix VI) I have included part of a school policy document on
discipline from Moonee Ponds West Primary School (Victoria), one of
the many schools that have successfully developed a school-wide policy.
I also wish to thank The Pines School in South Australia, Hare Street
Infant School (UK), Mousehold First School (UK), St Scholastica's
(Victoria) and Ardeer Secondary College (Victoria).

Many colleagues have supported me in this project. Particular thanks are
extended to Cathie Whalen, Rob Barnes, Toby Whalen, Harry Pearce,
Colleen Murphy, Debbie Barnes, Ros Daniels, John Robertson and Christine Mulligan.

Contents

About the author

Bill Rogers' concern with discipline and behaviour management in schools began in the classroom. As a young teacher he was troubled by the absence of training in discipline strategies and by the lack of support given to teachers in this difficult aspect of an already demanding job. As his career and studies progressed, he began researching the issues of discipline, classroom management and teacher stress. His Masters degree concentrated on conflict and conflict resolution among pre-adolescents.

Bill now works as a consultant in all areas of education (primary, post-primary and tertiary), running inservice programs for teachers, lecturing at universities and working with parent groups and students. He lectures widely on discipline, classroom management, stress and teaching, developing peer-support programs for teachers, and developing community-based policies on discipline and student welfare. He has run many demonstration classes in Australian and British schools, and has worked with over 300 000 teachers throughout Australasia and the United Kingdom in the last ten years. During the last eleven lecturing tours he has conducted six summer schools at Cambridge University. He is currently researching the issue of colleague support among teachers.

Bill Rogers holds degrees in theology and education, and was a parish minister in the western suburbs of Melbourne for seven years, a role which included chaplaincy in hospitals and schools. He has published several books and a number of videos on behaviour management and classroom discipline.

Preface to the British edition

A DECADE AGO I visited the United Kingdom as a fortunate recipient of a research scholarship. I was looking at the issue of teacher stress as seen by colleagues there. Apart from some formal lecturing I visited a number of schools in England, Wales, Scotland and Ireland, and I've since been back many times to the UK to conduct INSET with schools and universities.

Whether in the UK or Australia, whenever students and teachers are together in classrooms or playgrounds, it could be anywhere – local accents notwithstanding!

In western culture, at least, teachers face daily the same behaviour-management concerns. Students are more conscious and vocal about 'their rights', less 'compliant' (much less) to adult authority *per se*, more streetwise ... all of which present significantly different climates for discipline in schools from when many of us were students.

I've written this book as a teacher, for teachers, at every level in schools. You will easily recognise and tune into the student/teacher scenarios described here.

Some of the terms may need some explanation. When, for example, you read *Good on You* you're reading a common Australian expression. It's a cross between 'well done' and 'I'm pleased with your effort': it may even act as an expression of thanks. It can engender a rapport in the working relationship between teacher and student.

Fair Dinkum in the mouth of student or teacher most often means an expression of truthfulness. It can be used also as an epithet for frustration: 'Fair Dinkum!' (a way of saying 'Come on! You know what you should be doing, and if you don't, you should!'). It can be used to question if something is true – 'Fair Dinkum?' (i.e. are you telling the truth?)

Dob means to 'tell-tale' on someone. (Of course we need to teach students the difference between legitimate – and necessary – reporting to an adult and telling tales simply to get someone into trouble or gain attention.)

Terms like 'post-primary' refer to students from 12–17 years of age. Australian schools tend to use the term 'year-level' to describe a student's year place in school. Prep. Grade is a child's first year of life in school (rising five in age). 'Relieving' teachers are the equivalent of supply teachers in the UK.

Apart from these few qualifications you can easily read, hopefully laugh at, enjoy and adapt the strategies and approaches outlined here. Good on you!

Bill Rogers
November 1997

Introduction

> *The secret of success is the ability to survive failure.*
>
> Noel Coward

Form 4, 1960

When I was at secondary school, one particular student had the reputation of being the school tough, the school bully and the bane of the teachers' lives. He once half-hanged a Form 4 boy upside down by a rope from a tree just for refusing to do a job. He was caned in front of the whole school on several occasions. Every child watched while he and some of his mates received their canings on both hands by the principal or the senior science master. On the last occasion he was publicly caned the whole school watched him walk on to the school stage (after public singing, school anthem and motto—1960 remember?). The principal, dressed in his black gown, twitching eyes behind his thick glasses, lifted the cane to belt the impassive student, who stood facing the whole school. It happened so quickly! Down whooshed the cane. As it hit the student's hand, he grabbed the cane from the principal and with great aplomb broke it across his knee, threw it on the floor and marched off the stage. A few seconds later the Form 4, 5 and 6 classes began to cheer. It took the school staff five minutes to restore order and that was mostly by yelling threats.

Who won? And what was the battle?

It was our weekly music class. I was fourteen at the time. The music teacher was a thin, hirsute man; nervous, with a shock of Beethoven-style hair. He had a reputation in the school for being a 'weak disciplinarian', his classes ranging from moderate to extreme disorder. From time to time, during music, I managed to score a seat next to a rather pretty girl (in 14-year-old terms). Okay so far, except for the aforementioned school bully who was nearly as tall as our de facto Beethoven, but twice as broad. He smoked like a chimney, had freckles and flaming red hair and threw a punch like a heavyweight boxer.

It was the first few minutes of settling in before we were to begin another music lesson. The bully came over to me and said, 'You sit over that side Rogers. I sit here.' Very cool. Not only did you not say 'no' to him, you also didn't waste time with discussion. I did as he said.

The music teacher saw this 'seat cross-over' and called out to the student to get back into the seat from whence he had come. He, of course, just refused. He sat and smiled at the girl and at me. (I gave an 'It's nothing to do with me, sir' look.) This was, in effect, a minor contretemps. Clearly our music teacher didn't see it this way! The teacher marched up to the bully's seat and demanded that he move, 'Now!' Freckle-faced and fearless, he simply replied, 'Make me!' So calm, so cool.

'Don't you defy me!' screamed the teacher. 'If you don't get out now, I'll make you!'

'Yeah, you and who else?'

The teacher grabbed him and tried to pull him out of the seat. In the ensuing scuffle, chairs went flying and soon a ring of Form 4 children watched as teacher and student actually wrestled on the floor. A couple of girls raced to the staff room in tears and the science and geography teachers managed to drag them apart.

To get back at the teacher, the bully let the tyres down on his car. He was finally expelled and ended up in a boys' home. The music teacher left at the end of term.

Public canings, I recall, diminished within weeks following this famous incident.

How would this student fare in the 1990s, in a society that aims for social justice, elimination of sexism, democracy in schools and the abolition of corporal punishment? Psychologists and social workers would, no doubt, explain his behaviour as the result of social or emotional deprivation, or economic disadvantage.

Fortunately there are few students like my 1960s class 'mate' in our schools, though the level of socio-emotionally disturbed (and disadvantaged) students may be as high as from three to five per cent across the school population (Wragg, 1989).

There are, however, many students who are more 'up-front' with their disruptive behaviour these days. There are many students who will not do what they are asked the first time, or simply because the teacher said so. They will argue, answer back, challenge, procrastinate, debate ... In the UK report *Discipline in Schools* (1989) it was indicated that 'talking out of turn', 'distracting others', 'making unnecessary (non-verbal) noises', 'getting out of seats without permission' and 'general rowdiness' most concerned teachers, and that these behaviours occurred right across the school spectrum.

What is certain, in the 1990s and beyond, is that the protest song of the 1960s has borne fruit: 'Your sons and your daughters are beyond your command'. The relative power and authority that teachers once 'enjoyed' is being eroded by students whose behaviour demonstrates that they want fundamental rights, such as the right to fair treatment and a say in what happens to them at school.

7B, 1990

It's just after lunch. The bell has rung and 7B charge down the concrete path to their home room.

Mr S is nearly knocked down by a dark-haired runner wearing jeans. 'G'day, Sir ... gonna let us in?'

Already, half a dozen kids crowd the door so Mr S has to push through them to open up. 'C'mon fellas, give us some air!' he pleads. Once open, the teacher and the half dozen move smartly, into Room 17. The students *appear* to have no manners whatever as they yell, cavort, tap, hoon and swear at each other for five minutes or so until their teacher says, 'Can I have your attention please?' (He sounds tired, fed up, as if he doesn't believe that what he says will make any difference.)

Calling out is legion. One boy is half-lying across the desk. A boy with a crewcut and rat-like features has been tapping loudly with his pen for what seems ages; 'Get f——!' is directed at a crewcut minor (who is now sucking a lolly on a stick). More abusive missiles are hurled around the room between these charming lads: 'liar', 'crap', 'sh——', 'dickhead', 'Don't you sit near me, you prick!' Mike, a lad with terminal acne and a jean-jacket bearing a swastika and other motifs jumps up and runs after a small, fat boy who has apparently taken his sunglasses. 'Gimme them back now!' he yells, 'or I'll kick your arse!'

The teacher is oblivious, deaf, powerless, having a bad day, or feels he can do nothing except yell again, 'Now settle down! I'm trying to mark the roll!' This is Mr S's regular burden. They never prepared him for it at university.

'Hey Sir! Sir! Paul's away.' Apparently David cannot speak at a normal pitch. He shouts across the three metres separating him from the teacher's desk. Paul spits his chewy, loudly and with gusto, across the room and misses the bin. He grins. Mr S doesn't. He's had it. 'Look, shut up you lot, you can see I'm trying to mark the roll!'

All this in the first ten minutes of the session. Why do these kids act so rudely and disruptively? Perhaps you have never had a class like 7B or have never had to contend with someone like the bully mentioned earlier. Perhaps the disruptions in your class are minor ones—a bit of calling out, a few students without pens or some low-level answering back. Spare a thought, however, for those like Mr S.

Of course the kids described here come from socially and economically depressed areas. Of course they watch hours of TV (much more than the time they are on-task at school). Of course many of the kids think school is a wag—perhaps they're right in some respects. Of course many of them act disruptively as an expression of 'belonging' to the social group. They've found that A-grade hooning (attention-seeking, defiance, teacher-baiting) gives them a fundamental sense of 'belonging' in classroom life. But when kids regularly muck up in a class like this, something else is happening.

Sane order, purpose and management of a class are significantly related to the methods of behaviour management a teacher employs and to the presence they have in the daily classroom interaction. Kids are not naturally well ordered or well managed or well anything in a group. Without clear direction and leadership from a teacher, the class members will find ways to take over. It's unfortunate, but children are not naturally democratic; and ideologues who have either forgotten what a robust Year 7 class is like or, more likely, never been in one, don't help by peddling slogans of 'relevance in the curriculum', 'democracy in learning' and 'student participation'—as if these were the answer. They are not.

While student rights, a democratic curriculum, cooperative learning, participation and equity, access and success are worthy goals of education, those goals need to be supported by a clear structure. Discipline is one way to develop that structure. Not autocratic discipline, not the martinet-style that many of us knew in our schooling, but democratic leadership. Times have changed, students no longer easily or naturally respect the teacher role. Even that universal culprit, society, no longer rates teaching as a significant profession. It is certainly a stressful profession, and more demands are being made on teachers all the time: with Departments of Education governed by economically rationalist constraints, there are larger class sizes, and teachers have more evaluative and appraisal criteria to process.

Many teachers, finding discipline difficult, complain that their college or university did not adequately prepare them for what they have to face. Many teachers plan well for curriculum but tend not to plan rigorously for discipline, even though they know what the common disruptions are.

I believe we ill-serve trainee teachers if we do not give them discipline and management skills. While thorough preparation of curriculum is essential, so is preparation for discipline. We need to discipline even if it's only calling out, chattering and 'mobility' we have to contend with. With some of the 'worst case' scenarios discussed later in this book, a thorough, detailed discipline plan is vital.

When I became a teacher I quickly realised the need for discipline skills. I read, I practised, I evaluated, I failed, I revised and, in time, I began to discuss successes and failures with interested and supportive colleagues. One of the more optimistic signs in the current educational climate is the emphasis on colleague support; a move away from that assumption that a teacher is weak or inefficient in wanting to discuss discipline concerns and to access mutual solutions. Teaching (unfortunately) has the structural potential to be a lonely profession.

When I became a consultant, I used this approach in schools through peer-support groups, team-teaching new ideas and skills with teachers in their classrooms, and through professional development at inservices and seminars, and at university.

Discipline (as a major facet of classroom management) is not easy. It is taxing emotionally, straining relationships between staff and students and even between members of staff. Making discipline a *positive* feature of teaching practice, and school life, such that students have maximum self-control and responsibility with minimum damage to self-esteem and the due rights of all, is no mean feat. It requires skill, planning and colleague support.

There are no magic ways of achieving effective discipline, nor are there any guarantees. It takes hard work. But that work is made easier with knowledge and skills. I have seen countless teachers use the approaches developed in this book with success. That success has required changes in organisation, as well as changes in behaviour and approach by the teacher, which in turn has changed the working relationship between students and their teacher.

It is my hope that teachers, however long they have been in the profession, will benefit from using the ideas, skills and resources in this book to build more positive, workable relationships that enhance the educational climate of our schools. After all, isn't that the fundamental goal of all behaviour management and discipline?

No one should be without peer support

Discipline: definition and protocols

I am the decisive element ... my personal approach ... creates the climate ... As a teacher I possess tremendous power to make a child's life miserable or joyous. I can be a tool of torture or an instrument of inspiration. I can humiliate, humour, hurt or heal.

H. Ginott, 1972

When I sported thin white legs with knobbly knees, a baggy pair of shorts, and blazer with cap to boot (circa 1950), *discipline* was a 'thick ear', respect for our masters, a cane across the hand or legs, or the dreaded trip to the principal's office. *That* trip was a narrow flight of stairs, a pronouncement of doom by this fearsome, awesome, black-robed stranger and the holding back of tears as he lashed out across the back of the knees or across the open hands. I was caned at school for lateness, breaking a pencil, 'answering back', and going out of the school grounds to the shops at play time. It did not teach me to respect my elders, the system or authority.

The application of corporal punishment may have relieved the frustration of my teachers but their behaviour totally disenfranchised me of my due rights. Many children in the 1950s were not aware they had such things as rights.

Corporal punishment

Corporal punishment (hitting, striking, pulling of ears or hair, pushing and shoving, beating, teaching-him-a-lesson-down-the-back-of-the-bike-shed), is now discouraged in most democratic countries. This does not mean that frustrated teachers do not occasionally hit, strike or poke their students when they display disruptive behaviour. It does mean that such behaviours may be against the law. By the 1980s, Australia had followed the lead of the United Kingdom where prevailing opinion was that the exercise of corporal punishment was incompatible with democratic education. This was in tune with the 1982 report to the General Assembly of the United Nations on a student's right not to be physically punished as 'an educational or disciplinary measure' (Boer and Gleeson, 1982).

The questioning of corporal punishment coincided with the emergence of a more open, less repressive society in the West. However, there are still principals and teachers who pine for the 'good old days' when they had 'real' power over children, when they could 'teach' them via the strap or cane. I still hear the asinine statement, 'They've taken our power away'.

There is a view still common in the media and among some teachers and parents, that corporal punishment is a necessary, fundamental tool. Whenever I speak to parents (especially fathers) about discipline, I often hear statements like, 'I know what I'd do with some of these kids ...' The suggestion is that control by force is a *necessary* ingredient in discipline. The basic argument still tendered for corporal punishment is that it *shows* that the child is wrong by associating pain with unacceptable behaviour. It is also supposed to act as a 'red light' to the other students and, of course, it relieves the frustration of the teacher. It *looks* as if something is being done.

Corporal punishment may solve the situation temporarily but it is ineffective in the long term, especially with those students whose background is already one of socio-emotional deprivation or aggression and hostility and who are under stresses often not of their own making. If a child is already being maltreated or emotionally 'bastardised' at home, how will further adult physical punishment help the resolution of inner turmoil? What do students learn about problem-solving if teachers use physical force to deal with external conflicts? Is it not teaching them to solve a problem *by force?* Corporal punishment does not work for the 'harder' student—the recidivist. It teaches such students nothing about the *resolution* of inner turmoil or conflict. Most of all, it teaches students nothing about the positive social or educational-task behaviours that they should be employing to cope effectively at school. A policy of accepting the consequences for one's actions, as distinct from punishment by pain, seeks to enhance accountability and self-control. Even if corporal punishment temporarily works, it doesn't make such discipline *right.*

In schools with serious behaviour problems some teachers will still say that corporal punishment is necessary 'because it's the only language those kids understand!' Again, what does such a teacher attitude convey about power relationships between an adult and a minor? About the nature of authority? About 'class' attitudes towards children whose background often predisposes them to poor social behaviour patterns?

When physical pain is being used as a form of control, the recipient needs to be passive. The degree to which, in the past, even recidivist children submitted to hair-pulling, caning, belting around the ear, was staggering. Such behaviours exhibited today would not only be (rightly) resisted by students, they would be tantamount to child abuse. It is very difficult to smack a struggling, resistant child.

It is my view that those who still hark back to the 'good old days' forget how degrading it is to hurt another human being in order to discipline them. Are there no other options? Are we so bereft of discipline and management skills that the touting of physical punishment is still seen, by many, as a panacea for behaviour problems? There is no convincing evidence to demonstrate that physical punishment (as distinct from behaviour management built on rights, rules, responsibilities, consequences and support for behaviour change) leads to self-control and self-discipline. It has been my experience that teachers (and parents) who call for the reintroduction of corporal punishment often betray a singular lack of skill in the areas of discipline, classroom management and curriculum planning.

We can no longer expect to walk into a classroom and automatically be given respect because of our role. Many children *will not* just sit still and do as they're told. We have to learn to work with our students and discipline them in a way that makes it clear that self-control and respect for rights are the norm in the classroom.

Discipline—as used in this book

The word 'discipline' is used in this book in three ways:

- *Preventative discipline*: is concerned with basic rights and clear rules and consequences, contracting with students, room organisation, curriculum planning, time-out etc.
- *Corrective discipline*: teacher actions are carried out to correct disruptive, antisocial or deviant behaviour.
- *Supportive discipline*: ensuring that 'correction' is received as fairly as is possible and working relationships with disciplined students re-established.

Preventative discipline

- clear rules and routines established with the class
- clear expectations about learning, tasks etc.
- attractive environment
- well-planned room organisation (seating, movement capability, access to equipment, clearly labelled cupboards, etc.)
- setting up of time-out area in the room (age appropriate at primary level) and beyond the classroom
- adequate resources
- organising curriculum to cater for mixed abilities

Corrective discipline

What we say, how we say it, when a student is disruptive or off-task.

- tactical ignoring of some behaviours
- reminding or restating classroom rules
- simple behavioural directions or warnings
- casual or direct questioning
- defusing or redirecting potential conflict

- giving simple choices
- directing students away from the group
- using time-out in class and out of class if necessary

Supportive discipline

- developing and maintaining a climate of respect
- building a positive classroom 'tone'
- following up disruptions later when the initial 'interpersonal heat' has subsided
- re-establishing working relationships with a 'disciplined' student
- encouraging students wherever possible
- developing behaviour agreements with a student
- applying a team approach to solving discipline problems

Discipline is a teacher-directed activity whereby we seek to lead, guide, direct, manage, or confront a student about behaviour that disrupts the rights of others, be they teachers or students. This teacher behaviour has *goals* beyond retaliation or punishment. It aims to lead a student towards self-control and personal accountability. In fact, the *test* of good or positive discipline is this: how does what I do and say enable a student to reach socially responsible goals?

Goals of discipline

- To develop students' self-discipline and self-control.
- To enable students to be on-task with their learning.
- To enhance students' self-esteem.
- To encourage accountability for behaviour.
- To encourage individual students to recognise and respect the rights of others.
- To affirm cooperation as well as responsible independence in learning.
- To promote the values of honesty, fairness, respect for others, etc.
- To enable rational conflict resolution.

Discipline is concerned with the following:

▌ Socialisation of individuals.

It is important that children see stability, and develop stability, in social conduct. Respect for the rights of others, accountability for one's actions as they affect others, cooperation, self-direction, achievement of a balance between freedom and restriction, and tolerance are important social realities that can be usefully learned in a classroom and school environment. One of the essential skills of life is the ability to get on with others. We, as teachers, need to model that and teach it. We need to teach some students how to live with inner conflict and tension. Of course we don't always have a lot of time to do this but by the *manner* of discipline we choose to exercise, we can give students better options for taking control of their behaviour.

▌ Personal maturation.

Children need to develop a sense of responsibility, tolerance for the frustrations of learning and social relationships, a sense of individual effort, and fair pride in themselves and their potential.

▌ Moral development.

This is bound up with the socialisation process. Manners, standards, rules, boundaries of right and wrong are required to enable all members of a group to enjoy their rights. This assurance comes about when children know what the clear, fair rules are and why those rules are in place. Children care very much about justice, and discipline will be better received when it is seen to be just.

▌ Emotional security.

Discipline can provide that sense of security which enhances effective learning. We learn best when we feel good about ourselves, which is why self-esteem is an important goal of discipline. Encouragement, positive reinforcement, helpful guiding, questioning and listening are the sorts of teacher behaviours that assist the achievement of this goal. Even when a teacher needs to be firm, assertive or angry, it is possible to discipline and still affirm this laudable goal.

Discipline is not merely an end in itself. It is a process to enable students to come back on-task with their learning, allow self-control and give a sense of 'choice' over their own behaviour. It is more than mere punishment. If we want to punish someone, let's call it by its right name; discipline is about longer term goals. In this sense, corrective discipline can be both corrective and guiding *and* still positive. If a student (primary) asks if she can do her project on the word processor, a teacher might say, 'No, you haven't even started your first draft', or he could say, 'Yes, when you've started your first draft'. One approach is more invitational than the other (depending, of course, on the teacher's tone of voice, body language and the quality of the relationship).

Discipline is needed in a classroom for the security and protection of the rights of all its members. It is necessary that a class run as smoothly as possible so that all students can benefit from the learning environment. However, discipline *technique* is not an answer in itself. Technique is only as good as the human relationship in which it occurs, and techniques are not value-free; if we believe that the dignity of the individual is important, we will eschew discipline that uses humiliation, sarcasm, ridicule, verbal aggression and put-downs.

Discipline occurs in a dynamic relationship in which relationships are sometimes strained (at times seriously strained). Technique, without due consideration for the fact that we are dealing with individuals, will often increase the conflict and further strain the relationship. I once saw a teacher drag a Year 4 student out of his class, pin him by his arm and repeatedly push him against the corridor wall. He yelled at this admittedly difficult child, 'I'm sick (thump) and tired (thump) of your stupid, idiotic (thump) behaviour. How old are you?' Across the passage, my class went deathly silent, then ... they laughed!

I've seen teachers put children in rubbish bins and tell them they're 'rubbish'! I've witnessed countless acts of deprivation and had many more drawn to my attention. Surely no one who understands anything about child development and teaching can sanction *that* kind of teacher behaviour.

Protocols of discipline

Everyone has a view about discipline; everyone has been 'disciplined' at some point in their life. The case for discipline can be argued on a continuum, from physical punishment to maximum freedom, as has been demonstrated by experiments such as Summerhill (Neill, 1960). It means different things to different people. Even within the teaching community, within faculties of education, there can be wide variation of opinion. When we act to correct or address unacceptable behaviour in our students, we act on the basis of certain beliefs or philosophical assumptions. These assumptions may be stated or unstated but they are certainly there in our actions.

If we believe children *must* respect their teachers, our behaviour will be different when a student says, 'this work sucks!' from that of a teacher who believes that we earn respect from our students by the kind of leadership we display. The teacher who believes that intentionally embarrassing students in front of their peers is okay will act very differently from the teacher who believes in giving students their due rights, especially the due right of respectful treatment.

There are several major approaches taken to discipline in the published literature. See Charles (1985), Wolfgang and Glickman (1986) and Tauber (1990) for discussion on the various models of discipline in the literature. These reflect the degree of intervention teachers believe they ought to exercise and how that intervention is practised. Behind each 'position' is a philosophy of human interaction. This book is not a discussion about those approaches or philosophical positions.

It is my argument, an argument that will be sustained through every practical example of discipline given, that there are central protocols of discipline. These protocols are, in a sense, the 'bottom line' when it comes to *how* we discipline. They reflect the kind of discipline that endorses and maximises the due rights of all parties in the education stakes.

Of course there is a philosophical position behind these protocols. (No teacher's professional practice is free from values. Even if they are 'unstated' they can be seen in the characteristic practice.) I will need to leave my philosophical position undefended at this point and allow the protocols and practices to defend themselves, save to say that I hold the dignity of the individual and the fundamental nature of human rights to be pivotal in the practice of effective discipline (see Chapter 3). The protocols outlined here enable a value position to be held even if, for example, a behavioural approach (say behaviour modification) is used. When we embrace due rights, ensure the minimising of embarrassment, maintain respect, and give appropriate behavioural 'choices' we maintain the dignity of the individual. Even if we have to be highly assertive with a student or display appropriate anger, if we embrace these protocols we have done the best we can do in the human transaction.

These protocols are the starting point for a positive teacher–student interaction that supports goals (see p. 11). They do not always make such discipline *easier*. They make the practice of discipline with dignity achievable.

1 Approach all discipline from the perspective of joint rights, responsibilities and rules

This means that the focus of discipline is not merely the teacher's relative power and authority (earned rather than imposed), but the joint rights of all members of the class. The most fundamental rights of a classroom member are those of respect and fair treatment. These rights are not automatic. They relate to due responsibility, and fair and agreed rules (see Chapter 4). This 3Rs focus provides a positive and just basis for any corrective discipline. Teachers need to discuss, up-front in the establishment phase of the year, the basis of classroom life and how due rights will be enjoyed in the classroom. A clear understanding and practice of rights, rules and responsibilities is the basis of preventative discipline.

2 Speak and act in such a way as to minimise embarrassment, undue confrontation and hostility

Sarcasm, put-downs and critical or caustic language are unfortunate features of some teachers' disciplinary style. When verbal and non-verbal hostility (slamming hands on desks; snatching up objects such as pens, food, toys; waving a pointed finger; yelling; throwing objects; waving fists at students, etc.) is a feature of discipline style, it not only reveals a tragic professional weakness, it models a distinctly unprofessional approach to conflict resolution. Witness the teacher who screams at the student, 'Don't you dare scream at me!'

Emotional management is never easy but it is possible to speak firmly and assertively without unnecessary or intentional hostility, even when frustrated or angry. It is a basic maxim of respectful conflict resolution that one person can assert her rights without trampling on the other person's rights (see Chapter 8).

3 Use a least-to-most intervention approach

When walking down the corridor one morning I saw a colleague stop a student who wasn't wearing a tie. 'Oi! Why aren't you wearing a tie? Eh?' I could hear him ten metres away. He didn't even address the student by name, or ask him to step to the side of the corridor and then keep his voice down while addressing the no-tie situation. It could have been far less intrusive if the teacher had beckoned the student quietly to one side and said, 'David, I notice you're not wearing a tie ...'

'Yeah ... like I forgot.'

'So, what do you think you can do about it?'

'Go home?'

'Anything quicker?'

'I dunno.'

'I've got a spare tie box in my office. Meet me there in five minutes ...'

I had a colleague march a student up to me one day with the words, 'Tell him, go on, tell him ...' (pointing to the student and then to me) 'tell him what you said to those students out there!' (He pointed to the student and then to the playground.) My concern was as much with *his* lack of social skill as with what the student had done (swearing). He didn't even introduce me to the student or invite her to cool down while we had a brief chat. It was as if the student didn't exist, as a person, while the teacher vilified her in front of me.

I've seen colleagues reach over a student's desk, tap several times with forefinger on the student's work and interrogate them. 'Why haven't you done a margin?' or 'What do you call this then, eh?' Don't they realise how confrontational and intrusive such actions are?

Imagine if the experience was reversed, if a head teacher were to treat a fellow staff member in the same way. They would rightfully be angry—even livid.

The teacher comes up to the Year 2s sitting at their work area, using play dough, scissors, paper etc. 'Look at this mess. Why is it so messy, eh? And look at the play dough everywhere. Why isn't the lid on, eh?' Quite apart from the use of the interrogative 'why?' the teacher then adds, 'Look at this mess. When the lid's off the play dough container it gets hard, doesn't it? And who makes the play dough, eh? Not you. And those textas ... they cost money, don't they, how long are they going to last if you leave the lids off?' Most children will turn off after the first question. This teacher may not mean to be a nag but that's how it sounds to the children. Also it's too many words; they can't take it all in. It might have been more effective to remind them: 'Remember to ...' (be specific and brief) or use a direct question, 'What do we need to do to keep the felt-tip pens working well? And to keep the play dough workable?'—here the teacher gives a non-verbal signal demonstration of pliability using two hands. (See Chapter 3 on the language of correction.)

This approach doesn't take any longer. It has kept the correction unobtrusive and positive. This approach is also more invitational to the student and still enables 'ownership' of behaviour.

4 Give appropriate choices when disciplining students

It is an important feature of positive discipline that teachers seek to direct students to responsibility for their own behaviour. Teachers can do this by using language that emphasises the student's 'choice' rather than the teacher's threat.

Jarrod (7C) had a pile of tazos (small coloured discs of cardboard with pictures on) on his book during classwork. I approached Jarrod, had a brief chat about the tazos and asked him to put them '... in his bag or on my desk. Ta.' I walked away to give him take-up time. He grumbled a bit but put them away in his bag. I could have just taken them. I chose to give him a simple (and fair) 'choice'. This approach is explored more fully in Chapter 3. Even when speaking to a child aside from the group, the teacher should seek to enable the child to:

▌ examine her behaviour and seek to act responsibly, and 'own' her behaviour

▌ move into a solution-oriented focus that puts primary responsibility on the student choosing the better options.

When we give appropriate choices, we develop an approach to discipline that emphasises self-control rather than merely teacher control. 'I said move!' is different, in kind, from saying, 'David, you can either work quietly here or I'll have to ask you to work over there.' Expressed as a choice, it gives the student an option, or options, *within the rights–rules framework.* Apart from students involved in ongoing disruptive behaviours, physical fighting or unsafe behaviour, it is better practice to give a 'choice' before imposing consequences such as relocation in the room, or time-out. Our interaction style ought to try to help students choose the better option or 'wear' the consequences of their actions. Sometimes the consequences will be deferred (at the close of the lesson, or when the interpersonal heat has gone down). When a male student referred to a Muslim girl's head-dress as a tea-towel the immediate discipline was a firm corrective assertion (his put-down had been heard by all). 'Lee, that's a put-down and that hurts.' He argued that it was just a joke. I replied, 'It may have been a joke to you; in our class that's a put-down. I'll speak to you after class.' He (indeed the whole class) could hear the assertion in my voice. Later, at the close of the lesson, I asked both students to stay back and we had a short 'accountability conference', at which the female student was able to put her feelings and perceptions to Lee (see p. 105). In the heat of the moment it would have been counter-productive to force an apology.

5 Discipline students respectfully, especially the annoying, frustrating ones

It is easy when faced with difficult, testy, 'pain in the neck' children to act from feelings of dislike. Conversely, it is easy to act fairly, kindly, reasonably, affirmatively towards those we like. This is natural. It can be observed in countless classrooms and often guides actual teacher behaviour. Some teachers rationalise their different treatment of students by saying, 'Why shouldn't I give Jason a hard time? He's a pain in the neck! He deserves it.' To discipline *respectfully*, however, we need to concentrate not so much on our feelings or likes and dislikes but how we can discipline (guide, direct, motivate, lead) without resorting to rancour, sarcasm, put-downs, or embarrassment. Respect means employing a verbal repertoire that models what we want, and expect, to see in our students.

Respectful discipline also means making an effort to notice (affirm, encourage or merely speak humanly as we pass by their desk) the normally 'painful' disruptive students when they show evidence of on-task behaviour. In this way the student can begin to relate to the teacher at times other than when he's being disciplined. If the only time I visit Jason is when he is a 'pain' then I have a very limited and unproductive working relationship with him. To speak regularly, individually, with every student, takes a lot of effort— especially the effort of respect. It is worth it.

Ultimately respect is a relational exercise that seeks to:

I model dignity in treatment
I not hold grudges
I re-establish positive working relationships as soon as possible with the disruptive student
I give the student a 'right of reply' when it is appropriate (see especially p. 102).

Even when a child has to be exited from the room for significant disruptive behaviour, such an exit can be carried out respectfully without screaming, yelling or last-minute grandstanding.

6 Be aware that we often get what we expect—so use positive corrective language where possible

8D can be painful on Friday afternoon; 9E are no picnic either and a prep class, first term, is equivalent to digging the roads from 6.00 a.m. until sundown! Notwithstanding pay, conditions, and public perception, if we expect 8D to be dreadful we may well find our expectations returning to us. The maxim 'children rise to the level of our expectations' is not a plea for Pollyannaism but a recognition that what we may be saying, believing and reflecting about our students has a 'boomerang' effect. I have seen and heard teachers

Defuse conflicts

stand in front of a class and berate them in a long and demeaning lecture. 'You're the worst class I've ever had, you are. Yes, you and you! You never listen, do you? Look at you, you'll leave here and you won't care what I've said, will you—it won't make any difference. You never listen to me, do you—unless I shout! What's wrong with you?' Next morning, 'I hope you're not going to be like you were yesterday! I had valium and Aspros because of you! So watch it, just watch it!' Expectations can so easily be communicated unconsciously by the teacher. Children pick up fairly quickly what we expect of them from our actions. Better surely, to communicate expectations more reflectively, purposefully, even overtly in a positive way.

We have a difficult and at times demanding job. A judicious sense of humour is clearly needed (and appreciated by our students) if we are to keep our sanity. A smile, a joke, a laugh now and then says we are human. Even when we have to discipline, humour can have a place. One of my Year 7 students was getting frustrated with his written work and sighed, adding loudly, 'F—— this work.' Looking at him with mock seriousness I said, 'I didn't know you could do that with your work.' He raised his eyes, furrowed his brows and wryly said, 'Sorry', adding a grin. I also had a brief chat with him after class (see p. 96). Certainly self-humour, not taking it all *too* seriously, is a useful antidote to the routine stress of the chalkface life. And there is plenty to laugh about in our profession.

7 Follow up issues beyond the classroom

One of the marks of consistency is keeping track of ongoing disruptions. If we say to a child we expect her to stay back after class (for detention, logical consequences, behaviour contract, or time-out) we need to ensure it happens. It's so easy when the coffee break looms to ignore it or pass the issue on to a senior teacher. Follow-up (and follow-through) is important because ultimately, the disturbance of Trish in *my* room, while benefiting from senior teacher intervention, is still a problem to be resolved between Trish and *me*. *We* are the ones who have to work together in Room 17 1our times a week, or all day if it's a primary-age class.

Following up with behavioural consequences demonstrates concern as well as consistency, justice as well as accountability, and models the fact that we will not easily give up on them even when they are a 'pain'. At this level of discipline, though, we will often need colleague support beyond the classroom.

8 Try to ensure that there is a logical relationship between behaviour and outcome

Emphasise the certainty rather than just the severity of the consequence; keep the respect intact.

9 Seek colleague and parent support

If we are struggling with a particular student, or a group or even the whole class, and our personal 'plans' are not working, it is in the interests of all to:

■ seek help from trusted colleagues

▌ seek out senior teacher support
▌ call on parents to assist by mutual understanding and resolution.

There is no virtue at all in social and professional isolation and pretending all is going well. A good deal of teacher stress arises because, as teachers, we tend not to communicate our feelings, problems and concerns. When we do, we often find how similar our problems are. One of the difficulties for *some* teachers is that they feel that disclosure of classroom discipline (and control) problems is an admission of weakness. Also, offering colleague support is sometimes seen as implying that the (other) colleague is a weak, or unprofessional, teacher (see Rogers, 1992; *Discipline in Schools*, 1989). A *whole-school* approach to discipline will provide regular opportunities to share problems, identify needs and have a shared focus in exploring solutions and support. There are nearly always one or two teachers that we can share with (see Rogers, 1995 on a whole-school approach).

These protocols are a guide and, coupled with the skills discussed in Chapter 3, a means of 'testing' how positive our discipline style is. In fact, where teachers seek to build such protocols into their practice, they find that their working relationship with students is more positive, less demanding and more productive for all concerned.

Protocols of discipline

▌ focus of discipline is the common rights, rules, responsibilities
▌ avoid unnecessary confrontation/embarrassment
▌ use a least-to-most intervention approach
▌ give appropriate 'choices' within rights/rules
▌ discipline respectfully
▌ use positive corrective language where possible
▌ follow up and follow through
▌ use related consequences where possible
▌ seek colleague and parent support

Summary

The concept and practice of discipline has suffered roundly from an over-concentration on punishment and teacher control. It should be seen in terms of what it is trying to achieve, namely self-discipline, self-control and respect for others' rights.

Such 'discipline' requires a conscious effort by teachers to embrace a philosophy and practice of teaching and behaviour management that:

■ emphasises due rights, responsibilities and rules
■ allows appropriate collaboration with students in formation of some rules and responsibilities
■ minimises hostility and embarrassment in teacher–student interaction
■ develops and maintains respectful treatment
■ develops a climate of choice within a rights–responsibility framework
■ provides due right of reply to the student
■ follows up and follows through with disruptive students
■ includes as wide a support base as is necessary to improve and enable a positive working and social environment for student(s) and teacher alike.

Questions to consider

■ How can I be corrective, and appropriately confront disruptive behaviour, while giving due rights to myself and students alike?
■ How do I define appropriate authority and status differences between teacher and student?
■ How do I exercise that fundamental humanity that children of all generations have wanted in their teachers, yet still maintain a well-ordered classroom that enhances learning?
■ In disciplining students, how can I enable them to get back on-task as quickly as possible:
   – without long-winded discussion?

– without intentional embarrassment?
– with minimal audience attention?
In reflecting on this question how aware am I of my characteristic discipline language? (See especially Chapter 3.)

■ If someone were to observe my characteristic discipline style, what sort of things would they note?

■ What is my school's working definition of discipline?

■ Do I consciously discipline students with particular *goals* in mind? What are these goals?

■ In what way do I modify my behaviour (discipline behaviour) to make the attainment of those goals (say self-control) a possibility?

■ What are the protocols by which I discipline? How do they relate to the protocols discussed here?

Disruptive behaviour and teacher management style

A plank in reason broke.

Emily Dickinson

Disruptive behaviour

Every classroom has its share of disruptions. Of course they may be only low-level disruptions, such as talking while the teacher is talking, seat-leaving, gum-chewing, calling out, not having equipment, or uniform misdemeanours. We no longer hear the respectful and dulcet tones of 'Please Sir', or 'Yes Miss'. More likely, we'll hear, 'This work sucks!', 'Gees this is boring—fair dinkum!', 'You can't make me!' and 'I don't care'. Add to this aggression, sulking, insolence, swearing and defiance, and it's easy to see why teaching is often rated as a highly stressful profession.

The causes of disruption

Children disrupt for a number of reasons: boredom, 'fun', immaturity, inability to master the curriculum, low tolerance to frustration, or an emotionally disturbed and dysfunctional home situation. These days we are seeing more and more children whose home environment is seriously affecting their ability to cope in a 'formal' social setting like school. If Johnny's current male caregiver is unemployed, belts him regularly, has a 'drinking problem' and often 'shoots through'; if mum has five other children under 15; if there is regular screaming, shouting and put-downs at home, this will have an effect on Johnny's social behaviour at school. If he comes to school with significant inner conflict that he can hardly comprehend, and then meets an intransigent, petty teacher whose verbal repertoire is limited to hostile and embarrassing interaction, there is already a context for disruption. This is a particularly bleak picture, but variations of this situation will be found in many schools.

Johnny comes to school late (yet again) and meets Mr D at 9.40 a.m. for maths. 'Listen,' says the teacher, 'I'm sick and tired of you coming late to my class. Where's your late pass? I suppose you haven't got one again. What's your excuse this time?' Of course, by this time, the whole class is focused on these two (it's much more interesting than maths). Johnny is feeling 'screwed up' inside. Already that morning, his mum has screamed at him about his mess in the bedroom, he's had a lousy breakfast, he's fought with his younger brother. He had to run to the chemist at 9.00 a.m. to get some painkillers for mum who had another of her headaches. He reacts angrily to Mr D. 'Don't sh—— me! You're always picking on me. What about the other kids who are late?' He throws his bag on the floor. Mr D yells back, 'Who the hell do you think you are speaking to me like that—get out, go to the office! Go on, get out now!' Johnny turns and when he is three metres away, slyly pokes his finger up at Mr D.

Who won? Was it worth it? Johnny doesn't have the social skills to say, when he's angry, 'Excuse me, I'm late for a good reason. I wish you wouldn't speak to me like that.' The situation could have been handled differently and the level of the disruption could have been changed by the approach used. Further, how is Johnny going to fit into a class where the teacher has no interest in the problems that contribute to his performance? How is Johnny going to sit there and lap up maths, or history, when all he's thinking about is home problems? Some teachers argue that kids like Johnny shouldn't be at school. Where should they be? At home? Of course we have little or no control over our students' home environment. Some students' backgrounds are pitiful, even tragic. We can rarely step in and modify them, but we can modify the environment that we have relative control over at school.

There are many students like Johnny attending our schools and they don't all go to the local state school. St Smiggins private girls school has its fair share of emotionally stretched students too. Defiance, persistent tantrums, even swearing are not the behavioural prerogative of the so-called disadvantaged schools.

Tom comes late to class; his home environment is not dissimilar to Johnny's. He swaggers in with some attention-seeking; he has no pen, no books. The teacher is halfway through explaining the lesson topic. He greets Tom, 'Good morning Tom, welcome.' This teacher is not Tom's regular teacher. Tom says, 'You're not our normal teacher', and frowns. 'There are no normal teachers, Tom.' The class, and Tom, laugh. 'I'd like you to take a seat over here.' He points to a seat in the front next to Daniel. 'But I normally sit next to Corey and them.' Tom looks at the back row—all seats are taken.

Rather than argue with Tom ('Look, don't argue with me, you'll sit there!'), the teacher points to the spare seat, saying, 'The back seats are taken Tom. I'd like you to sit here for now, thanks.' His body language is relaxed, his voice confident. He breaks eye contact with Tom and carries on teaching *as if* Tom will comply with this simple request. Tom does.

Later, during the on-task phase of the lesson, the teacher notices Tom hasn't started the activity. He comes across to Tom and Daniel's table and notices the picture on Daniel's diary that Tom and Daniel are chatting about. 'How's it going then?' He has a brief chat and says to Tom, 'Tom, I notice you haven't started.' He describes without judging (not *'Why* haven't you started?') before he asks Tom if he needs help. Tom replies, 'Yeah, well I haven't got a pen, have I?'

'There's one in my yellow box, Tom.' (This teacher always carries a box with pens, rulers, pencils, a roll of A4 paper, plus his own chalk, whiteboard markers, tissues, etc.—preventative management). The box is yellow in colour (small); each ruler, pen, pencil etc. is tipped with yellow tape to 'track' it back to the box (this helps the visual learners). Tom's a bit persistent; 'I haven't got a ruler.'

'There's one in the yellow box, Tom.'

'Gees, I haven't got any paper.' Tom leans back in his chair with a sigh. 'There's paper next to the box, Tom.' Tom mutters, 'Sh——'. The teacher replies, 'No, Tom—I don't think there's any of that in there.' He leaves Tom's table to go and work with other students. As he leaves he smiles, saying, 'I'll come and see how you're going later, Tom.' He's found it helpful to leave students like Tom with a task-related reminder or direction. Sometimes he'll leave the student with a task-related question, for example 'What are you supposed to be doing at the moment?'

You can imagine a different scenario within the same context: 'Why haven't you got a pen? The other students have a pen, don't they? Use your brains and get one!' We can understand a teacher's exasperation with students like Tom. The ambiguous direction 'get one' might see Tom walk right across the class to one of his mates in the back row. 'Eh, give us a pen, Corey.'

'Gees, I ain't giving you a pen, I didn't get the last five back!' Or Tom might walk out of class.

'Oi, where are you going?'

'You said I could get a pen. I'm going to me locker, it's only half a kilometre away. Won't be long!' Before the teacher can stop Tom, he's off. It does happen.

I use the yellow-box approach myself (I've had different colours over the years). It's called preventative management. If a student doesn't bring pens etc. over several sessions then I'll work on a one-to-one plan to help the student remember basic class equipment. I also find it helpful to have a few spare textbooks or photocopied sections from textbooks for those who forget.

Attention and audience

Whatever the causes of disruption, when a student comes into a group she immediately seeks to find some sort of 'social' place, to *belong* in some way to the classroom, in effect to her peers. One of the central needs a person has is to be noticed: to be attended to, to have contact with others. Most students fulfil this need in socially acceptable ways: they put their hands up, they ask for equipment instead of snatching, they wait their turn, they gain positive attention through the production of acceptable work, they participate cooperatively—they 'belong'. Their teachers and peers reinforce this acceptable mode of attention-seeking.

Mary gets her attention differently. If she is asked to 'settle down', she pouts and tosses her head around like an irate horse. It works.

Her teacher comments, 'Look, I asked you to be quiet, not to snort like a horse! What's wrong with you?' Mary answers back, 'Others are talking as well, why d'you have to pick on me?'

'I am not picking on you. I am telling you to be quiet or you can move out of that seat now!'

What a lot of words. What a lot of attention. Mary got what she wanted. Procrastination is something she learned in the supermarket trolley: the attention-seeking whine, the sulky 'notice me' pout, the extended 'come over and pity me' sulking routine.

The attention-seeker

Primary and secondary behaviour

Another way of looking at attention-seeking behaviour is to view the behaviour cycle as progressive: from the primary disruption through to secondary attention- or power-seeking behaviours.

Cameron has secretly brought his expensive ultra-light *Walkman* into class and hidden the cassette deck in his bag by his feet. The teacher notices his nodding, hears the faint music and 'twigs'. She directs him to take it off and put it away; she addresses the primary behaviour. Now Cameron (even though he's in Year 10 at a private school) does not say, 'Right Miss. I'll take it off straight away. Thanks for pointing it out.' Cameron employs typical 'secondary' behaviours. He grunts, sighs (to increase the feeling of 'notice how annoyed I am!') and says, 'Gee, Miss Davies lets me play it in art—

fair dinkum' (more sighs). His secondary behaviour is designed to change the issue of responsibility for his primary behaviour (having a *Walkman* on in class—or whatever) to an issue of 'justice' (comparing one teacher's standards with another's).

The problem with secondary behaviour is that it is so easy to get emotionally caught up with it, speak to it, and never really direct ownership to the real issue. 'Cameron, this is not Miss Davies' class. Now why have you got it on?'

'Gee Miss, I can still work with it on. I'm even quieter with it on, aren't I Harry?' He turns to his mate for back-up. And so it can go on. Procrastination, more secondary dialogue, avoidance of behaviour ownership. It can happen in almost any discipline transaction—if we let it.

Secondary behaviours include sighing, pouting, sulking, a range of 'tantrumming' behaviours, and eyes rolled to the ceiling. Students will sometimes answer back, procrastinate, or want to have the last word. The teacher quietly beckons a student to remove his hat in class. The student replies, 'Oh, come on (whine) other teachers don't care if we ...' The reply, and the tone, and the body language are all secondary aspects to the main issue of the rule about hats. Secondary behaviour may be habitual, the result of frustration, or employed purposefully by the child. It may even be a backlash by the student at what he perceives as unfair treatment by a teacher. Secondary behaviour can contribute to:

▪ over-attendance by the teacher to the student (and over-servicing)
▪ avoidance of responsibility for the real issue at stake—their primary behaviour (out of seat, calling out, having a comic on the desk, etc.)
▪ a feeling of guilt in the teacher, as if she shouldn't even be addressing the student about this behaviour. (This is where pouting, sighing, shoulder-shrugging, kicking-the-chair-in-passing are used for great effect as secondary behaviour—'I'll make you feel sorry!')

This teacher is well-meaning, but, through over-attention to Cameron's antics, her behaviour reinforces the very thing she is trying to eliminate. Even if the child does stop disrupting (having got his dose of attention), it is likely he will employ similar behaviour next time he's after attention. Some children make a career of it! It's easy to fall into the trap of just reacting to such attention-seeking because we feel frustrated, angry, or anxious. What we often end up doing is just what the child wants—'Notice me!', 'Attend to me when I want attention!'

The need for attention is fundamental in children, in all of us—it flows from the 'need to belong' to a social group.

Behaviours which indicate attention- and power-seeking

THE NEED TO BELONG: ATTENTION

'Notice me!'	'Make me!'
'Attend to me.'	'I will make you attend to me.'
▌ calling out	▌ blatant task refusal
▌ butting in	▌ defiance
▌ procrastinating, questioning work	▌ swearing ('get stuffed!' or variations thereof)
▌ sulking, pouting, tantrums	▌ 'can't make me'
▌ task refusing	▌ provocative gesturing
▌ clowning around, silly noises	▌ dumb insolence
	▌ challenging behaviour
	▌ aggressive behaviour

Attention-seeking children, in a group, find it easy to get teachers into an indecisive management mode when they become embroiled in long and fruitless discussions or pleadings in front of the class or when they get teachers involved in power struggles.

Teacher frustration

Teachers will note how frustrated they get with children when they call out, make silly noises, tap and the like. This is both a problem and a clue for what we can do when dealing with such behaviour. Because we are frustrated by the child's behaviour ('Attend to me',

'Spend time on me', 'Engage the group to notice me') it is easy to act in accord with the child's goal. In fact, the child may have learned how to trigger such attention from adults even if such attention is adult anger. 'Gee *I* can get him angry just by calling out!', 'I can make him come over to *me* by pleading.' Some children may not be consciously aware of their attention-seeking behaviour but the reinforcement they gain strengthens their attention-seeking or power-struggling behaviour, even if the attention is negative in tone or manner. It is essential in dealing with such behaviours to marshal thoughtful discipline responses.

Power-seeking is another form of attention-seeking. The power-seeking child is out to 'belong' by using challenging behaviour: 'Can't make me', 'Not gonna do this work', 'This work is boring', 'I hate you', 'I don't care anyway'. When such a child throws out a challenge, he is inviting the teacher to a contest. His belief may even register as 'I belong when I'm as powerful or more powerful than the teacher' or 'I must win, she must lose'.

When the teacher uses more force—'You'll do this work or else!'—she endorses the child's purposeful behaviour. There is also the added problem that there is a sense in which a teacher cannot make a child do any work. She can invite, ask, direct, apply consequences but cannot merely *make*. We can, of course, make a small child move from one place to another by physically 'helping' him. We can hardly do that with a robust Year 7 student who responds by saying, 'No, I'm not gonna move and you can't make me.' What are we going to do? Drag him out? Fight him? There are more effective ways of dealing with power-seeking students than merely giving them the easy win–lose perspective they seek.

Power-seeking children 'feed' off force, which is why it makes good sense to avoid such a reaction. The teacher's response (rather than reaction) can reinforce a child's inappropriate behaviour as much as anything else.

Awareness of disruptive behaviour patterns

If we are aware that some children's misbehaviour is *purposeful* in seeking attention or an exchange of power, we can better plan how to manage disruptions that arise from their behaviour. If a child is actively seeking attention in off-task, clownish, annoying ways, it is counter-productive to let him achieve such a goal at the expense of our frustration: 'I won't tell you again!', 'Just sit down will you!' If we are aware of the behaviour that signals attention-seeking, we need to be consciously prepared not to over-attend or fall into power exchanges. If Johnny is purposefully baiting the teacher with a whining 'This work sucks', it is clear that an angry retort from the teacher will only reinforce such behaviour. This child may never have successfully learned cooperative ways to belong but he gets an 'A' for being a 'pain'. We may be the ones giving the marks!

Effective discipline approaches will seek to minimise a child's inappropriate ways of belonging through attention-seeking and power-play, and maximise appropriate ways to belong. The way we do this will depend on our teaching style and what skills we bring to bear. Such skills need to be developed in a planned and purposeful way. The combination rarely occurs accidentally (see Chapter 3).

Styles of management and teaching

Teaching and management styles significantly affect classroom climate. Any visitor to a classroom could, after several visits, pinpoint a teacher's characteristic style: authoritarian, decisive, autocratic, indecisive …

In the late 1930s Kurt Lewin experimented with teacher style and classroom leadership and observed and documented three basic management approaches: *laissez-faire*, autocratic and democratic (Lewin, Lippitt and White, 1939; Lewin, 1948). He hypothesised that all teachers fit somewhere along a continuum embracing these positions.

The *laissez-faire* teacher appears to let the children do virtually what they want. The results can range from inconsistent application of rules and inconsistent corrective management, to virtually 'giving in' to students just to keep the peace. In the worst extremes the result can be marginal chaos.

The autocrat basically tells children what to do, with most children being compliant (not necessarily happy, not necessarily engaged in effective learning, but compliant). This approach relies on overt power and constant teacher control. The trouble with the autocratic teacher is that all is 'under control' (no noise and heads down) but only when the boss is there. In extreme cases of auto-cratic control, the vertical tyranny of the adult is often accompanied by rough or unthinking verbal treatment.

The democratic leader seeks to win cooperation rather than demand compliance, and is prepared to discuss and assist in a child's own decision-making even when the child is being 'disciplined' (corrected, challenged or directed) about off-task or disruptive behaviour. Children are challenged, spoken to and assisted in such a way that independence, self-motivation and self-control are the most likely outcomes.

Hoping for compliance: the indecisive teacher (*laissez-faire*)

'I've got to teach number and line today—how can I do it?' Ms A is in her second week at Styx Rd, a large post-primary school in an area demographically described as being of low socioeconomic status. This was not the school of her choice.

Because she is new to the school she has been given four periods of maths with 8E in a portable classroom! (This is an unfortunate practice in some schools where the last teacher in gets the 'worst' classes and classrooms. It says a lot about teacher welfare.) The portable is a 1970s reject, with lousy seats and desks, cupboards that don't open properly and windows that jam.

8E are filing in as Ms A seeks to start a new day, another lesson. She is nervous. She knows what she wants to do in the lesson but is uncertain about how to handle the inevitable disruptions. With the best of intentions, she wants these students to like her. It is quite noisy at the beginning of the lesson; that's normal. Her eyes dart around the room. Several times she says, 'Shh please' or 'Settle down now'. One boy calls out, 'Miss, can I go to the toilet?' and grins. The question races through her head, 'What will I do?'

'Oh Craig, can't you wait please? I'm trying to start the lesson.'

'Gees Miss (grin), I didn't get a chance before. I'm bustin'.' He looks around and grins again. She wants to keep the peace, she doesn't want to lose face, she doesn't want to be aggressive but is equally unsure about how to assert her due rights. 'Craig, can't you wait till I've finished this explanation?' Ms A's body language com-municates uncertainty, and possible defeat. She is hoping (against hope) for compliance. Craig folds his arms and, in mock frustration, sticks his legs out: 'umph!'

Bravely Ms A soldiers on with the up-front teaching. Drawing a train line across the board, she proceeds to draw a train on the tracks. She puts a zero on the tracks and then the negative and positive numbers on either side. Each time she faces the board the students start talking. She is getting more and more concerned and edgy. As she completes the drawing she begins to explain the theory of negative numbers. The class wag notices she hasn't drawn any wheels on the train and leaning back in his chair calls out, 'Hey, Miss, can't you draw wheels on a train or something?' She turns and says, 'Who said that, come on who said it? Be fair. What does it matter that I left the wheels off? Was it you who said that Bilal?' (She's angry now.)

'Me (stupefied look) Miss? Me? Why do you always pick on me?'

'I don't, but why do you have to be rude?' She starts a public discussion with Bilal in front of his peers. He leans back, enjoying the peer attention this exchange is giving him.

Ms A finally manages to write up some problems on the board, answers several students who call out and then sets them to work. During the on-task phase of the lesson, Maria calls out. 'Miss, can you come here? I need your help.' Ms A is already working with Richard, who displays no interest in number lines. She walks across to Maria and says, 'Maria, please can't you see I'm trying to work with Richard?' (Her tone has a pleading quality about it.) At this juncture Richard calls out, 'Hey Maria, can't you wait your turn?' She turns back to Richard. 'Please Richard, *I'm* talking to Maria not you!' She's starting to get very frustrated. 'Gees, I was only asking a question' says Maria, who leans back in her seat, pouts and folds her arms.

'Well, can you wait please?'

'Doesn't matter now!' comes the reply, as Maria again pouts at her teacher.

'Why did I choose teaching?' thinks Ms A, as she goes back to Richard. Paul gets out of his seat to wander over to his mate Dimi. She can see and hear that they are way off-task. Her shoulders slump, a signal of her Herculean task. Not another problem. 'Paul, why are you out of your seat?'

'I'm only asking Dimi for a pencil, Miss.'

'But you've been talking Paul, I heard you. I'm trying to teach over here.'

'C'mon! Other people get out of their seats and you don't tell them off.' (It's Paul's turn to pout.)

'Now be fair, Paul. I wasn't picking on you. I only wanted to know why you were out of your seat.' She is naturally frustrated yet trying to be reasonable. Dimi jumps in. The rest of the class are watching.

'Yes you do Miss, you do pick on Paul!'

She turns; now she *is* frustrated. 'Look Dimi, all I asked was a civil question. I wasn't talking to you anyway!'

Of course this is a challenging class, of course the school has been unfair in its timetable loading, of course there are students here whose main goal in life seems to be feeding their egos, who compensate for their struggle in learning by engaging peer and adult attention in destructive ways. When pushed to the limit with children like Paul or Richard she says things like, 'Do I have to get angry with you Paul?' Inside, Paul will say, 'Yes—of course you do!' In many of the discipline transactions Ms A is engaged in, she never really believes the students will be compliant. She hopes they will, but her behaviour, verbal and non-verbal, clearly signals a lack of assertion, uncertainty and often indecision.

It doesn't help simply to label her an ineffective teacher when her training has not prepared her for the type of discipline problems she encounters. Her heart is in the right place. She just is not sure *what* to do. She plans well for her lessons but not for the things she needs to say and do when students are disruptive. She plays it 'by ear'; ever a dangerous stance in teaching, especially with 8E.

The indecisive teacher:

- has a non-assertive stance (passivity)
- has an overly discursive means of settling disruption, especially when concentrating on secondary behaviours (see p. 29)
- believes that it is wrong to impose the teacher's will on students and has a tendency to over-compensate for this by a tone of voice and body language that indicate vacillation

■ believes that it is wrong to use force in words or actions, but when pushed to the limit will get angry and yell and then later feel guilty about this behaviour
■ fears failure
■ allows the student to decide the agenda in a discipline transaction
■ hopes for compliance, believing that goodwill and friendliness are enough. They aren't.

Demanding compliance: the overly authoritarian or demanding teacher

In his Year 6 class Mr B has a reputation for toughness. He's not one to mince words. At the beginning of the lesson Mustapah is silly enough to call out twice. Mr B sits on this 'rubbish' quickly. 'Listen, I'm not going to tell you again. Don't call out. You got that?' Mustapah sulkily replies 'Yes!'

'And don't sulk at me!' Mr B will never ignore stupid behaviour (not even *tactically* ignore).

While he is explaining the lesson material, two students are talking up the back. He calls out to them, 'You, yes you two! Don't pretend you didn't hear me. You're not deaf, are you? Stop talking—now.' He eyeballs them for ten seconds. Mission accomplished. He carries on. The two at the back whisper. It's time for a scene. He walks over and all eyes focus on him and the two students. 'Listen, didn't I just tell you to be quiet? If you can't shut up now, then you can have a detention if you want. You have no right to interrupt my lesson.'

There is little calling out in his class but when there is, he will remind them, 'Don't call out in my class. I'm sick and tired of telling you.' If anyone dares make a smart-alec comment or butt in, he'll probably say, 'Listen smart alec, who's running this class? You or me?' He will often bear down on a student using his size to intimidate. As he's walking around the room he can be heard saying things like, 'Look, I'm not going to tell you again, I've told you how to do this before, surely you can understand it by now!'

Most of the time, during the on-task phase of the lesson, Mr B is at his desk. Now and then he'll move out to help a student. If he hears giggling or talking he'll tend to be over-corrective. 'You, yes *you*. Got a private joke have you?'

Such teachers may disguise such churlish or petty behaviour as 'discipline'. Kylie is wearing rather large earrings. In seeking to 'discipline' her Mr B goes up and says, 'What do you think these are?' He makes what he thinks is a funny remark about 'street girls' in a rather loud voice. Kylie is one of those students prepared to stand up for her rights. 'Just my earrings.'

'You know they're not regulation, now get them off—now!'

Kylie is prepared to stand her ground. 'There's nothing wrong with them—Miss D said they were okay.'

'Listen, I don't care what Miss D said, she's not your teacher, I am! Get them off.'

Kylie is determined. 'No, they're all right.' It's a power struggle. Mr B cannot afford to lose face, he's in too deep by now. 'Right, get out now. Go to the principal. Go on—move!' Kylie sullenly leaves the class, jangling her earrings as she goes.

Who has won?

I've heard teachers call girls 'sluts', 'cheap', or make snide remarks about a student's home background. Embarrassment and humiliation are among the worst forms of teacher discipline and, as research shows (Lewis and Lovegrove, 1985), among the most disliked of teacher behaviours. Jacob Kounin (1977) coined the term 'ripple effect' to describe what happens when the impact of a teacher's discipline on one student 'ripples' out to others. When Mr B argues with Kylie, using straight humiliation, his 'discipline' has an effect on the other students. Some sit up straight, some are frightened or concerned, others are clearly off-task, most are angry inside at his unjust treatment. One of the sad features of overly demanding teachers is their lack of respect and basic humanity as they insist on the power-status relationship.

I have seen petty, demanding teachers send Year 7 students to the back of the room with the direction, 'Right, if you're not going to listen, you can move to the back of the class. Go on! You're not part of my class! Now stand and face the wall.' What amazes me is how many students still put up with this kind of rubbish.

I've seen teachers throw books in the bin, slam their hands on desks, snatch students' hats off, or slam the metre ruler across the desk to intimidate a child or create the impression of power. The defensive stance often sees the teacher defining the transaction as *me* and *them* (the enemy), and the nature of resolution as *win* or *lose*. Such teachers get angry quickly. Sometimes the anger may not even be connected with the child's behaviour but arise from the demanding beliefs that the teacher *must* win in all discipline transactions and that students *should* obey and respect their teachers. Further, good teachers must be able to control their classes at all times. They are failures if they don't or can't. The hidden agenda of these beliefs is the degree to which they demand from reality that which reality (8D, 6A, the testy little preps) may not *easily* care to conform to.

'Look, she *should* just listen and that's that! I've set the work—she should do it!' But she doesn't listen, does she? 'But she should dammit!' But the reality is she doesn't (yet). How does our 'belief' in any way help our emotional coping or increase the likelihood of student compliance?

If we say, 'He *must* not swear. Children *should* not swear!', we will feel differently and act differently than if we say, 'I dislike, even strongly dislike, abusive swearing, but it is *not* the end of the world. I can cope. It is only awful if I allow the awfulness to overwhelm me.' This does not mean we excuse swearing; it does mean our working beliefs are realistic enough to recognise reality and respond appropriately, even thoughtfully (see p. 282).

Of course, a *demanding* belief (as distinct from a flexible and more realistic belief) creates as much stress as the disruptive situation itself. When a student fails to respond to the threat, the demand, or the power stance, then the belief itself creates stressful emotions of intense frustration or anger. It's a short step to easy blaming. 'It's his fault, that little creep; he made me so angry when he refused to do the work. Cocky little bugger!' It's almost impossible to embrace this style of discipline and still maintain a *rights* focus in teaching.

Teachers who are highly demanding and authoritarian (rather than authoritative) are often hostile and overly critical, rude, or in some cases plain aggressive. They make little or no effort to manage their own frustration, apparently not caring about the effect of their behaviour on others. Some are even proud of such a stance. The strap may have been abolished but the power of the tongue to damage should never be underestimated. An easy option is to explain away teacher style in terms of mere personality. While it is obvious that we differ in personality, we have a professional duty to eschew the hostile, rude and aggressive styles of discipline; not because they don't work but simply because of their in-built capacity to disenfranchise students of their due rights. There are degrees of demanding behaviour in teachers of course, but these are the characteristics of the authoritarian demanding teacher:

■ demands compliance ('I must have it')
■ has demanding beliefs about his role and student behaviour, rather than preferential or flexible beliefs ('I *must* win' rather than 'It's preferable to resolve this with minimum heat')
■ tells rather than asks or directs
■ threatens rather than gives 'choices' (within a fair rights and rules framework)
■ will resort to humiliation, sarcasm, even verbal aggression
■ minimises or disenfranchises students of their rights
■ uses a sharp, even caustic tone of voice
■ employs an unreflective, unplanned verbal repertoire in discipline: 'If I have to tell you one more time', 'I'm sick and tired of telling you', 'You dummy!', 'What's wrong with you?', 'I've told you a thousand times!', 'Can't you get it by now?', 'Are you thick or what?', 'Don't …'
■ makes snide comments such as: 'What kind of home do you come from?', 'Were you brought up or dragged up?', 'Don't they teach you any manners at home?', 'Wipe that smile off your face!'

Expecting compliance: the decisive teacher (democratic)

Ms C is a second-year teacher at a secondary school. It's Year 7, term one, week four. The students are still testing her out somewhat.

In the first week she developed clear rules for each of her classes, she explained the need for rules (to protect rights) and involved the students in the process of formulating them. In her classroom, the rules are displayed on one wall. Like the previous two teachers she faces a common range of disruptions from calling out, butting in and out-of-seat behaviour through to teacher-baiting and defiance.

However, unlike Ms A and Mr B, she has planned her management and discipline repertoire ahead of time. She knows, all too well, the disruptions which are, in a sense, inevitable and has developed a 'discipline plan' in concert with her lesson plan.

Her lesson on multiculturalism will include a class discussion, small group work and a written exercise. She settles the class down by consciously encouraging the quieter members, not in an obsequious way, but simply with, 'Thanks for settling down', as she looks in their direction. Finally only a few are still talking. 'Okay, time to start.' This arouses their attention. The class is looking up-front. She welcomes the class with a 'good morning everyone' and explains carefully what they will be doing that lesson. She has a chart on the board with key points for 'visual learners'. She regularly uses language such as 'we will', 'our class', 'our assignments'. This is not accidental. She believes that each class is a community and this affects the way she relates to them, even in her choice of language. Damien is slouched back in his seat, leaning back against the rear wall. It's annoying, distracting. Ms C briefly cues him with a non-verbal signal: she makes eye contact and extends her first three fingers down, with thumb, to indicate 'four on the floor'. On day one she had used this cue with a brief verbal reminder, 'Damien, "four on the floor" thanks.' Today the non-verbal cue is enough. She will have a chat with him after class if he continues to seat-lean in a disruptive way.

The inevitable calling out is prefaced by a general whole-class rule reminder as she scans the class. 'Okay, you all know our rule for communication. Let's use it thanks.' Ms C then quickly looks for a hand up to reinforce the rule. If a student is calling out she will either *tactically* ignore (if just one or two) or give a brief, clear reminder of the rule, or simply direct the student to act fairly. 'Stella, you know our rule for communication—use it thanks', or 'If you want to ask a question put your hand up. Good on you.' The little phrase 'Good on you' is used to communicate, 'I know you'll comply. I expect you'll comply.' She speaks firmly, with eye contact, *expecting* compliance. She will then confidently resume the flow of the lesson by giving 'take-up time' (see p. 57). This conveys her expectation and authority to lead and teach. As Kyriacou (1986) and Robertson (1996) note, the tone, manner and body language when

delivering instructions can convey and imply an expectation that students will accept the teacher's authority. The teacher's tone, manner and kind of (and use of) language determine whether the teacher's style is authoritarian or authoritative. When an authoritative approach is matched with interest and enthusiasm for subject, topic and lesson, and caters (as far as one can) for differences in ability, then the management dynamic is far less stressful. 'If one behaves as though one has authority, it is surprising how far this attitude exerts a momentum of its own, leading pupils to behave accordingly ... effective teachers are able to take account of subtle signals and cues to know when a clash of wills with a pupil should be engaged in and when averted' (Kyriacou, 1986, p. 132).

Usually a simple direction or rule reminder is enough. Ms C doesn't preach or over-attend but is economical with her words. She has learned that it is important to be:

∎ brief (minimal attention)
∎ clear
∎ rule-focused
∎ calm but expectant
∎ assertive where the situation requires it.

When Jason starts tapping his book she tactically ignores it for a while. When it doesn't stop she addresses him. 'Jason I'm trying to teach. I can't teach with that noise. Ta.' That's all. No big deal. Just a hand extended and then very quickly she focuses on on-task students to bring attention back to the lesson.

Maria comes in late for the third time in two weeks. Ms C knows there are some home problems. Maria slams the door, throws her bag down. The class, naturally, turn to check this out. Ms C walks over. Maria quickly blurts out, 'The bloody bus was late, I tried to get away early!' Ms C doesn't waste time arguing about the veracity of the story or the 'bad' language. 'Look, I can see you're uptight. Grab a seat, I'll be with you in a sec.' Later in the lesson she'll have a quiet word with Maria about a late pass and team her up with a peer to conference the work she has missed.

There are several more calling-out episodes. Most she plainly ignores, a couple of persistent students she gives brief directions to. Winding up the class discussion she explains the set written activity and sends them off in groups for the on-task phase of the lesson. Nicko comes up immediately, as the class reorganises itself and says, 'Miss, I haven't got a pen!'

'What are you going to do then Nicko?'

'I can go to my locker Miss! Won't take a minute (grin, grin)!' Is he after a free five minutes? 'Well, you know the routine Nicko. You can borrow from a mate or borrow one of mine.' (See p. 27.)

'But Miss, it won't take a minute!'

'Your choice Nicko.'

'Gees, it's not fair.' He walks off sulkily. She ignores him, having already moved off, *expecting* compliance. She makes no comment about his sulky behaviour. She doesn't feed his procrastination. She leaves him with a clear, simple, fair choice.

Ms C would like to sit down and have a break but she realises the importance of moving around the room to direct, encourage, assist, redirect, correct and support her students. She musters as much enthusiasm and humanity as she is able. At all times she seeks to model respect even with those few students she doesn't actually like. Walking past Danni she sees her (out of the corner of her eye) leaning back provocatively on her chair. She could simply direct her, 'Sitting, thanks Danni' or remind her of the rule, but has decided to *tactically* ignore her. She uses a lot of tactical ignoring for low-level attention-seeking. Because she has that crucial teacher skill of being able to notice what students are doing without making direct eye contact, she is able to see *when* Danni stops leaning back on her chair. She then walks over and causally asks her, 'How's it going then?' In other words, she looks for as much on-task behaviour as possible and *then* visits the student to encourage her.

If she wants to see a student's work she doesn't snatch it, poke at it, or even just pull it towards her. She asks politely, 'Can I have a look at your work?' or 'Where are you up to?' or 'Having trouble, need a hand?' She doesn't invade a student's 'personal space' or 'territory' but respectfully asks them to turn the book, or work so they can both see it. If she meets a (rare) student who says, 'No, you can't see it', she simply says, 'Okay, when you're ready' and moves off. She doesn't over-attend to such students, who often use tactics like this as a form of attention-seeking, rather like the child who says, 'I'm dumb!', wanting the teacher then to say, 'Oh, don't say that, of course you're not.' She will, however, always speak to these students after class or make an 'appointment' to speak with them about their classroom behaviour to work through the issue as early as possible (see p. 96).

As the teacher continues moving around the room, Jason, keen to get her help, employs his get-the-teacher-here-quick routine. 'Miss, hey Miss!' he calls out across the room as the teacher is assisting two other students. Should she go over to Jason or ask him to wait? If she does either she may easily be saying to Jason, 'Your calling out will be noticed and attended to any time you try it on.' She decides to tactically ignore Jason. She neither looks in his direction (though she can see him out of the corner of her eye) or comments on his behaviour; she continues working with the other two students.

Jason calls out again. 'Miss, come on, Miss. I need your help!' Ms C decisively continues the tactical ignoring. She moves off to work with another student. As she is talking to Boris, Jason starts clicking his fingers and sighing. 'Gees, Miss, what's wrong? I only want to ask a question.' By tactically ignoring Jason, she sends a message saying, 'Yes *when* you are on-task, quiet, I'll come over', or 'When you put up your hand *without* calling out then, yes, I'll come over, I am not at your instant beck and call.' Ms C seeks to communicate all this by her tactical presence. Students quickly pick up this silent, but decisive, semaphore.

Jason sulks for a while. Ms C keeps on doing the rounds. She notices, in passing, that Jason is now writing. She goes up to him and casually asks, 'Can I have a look at your work? How's it going?' and reaches down to turn the exercise book so she can view his work. Jason moans, 'Why didn't you answer me before?' Instead of getting into a debate with Jason, she simply, quietly, reminds him of the rule. 'When you put up your hand and wait, then I'll happily come over.' Smiling, she quickly directs Jason back to the written work. In time she will develop a conferencing/teacher-assistance roster. It is important to clarify routines for getting reasonable teacher assistance.

If this calling-out behaviour had occurred in a primary setting with prep to Year 3 students, the teacher may have said, 'Jason, *when* you can put your hand up and wait, then I'll come over and help', and *then* tactically ignored any subsequent calling out.

Ms C is also conscious of a contingency plan for Jason's calling out. If tactical ignoring and positive reinforcement are ineffective, she will give a firm rule reminder, or restatement, or a clear, simple direction. 'Jason, if you want to ask a question, use the rule please.'

As she continues her rounds she sees Sally and Marisa teasing Antonella. The noise level rises quickly and can't be ignored. Seeing Antonella crying, she calls across firmly, decisively, to the other two, 'Sally, Marisa, I'll see you over here *now*.' She pauses, establishing eye contact and extending her hand as if directing them to the rear of the room. '*Now*, thank you.' The teasers sullenly move off down the back of the class, the rest of the students resume work, watch, or whisper.

Ms C takes the teasing students aside to minimise any embarrassment to Antonella, but also to reduce blame shifting and hostility with the teasers. Ms C walks to the back of the room and asks the question, calmly, quietly, 'What's going on? You can see Antonella's upset.' She uses an approach that puts responsibility quickly on them by asking, 'What are you going to do about your behaviour?' She doesn't have time for the full story but simply asks the question firmly to engage responsibility now. By taking the students aside, she can afford to be more discursive. She will also follow up after class (see p. 96).

Later in the lesson, Michael wanders out of his seat to talk with Alex. The two of them are talking quite loudly. She finishes what she is saying to Maria (the student who came in late) and decides the Michael–Alex noise incident can't be tactically ignored. Walking past a gum-chewer, she merely indicates with her hand to the mouth, 'In the bin thanks.' She winks at Paul, who drags himself off to spit his chewy into the bin. As she comes over to Alex and Michael she establishes eye contact by firmly saying, 'Michael, what are you doing?' Most students say, 'Nothing!' Michael, however, is a bit of a 'hot shot'. 'What's it look like I'm doing?' She doesn't take his bait. She focuses in on his behaviour. 'It looks like you're out of your seat and talking loudly to Alex.' 'I was just getting a rubber—fair dinkum!' Again, she doesn't take the bait, she merely asks, 'What should you be doing?'

'I told you I was just getting my rubber.' Rather than argue, she simply repeats the question, 'What should you be doing?' She knows all too well the fruitless, pointless procrastination game. She asserts, by her question, the clear implication of responsible behaviour, expecting (not demanding) compliance. Michael gets up to move off. The moment he moves, she walks away as if to say, 'I knew you'd cooperate, I'm not going to stay around to push you!' He could, of course, refuse to move. I have had many students say, 'No, you can't make me.' Like Ms C I usually say, 'True—it's your choice. If you don't move now, I'll have to ask you to stay back and we'll discuss why later.' Most students do move.

This is an important stance to take with older students. If we merely stand with folded arms and a foot tapping, we communicate that we believe they'll only move, obey or respond because we are there. With younger students, kindergarten to Year 2, we may need to stay close, establish eye contact, repeat the rule if necessary. But, again, the moment they go, move off to work with other students.

When he gets back to his seat Michael sulks and folds his arms. Now and then he grunts and scrapes his chair on the floor. She ignores this regressive sulky behaviour. In fact, she will purposefully ignore it until he picks up his pen again. She knows that if she goes back either to coerce or plead or 'make' him work, she is giving attention at the wrong time.

Ms C combines several approaches in a dynamic way. At one moment a simple direction, another time a rule restatement. She may distract or divert a potential disruption by moving alongside a student, asking a question, or giving a task. If behaviour becomes disruptive beyond a simple direction, warning or question, she will then give a simple choice or take the student aside. It is not easy. She has to think ahead to ensure that her behaviour is appropriate for the disruption. For example, when Lee drops her pencil case and swears, she will deal with it differently from when Lee swore at her in one of her temper tantrums.

Maybe it would be easier to shout, yell, intimidate, to be sarcastic, cruel or immature towards her students, but she realises that giving in to mood, chance or circumstance creates a poor learning environment and models the very thing she is trying to work against. There are no short cuts to good discipline.

Ms C also works hard at establishing good working relationships with her students. It is easy to miss the significance of this. If we only ever visit the difficult students to 'discipline' them, then the relationship becomes lopsided. We need to be scanning the room to pick up those times when a student *is* on-task. In doing this, we encourage the student to build on small successes and consolidate those appropriate behaviours.

Like the other two teachers (indecisive/*laissez-faire* and authoritarian/demanding), Ms C still gets frustrated and angry from time to time but she has learned to use those emotions to her advantage. She doesn't deny them or bottle them up inside but uses the emotions to respond. She has learned to recognise how the emotion comes and then to reassess the threat quickly as she perceives it and respond appropriately (see Chapter 8).

Dean, the class 'toughie', swore at her on the second day. She communicated her anger assertively. 'Dean, I don't speak to you like that, I don't expect you to speak to me like that. Ever!' She was tense, but controlled. There was unambiguous anger and assertion in her voice. Later, at the end of the lesson, she called him over to discuss his behaviour and obtained the apology she would not have received if she had demanded it at the time of the outburst.

Uncontrolled, irrational, undisciplined anger ('You idiot, you dummy you!' 'I'm sick and tired of your stupid, idiotic behaviour—

get out!') or internalised, repressed anger is damaging to both health and personal relationships. We can't eliminate the emotions of frustration and anger but we can learn to utilise them. We can only do this if we plan the discipline environment rather than react to disruptions as they arise.

Decisive discipline is marked by these characteristics:

▮ a focus on the due rights of all
▮ an intervention style characterised by a least intrusive to most intrusive approach, with an emphasis on a wide language repertoire at the least intrusive level of intervention, only moving to most intrusive as circumstances and situation really merit
▮ an assertive stance—neither aggressive and hostile nor passive and capitulating to student demands (Essentially, assertion communicates one's own need and due rights without trampling on the other parties' rights.)
▮ a refusal to rely on power or role-status to gain respect
▮ speaking and acting respectfully even when frustrated or angry
▮ choosing to respond to discipline incidents (from prior reflection and planning) rather than reacting to incidents as they arise
▮ planning for discipline as rigorously as any aspect of the curriculum, especially in terms of the language used and non-verbal behaviour.

When actually disciplining, a teacher with a decisive approach engages the student by:

▮ establishing eye contact
▮ speaking clearly with appropriate firmness
▮ speaking briefly, addressing primary behaviour and tactically ignoring as much of the secondary behaviour as is possible
▮ conveying an expectation of compliance rather than demanding or merely hoping for it
▮ re-establishing working relationships as soon as possible.

Contrasting teachers

I like to draw—I've always liked to create visual images, cartoons, picture stories. At school I used to 'secretly' draw pictures during a lesson, or draw little pictures up and down the margin of my class book, especially when I was bored. I'd show it to my mate sitting next to me and whisper (it had to be whispers in those days). I recall one teacher marching over to my desk and poking me in the shoulder saying, 'Were you brought up or dragged up, Rogers?' The class went quiet, all eyes on us. I was angry with the implied put-down of my family; I stood up facing the teacher and said, 'It's none of your bloody business', and walked out of the classroom, my heart racing, every eye on my back as I made for the door. He, and the class, stood in 'dumb silence' (a few were grinning—silently cheering). I was 15.

Some of the other teachers used to tear a page out of my book, even throw the book in (mock?) rage across the room, 'This is not an art class, Rogers!' If we were late, we were publicly embarrassed in front of our peers. Some teachers even managed to get the class to laugh at some unfortunate 'disruptive' pupil as a form of 'public discipline'.

I can remember the teachers I liked, respected and related to. My art teacher encouraged me in my drawing and painting even though I was colour-blind. She never put me down, made fun of me, or criticised me. She did give me *feedback* on my strengths and weaknesses (see p. 231). I sat a national art examination on the strength of her encouragement—and passed! I enjoyed art.

One of my English teachers saw me drawing in my English book one morning. She leaned over and said, 'Billy (like my art teacher, she always used my first name) that's a very interesting drawing. Look at the features on that bird! (I'd drawn some birds flying across my 'English'.) Wow! I didn't realise how well you drew ... but (here she gave me a friendly frown) what are you supposed to be doing?'

'My writing, Miss.'

'Well, I tell you what, Billy, if you leave the margins for me to write in, and only draw when you're supposed to I might have a special art project in class for you to do for us.' (I was 11 at the time.) I worked flat out for her. My 'reward' was (whenever I'd finished my formal work) to work on a large poster of the houses of Parliament and Big Ben with the River Thames. It took me ages.

I was late to science one day. I was 15. I rushed into class, puffing, and the white-coated teacher walked across to me (the class were working on displacement of liquid by mass—the Archimedes principle). 'Hello Bill. You sound a bit puffed, eh?'

I panted out a 'Yes, sorry, the bus was late.'

'That's okay Bill; we're still working on the topic, you know where we measure the displacement of water? But get settled and then team up with Malcolm, that okay?'

'Yeah.' I immediately *felt* better, worked better and even remembered the topic.

Teachers can, and do, make a difference when they:

▌ demonstrate interest in the student, as a person
▌ demonstrate and show some enthusiasm for the topic and lesson
▌ tune in to how the student might be feeling
▌ recognise the student's 'individuality'
▌ keep the respect intact—even when they have to discipline or 'punish'
▌ don't hold grudges and give the student a right of reply and a fresh start
▌ support the student (I remember Mr Randall particularly helping me with some references for employment. He spent a lot of time getting them just right.)
▌ encourage the student.

Classroom management: planning and skills

A theory must be tempered with reality.

Jawaharlal Nehru

The specific skills advanced here follow on from those explored in the case study of the decisive teacher (see pp. 40f). For these skills to be effective in the dynamic setting of a classroom, a teacher will need to recognise the crucial importance of fundamental discipline protocols (see pp. 14f). These skills are discussed in the context of typical classroom disruptions from 'low level' to 'high level'.

It is worth restating that the purpose of these skills is to enable the teacher to act in a more decisive, non-aggressive way; to use those forms of discipline that are more likely to encourage some degree of self-discipline in the student and enable on-task learning to take place. Discipline has an educational focus; the aim is to create the least stressful, most positive environment for teaching and learning.

Levels of disruption

It is not easy to rate a disruption as 'low', 'medium', or 'high level'. To one teacher, pen-tapping may be no problem; something which can be ignored. But if it is persistent, pen-tapping, on a hot day, in the middle of an important explanation by the teacher, can be quite a different matter. How disruption is perceived is also important. 'Do I perceive it as a threat to me personally?' 'Is my authority in question?' 'How seriously does it affect my right to teach or other students' rights to learn?' 'How frustrated am I feeling when …?' Teachers have different levels of tolerance to frustration. One teacher may effectively deal with some calling out by the use of tactical ignoring and reinforcement, while others feel compelled to 'shh' at every instance of rule-breaking or constantly remind those who call out of the rule. Teachers' ability to effectively manage disruption will depend on the degree to which they can effectively cope with frustration, the sort of discipline skills they possess, and how confidently they can use those skills when required.

Children understand when we have bad days. If we're really feeling frustrated or even angry about something, far better we telegraph that to the class (or the individual) than hold it in and give ambiguous signals. 'Okay everyone, I'm feeling frazzled today. I'm not my normal, relaxed self! If I sound snappier you'll know why. I don't want to go into details. It's not your fault (well partly it is!). Let's move on.' They'll know from our body language that we're being honest.

Developing a discipline plan

Few teachers would enter a classroom without some sort of lesson plan. It is surprising that many teachers, even some of the very experienced, will enter a classroom knowing that calling out, butting in, students with 'no pens', restlessness and mobile behaviour may well occur, yet not strategically plan for them in the sense of seeking answers to the fundamental questions:

■ What will I do when …?
■ How can I best deal with X behaviours?
■ When is the best time to intervene in a disruption?
■ What will happen if my initial approach is ineffective?
■ What are my contingency steps?

Imagine these situations:

■ You've completed your description of metric number on the board and you ask for questions. Five students call out, two call out with their hands up. What do you do?

■ You've asked two students to settle down, and one of them starts to argue. What do you do?

■ Mia starts flicking elastic bands at Nadia during maths. What do you do?

■ A student wanders out of his seat for the fourth time. What do you do?

■ Andrew throws a tantrum. What do you do?

It is helpful to have a kind of hierarchy of possible interventions in mind; a repertoire of actions that will enable us to take a decisive stance in the demanding context of a classroom. It can stop us from falling into an unnecessary faltering or reactive stance when someone butts in on our lesson delivery, or when a student starts the game of 'let's see how long I can keep you discussing the merits of my case'.

The possible actions are best thought of as 'steps' to take, given certain disruptions. These steps would range from least intrusive teacher action to most intrusive teacher action, as the circumstance demands; that is, the degree to which the disruption is affecting others' rights. Each step or suggested action is set in the context of common disruptive incidents occurring in the classroom. The language of each 'step' can be modified to suit the age or maturity of the child but the basic purpose of each step is generally relevant at any age level.

The language of correction and discipline

Often, the last thing we plan for is what we'll say in discipline contexts. By planning ahead we can minimise (not eliminate) unnecessary arguments and no-win dialogue. Even in those rare situations when we have to exit a student from the room, some language approaches will be more effective than others. For example, rather than 'losing it' altogether ('Get out, go on get out! I'm sick of stupid behaviour. You're an idiot! You never listen do you? eh? Well I'm not putting up with it do you hear? You can get out of my classroom now! Go to the deputy principal. He gets paid more than I do!'). The teacher could direct the student aside. 'Michael (use the child's first name), it's not working. I've asked you several times to (or not to …) I want you to leave the classroom now and go to … I'll follow up with you later.' Of course this presumes the school (or faculty) has a well-thought-out and workable time-out plan (see p. 165). The teacher's voice is assertive and firm, not loud or aggressive. She is not pointing at the student or gesticulating or salivating. She does sound convincing, however, even though her voice is not raised. The student leaves, heading off to the office, muttering a few swear words. She tactically ignores this (see p. 59). She will follow up and follow through later (see p. 96). If the swearing had been loud she would have addressed it (see p. 295). Her approach is not accidental, nor is it 'merely' the product of personality or 'chance'. She chooses to discipline in this way.

I know I've said some stupid and unhelpful things when I've been angry but I've learned that I can make an assertive, and necessary, point (through language) without 'losing the plot', even when angry. It isn't easy—it requires some reflection, some planning, and practice. For some teachers it will also require some attitudinal change (see pp. 279f).

Non-verbal behaviour

I was watching a colleague address a Year 11 class one day. He was bouncing up and down on the balls of his feet. At the back of the classroom I noticed several boys involuntarily tracking the up–down movement of the teacher with their eyes. I've watched teachers pace the front of the classroom and students track the teacher's pacing (and consequently find it difficult to listen to the teacher).

A teacher gives the class a pack-up reminder before the bell goes. She is walking around while talking. '… and don't forget felt-tip pens, and also the chairs. Don't leave them out like last time …' She's lucky if half the class are listening because half are still working and some are watching her but not really listening. The class reminder would have been more effective if the teacher had gone to the front of the classroom, used an attention-getting signal, and *then* given some brief, specific verbal reminders. The position at the front of the room signals that here, up-front, is where we engage the whole class's attention, to direct, to remind or for active teaching or class discussion (see p. 185).

Non-verbal behaviour is a very powerful and significant factor in our classroom management style. I heard Robert Rosenthal (Harvard University) comment on this in a TV lecture: '... non-verbal behaviour is everything we do, omitting all the words.' That's a lot. Eye contact, proximity, tone of voice, tactical pauses, body language (big gestures as well as micro body language). The teacher who comes into a student's personal space 'face on', casually lifts the student's work from the table and stands reading it with a frown and sigh communicates a great deal—non-verbally.

When we come into a student's personal space it is important not to crowd, not to put fists on the table in some display of power.

Expectation, decisiveness, humour, jadedness, degrees of frustration or anger, confidence are all communicated non-verbally as well as through our words. Given a choice between non-verbal and verbal in terms of significance and 'weight' in a personal transaction, students will opt for the non-verbal meaning.

Positive language, the actual words, can be made negative purely by tone of voice (dismissive, cursory or sarcastic) and gesture. 'Yes ... you can go to the toilet when I've finished the story.' Try saying that in a negative or sarcastic tone with raised eyebrows and twisted mouth. You can see the weight that is given to a transaction by non-verbal behaviour. Conversely, a simple signal of thumb and forefinger turning (as if twiddling a volume knob) can be an effective non-verbal cue delivered across a classroom (see p. 65) to two students talking loudly during on-task learning. But if the same non-verbal cue were delivered with an aggressive body movement, it would destroy any positive meaning the cue might have had.

Indecision, a lack of confidence, non-assertion are all conveyed through body gesture and voice tone. Students can pick up very quickly how confident, serious, expectant we are by how our voice sounds, how we stand not slouched, or casually leaning against the board or sitting down during the instructional phase of the lesson in, say, a Year 9 class—sitting down is entirely appropriate during the instructional phase in an infant class.

Characteristic tone

It is the characteristic tone of our voice and body language that matters. Children know our humanity too well, and they know we're fallible (like they are). We have bad days, we lose (and find our temper), we nag, we say the inadequate, the inappropriate and (sometimes) the wrong thing.

We need to forgive ourselves and others for our bad days—and theirs. We also need to distinguish between bad-day syndrome and bad *habits* in our discipline style. If we apologise when we've said the wrong thing, or have been 'unthinking' about our behaviour and its effect on others, children are normally quite willing to accept and forgive.

The tactical pause

The tactical pause (…) is an effective way to increase attention when communicating. The first word said a little louder than usual, 'David', followed by a pause, says (non-verbally), 'I'm waiting for, and expect, your eye contact and attention.' When addressing a whole class the tactical pause also gives take-up time. 'Settling down. Thanks (…)' The pause allows that the class do just that. The teacher then steps her voice down (beyond the initial 'lift') and completes the whole class direction. 'Facing this way thanks (…) and listening.'

Take-up time

Take-up time is the expectational cue we give a student when we turn aside, or walk away a few steps, after having given a direction.

The teacher notices a student hitting another 'playfully' with a ruler during on-task learning time. She calls him over. 'David (…) I'd like to see you over here for a minute thanks.' The teacher then turns aside as if the student will come. She doesn't face him and eye-ball until he comes. This would convey unnecessary confrontation. The teacher gives a directed 'choice' to a student about the baseball cards on his table. 'Kyle … put them in your bag, or on my table thanks.' She then walks away (with peripheral eye contact) *as if* he'll do what she has asked. If he challenges she will refocus (see p. 87) then walk away, giving take-up time. With younger primary-age students she will stay a little longer with eye contact and move off as the student responds. Take-up time enables trust, maximises face-saving and can convey expectation.

A smile

A smile can disarm, defuse tension, encourage, motivate, humanise. At the most basic level it acknowledges the other person. A brief smile to a student or colleague can give a brief, humanising affirmation. Even a wry smile can acknowledge the mutual awareness of life's gristle. It can say (without words) 'You know, that I know you know I know ... I'm with you in spirit.'

Shouting

Shouting (especially frequent shouting) only reinforces that the attention of an individual or the class can only be attained in this way; it may even entertain! Also it establishes an unfortunate pattern of events, especially in the establishment phase of the lesson. Many of us can remember the self-defeating reinforcement of trying to shout a class down (Rogers, 1997).

There are occasions when we need to lift, or raise, our voice for effect—when the class is noisy at the beginning of a lesson, to call a student (or two) across the room so we can speak to them one-to-one.

On these occasions the voice is lifted with a focus word or two, for example 'Excuse me', or 'Class ...', or 'Everyone settling down', or the use of a student's name, 'David ...' The attention is sustained by a tactical pause (see p. 57) and then we can speak at an appropriate level for class or individual attention. Sometimes we'll need to repeat the first attentional cue a couple of times to get their initial eye contact so we can speak to both eyes and ears.

If a class is persistently noisy it will be important to develop a plan to address noise during instructional and on-task times. This is covered in more detail in Chapter 6. Suffice to say, here, that shouting trains the students to expect it. Invite a trusted colleague with some experience in working with challenging classes to assist with a plan. Do it earlier in the establishment phase before restive, loud, class noise is accepted by the students as the norm.

Attention-seeking and tactical ignoring

Nothing is more annoying than disruptive behaviour that seems set on raising a teacher's frustration level. Attention-seeking is a well-developed, learned behaviour pattern in some students.

Little Dean in Year 1 is an expert at home at getting his own way. He starts with a whine and builds it up into a tantrum. He's 'trying it on' with his new teacher. He starts off by calling out across the room while she's assisting students at another table. 'Miss ... (he whines as if he's in pain), come here, I need you!' He puts his hand up and down, up and down, to pretend he's within the class rule. 'Miss, Miss!' Not only does he have low frustration tolerance, he has 'learned' that this behaviour works for him.

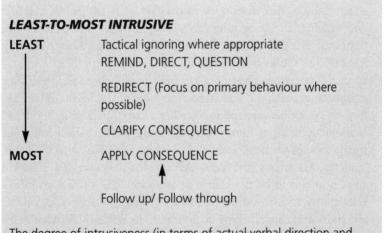

LEAST-TO-MOST INTRUSIVE

LEAST   Tactical ignoring where appropriate
              REMIND, DIRECT, QUESTION

              REDIRECT (Focus on primary behaviour where
              possible)

              CLARIFY CONSEQUENCE

MOST   APPLY CONSEQUENCE

              Follow up/ Follow through

The degree of intrusiveness (in terms of actual verbal direction and emotional weight) depends on how basic rights are being affected (see p. 120). In serious situations it will be important to move to a more intrusive level, say, in clarifying consequences as a *first* step.

Figure 3.1

What will she do? If she just accedes, what does he learn? Whistle dog—and she comes? Miss D cannot decide what Dean will do, only what she will do. She has thought out, in advance, how she can best deal with attention-seeking behaviours. She gives:

- minimal eye contact (at times none at all) and minimal verbal direction when the student is off-task.
- encouragement and attention when the student is on-task.

This is sometimes called 'negative' and 'positive' reinforcement and is found in its most systematic form in behaviour modification. It is discussed here as part of normal classroom discipline, as a form of *tactically* ignoring the child's off-task behaviour until she stops seeking attention in that way and elects to seek it in socially appropriate ways.

Miss D looks across to Dean (without going over to him) and says firmly, with eye contact, 'When you put your hand up and wait then I'll come over and help.' No more. That's enough. She then ignores him. He calls out again, 'Miss! Miss!' and grunts and snorts in a sulky fashion. She continues moving around the room helping, encouraging, directing. She can see out of the corner of her eye (without giving eye contact) what Dean is doing. 'How's it going Maria?' She speaks to a student at a table near Dean. She continues to tactically ignore Dean, hoping that he will then decide to seek attention by putting up his hand and waiting. He doesn't. He drags himself out of his seat and follows her around, pulling at her dress. Without looking at him, saying anything to him, she gently, but firmly, pushes his hand away and continues working with the other students. He tries again. 'Miss, Miss.' He's nearly crying now. He can't bear not to be the centre of attention. She tactically ignores him, gently, firmly pushing him away. After all, he knows the rule. If she starts preaching, yelling or pleading, she will only do what mum and dad do: reinforce by association.

He finally gives up and falls on the floor crying in tantrum style. She walks over to him and around him. He finally goes back to his seat, head in hands and sobs. When a few children say, 'Miss, Dean's crying', without looking at Dean she simply says, 'I know', then distracts them by redirecting them to their work. The other students are secure in the knowledge that their teacher knows what she is doing. The teacher has clarified what she expects and acts accordingly. With older children it can help to have a one-to-one chat about their attention-getting behaviour suggesting (through discussion) what their purpose may be in behaving in such a way.

It takes a lot of effort to tantrum and keep it up. This regression-to-the-cot routine doesn't end in Year 1. 'Tantrumming' is a behaviour many people use all their lives to get their own way. Tactical ignoring is one way of communicating to a child:

■ 'Yes, I'll notice you, talk to you, help you, *when* you're on-task with your social behaviour and your learning. I simply will not accede to your pouting, sulking, clowning, tantrums, or baiting.' (Teachers need a sense of confidence and perspective when using this approach. They need to be secure in themselves.)

■ 'When you are off-task, I will firmly ignore you (my decisive choice) or I'll give you a brief, clear, simple direction (I won't argue, or procrastinate) or I may refer you to the class rules. You can't make me argue with you. You have no infallible magic to ruin my day.'

■ 'In extreme cases of attention-seeking, I will ask you to cool off in time-out, or ask you to leave our room, or have you escorted from our classroom.'

The students in a class are not foolish. They are astute enough to know when a teacher is tactically ignoring attention-seeking behaviours. They know why teachers will let some behaviours continue for a while (calling out, butting in, sulking, clowning, tantrums). I find tactical ignoring especially effective for secondary behaviours (see p. 29). If, for example, I've asked a student to clean up some

mess he's left at his table and he sighs and pouts, yet still cleans it up, I'll tactically ignore the secondary behaviour (the residual sulking) give him take-up time by turning away (to sulk without me watching) and briefly acknowledge his effort when he's finished: 'The floor's clear of litter, felt-tip pens and pencils are away.' If I call a student across to me in the corridor, or playground, and he walks in an exaggerated fashion (with annoyed frowning and sighing), I'll tactically ignore his non-verbal behaviour and keep the focus on the primary issue that I've called him over for. Tactical ignoring has to be exercised confidently by the teacher for the rest of the class to go along with it. It is not an easy skill to use. To be effective a teacher needs to:

■ Use eye-scanning to monitor the disruption without actually looking at the disrupter: for example looking around or past calling-out students until they put up their hand. This is crucial, because tactical ignoring is only a means to an end. When Alison stops her silly noises, then we can include her in the lesson; when the sulker finally gets back to work, then we go over to speak to him; when the low-level clowning stops, we can then go over and ask how things are going. Teachers need to use eye-scanning effectively to make ignoring *tactical*.

■ Know what behaviours you are prepared to tactically ignore. Never, for example, ignore repeated defiance, blatant swearing, high-level noise, unsafe behaviour, offensive sexist remarks or abuse (see pp. 295f).

■ Know how long you will ignore before you need to say or do something. Know beforehand what verbal interventions you will use when tactical ignoring is not working. It is only when we are in control of ignoring that it becomes a tactical and useful tool in discipline. Tactical ignoring often needs to be combined with other discipline strategies and, though a difficult teacher skill to develop, it is a powerful strategy for effective discipline.

■ Recognise that tactical ignoring is inappropriate when several students are disrupting at the same time. In this case we have to use clear, simple, directions to required behaviours or even relocate students if necessary (see p. 86). Tactical ignoring isn't easy, especially when one is tired, frazzled, it's 3.00 p.m. and it's the fifth calling-out or the sixth time a whining student has come up to you asking, 'Did I do good work?' When we are using tactical ignoring to deal with attention-seeking the disruptive behaviour pattern may get worse before it gets better. One of my Year 3 colleagues had a student come over to her one day and whisper, 'If you ignore me I'll get worse.' The hardest aspect to the use of tactical ignoring is knowing when, and what, to ignore. Some teachers will ignore the behaviour they clearly should address and over-focus on behaviours that can be tactically ignored.

There are teachers who object to this kind of ignoring because it looks like the child is getting away with 'it'. 'I'll teach her!' they say. What will you teach her? That your shouting stopped her calling out, that your slamming of a hand on her desk and berating her proved you could get back at her? That every time she calls out you'll attend?

You may say, 'She shouldn't call out!' But she does, she did and she will probably continue to do so. 'I've got to make her learn?' Yes, but how? If teachers struggle with tactical ignoring because they have difficulty tolerating frustration, they are better served by using simple directions or rule reminders. Note, too, that tactical ignoring can often be employed with other verbal strategies.

Diversions and distractions

Part of effective discipline is preventing potential or likely problems from getting out of hand. If you know that Ilun is first off the mark when you ask questions, divert possible calling out by saying something like, 'I know some of you will know the answer almost before I've finished speaking. But I want you to hold off for a while to give others a chance. Okay?' Then, if they do hold off, 'Thanks Ilun and Jilli for waiting. I see you know the answer but I see Vlado has his hand up'.

The teacher has introduced the topic on positive/negative integers. A loud mumbler says, 'We did that last year—what do we have to do it again for?' She knows who mumbled it but diverts the focus by keeping the flow of lesson and 'using' the comment within the topic. 'Some of you may be wondering why we're doing this topic again. Well ...' She looks at the whole class as she says it without eyeballing the student. She hasn't allowed her to divert the lesson.

A Year 1 child was constantly fiddling with her shoelaces, turning to giggle at a friend, pulling at the carpet. I'd asked her to face the front twice. I decided to distract her. 'Isabel, I want you to come up here and hold this board-marker for me.' She giggled as she held it. I asked her to hold it, facing me (away from her friend). 'I'll need that a little later. Ta ... Hold it quietly—thanks.' It kept her quiet for the instructional part of the lesson. Later I took her aside and worked on a one-to-one plan for sitting on the mat during instructional or group time, which included not sitting next to Danni (see p. 180).

'Having trouble getting started Craig?' This to a student gazing out the window. The comment is made, positively, to distract the student back to the task (rather than saying, 'Oi, the work's here'—teacher taps the desk—'not out there!') The teacher then tunes in to what she suspects he might be thinking. 'It can be hard getting ideas started.'

Other ways of distracting or diverting possible disruption are to give a job, rearrange seating, modify routines, have work available for early finishers or, if there is disruption in the early phase of a lesson, call the child aside to speak quietly about his work. 'Sean, are you having any problems? Do you know what to do next?' Invite another student to work with Sean; stay close without giving due attention (tactical ignoring). Use the 'when' statement: 'Sean when you've finished your maths, I want you to give me a hand with this please.'

Sean is supposed to be engaged in a 'cooperative building game', putting a large wooden car together. He picks up one of the wheels and throws it against the wall. The teacher quietly calls him over. 'What are you doing Sean?'
'Nothing', as he hangs his head.
'You threw the wheel against the wall Sean. What are you supposed to be doing?' No answer. 'Come on, show me how you can put the wheel on the car with Maria and Simon.' This diverts his attention to the task at hand.

Non-verbal directions or cues

With some low-level disruption, a wink, nod, brief stare, or frown is enough. It is a form of non-verbal direction that says, 'You know that I know that you know.' It works effectively when the teacher has a good rapport with students. The non-verbal gesture acts simply as a reminder or reinforcer. One useful non-verbal gesture during calling out is to direct an extended hand towards the calling-out student (an open, extended hand like a traffic controller) without looking at the student, and continue on. It can often be combined with tactical ignoring. If students are calling out, I sometimes look in their direction and raise my hand (briefly) to indicate I expect to see a hand up. If a student is leaning back on her chair, I use a non-verbal 'cue' resembling four chair legs pointing down (right hand has thumb and first three fingers extending down). Initially, I find it helpful to give the verbal and non-verbal cues together. 'Ellen (...) four on the floor thanks.' I had a student say once, 'I got four on the floor.' (He had two chair legs and his own legs.) 'Go for six then.' He grinned as I turned away.

Simple directions and desists

A simple direction conveys a message to students that we are directing them to do something about their behaviour. A desist is a direction to students that we are telling them to stop doing something. To be effective, directions and desists should specify the expected behaviour clearly and simply with appropriate firmness.

When Paul, aged five, is out of his seat forgetfully we will direct him differently from Nikki, who has spilt acid on the floor for fun in a Year 8 science class. For Paul it is enough to say, 'Paul, back to your seat, thanks'. For Nikki, one of those rare, and consequently powerful, desists is needed. A raised voice is used to establish contact. 'Nikki, put that jar down—now!' Get the others settled and then get Nikki to clean up. A raised, *firm* voice is different from a shout or scream, which may unsettle or increase unnecessary arousal.

When students engage in dangerous or unsafe behaviour, don't waste time in discussion. Direct as a command. 'Jason! (...) Paul! (...) Stop fighting now.' At this point the teacher will direct the students to sit apart and refocus the watching audience. The teacher will then refocus the fighters: 'You can sort out your personal concerns at recess. We don't fight in class.' Most simple directions, however, can be delivered as reminders to self-control. Deliver the direction quickly and firmly, a few times if necessary. Keep the same form of words. Use the child's name. Mild desists are effective if the teacher has a good working relationship with the children. 'Michelle, use the scissors safely—they're not for playing with' is better than, 'Michelle! I'm sick of telling you ...'

In a busy classroom with competing demands for a teacher's attention, we don't, generally speaking, have time for extended discussions when we need to correct misbehaviour or lead students towards appropriate behaviour.

'There's a mess on the table.' (Describe the situation.) 'Clean it up now—thanks.' (Direct and expect compliance.)

'I can't work with that tapping.' (Express need.) 'Pen down, now—thanks.' (Re-establish eye contact with the whole class and continue on with the lesson.)

> Two students are busily and annoyingly chatting over a comic while the teacher is teaching up-front. It is too loud to be tactically ignored so the teacher gives a clear, simple direction. She addresses the behaviour she wants. 'Michelle, Lisa (direct eye contact, her hand extended towards them) do me the courtesy of facing the front and listening. Put the magazine away too, thanks.' She immediately resumes control of the lesson; expecting compliance, she doesn't invite discussion.

If these had been Year 2 students instead of Year 10, a simple 'Facing the front and listening thanks' would be enough. Sometimes it is enough to simply use the participle form when directing: 'Walking thanks' rather than 'don't run', 'Sitting and facing this way' rather than 'Don't fidget on the mat', 'Using your partner voices thanks' (to a table of louder-than-necessary Year 4s) rather than 'Don't speak so loudly when you're working.'

I saw a Year 8 girl running in the corridor (yet again). I knew her from one of my classes. I said, 'Lisa (...) walking thanks.'
'I'm in a hurry!' she frowned.
'Try power walking then.'
She responded to my smile with a 'toss of the mane', raised eyes and a power stride!

Use the child's first name, and a please or thank you. Adding 'thanks' to a direction (or 'ta') can convey expectation (even a bit of 'persuasion'). With older students, we can often add an 'I' statement with the direction to emphasise the non-confrontational but just nature of the direction.

Sally is fiddling noisily with her ruler during the teacher's up-front explanation. He tactically ignores for a while but it is too distracting. He eyeballs her and says, 'Sally, put the ruler down, I'm trying to teach. Thanks.' The implicit expectation is clear but also positive. He throws in the 'thanks' as a mitigator to the direction and as a statement of belief that says, in effect, 'I know you'll cooperate.' He then briefly smiles and turns immediately back to the class and continues the lesson. It is surprisingly effective.

With younger children

If small children are over-excited and appear not to hear a direction the first time, it may be necessary to establish eye contact and repeat it. Small children need very clear rules for behaviour and brief, clear reminders, not nagging dialogues. If the boundary is uncertain and unenforced, the children will be insecure and act out their insecurity via their disruptions. A teacher will need to enforce routines regularly for safety, movement, tidying up and so on, especially with small children. But, again, respectful treatment is the key; staying calm, but speaking and acting firmly.

There is no point arguing, discussing, debating with a five-year-old who is uptight, frustrated, anxious, angry or confused. What children need most from their teacher when they're in such a state is direction, even if such direction means removal from the scene of frustration for time-out. Remember:

▮ Keep the direction simple and brief. Focus on the *behaviour* expected rather than behaviour you don't want to see. Lee and Jason (Year 8) were fiddling with the venetian blinds during instructional time. 'Lee and Jason, leave the blinds and facing this way thanks.' Lee said he wanted more light. 'We'll organise the light later. For the moment, face this way and leave the blinds. Ta.' After a very brief pause, I resumed the lesson.

▪ Convey, non-verbally, that you expect their compliance.

▪ If necessary, with younger children stay close and repeat.

▪ Stay calm, unemotional, using a calm, clear voice—firmer when necessary.

▪ If they refuse, or become disruptive, make the consequences clear (see p. 86).

Observational language

The teacher is moving around the room (during on-task time). He notices bits of paper littering the work area and several lids from the felt-tip pens. 'Hannah (…) there are several lids off the felt-tip pens, and there's a fair bit of paper on the floor.' He says it quietly in passing. He could have asked why: 'Why is there so much mess here? And look at those pens. They won't last long like that, will they?'

Sometimes the observation can be given in a single word, in passing. 'Mike (…) pens.' 'Angela (…) floor.' This approach relies on the teacher having a positive working relationship with his students, and a pleasant tone.

Observational correction is often combined with behavioural directions. Several students are talking at the beginning of instructional time. The teacher looks in the direction of the talkers (without moving across to them and giving unnecessary attention) and briefly describes what she sees. 'Several students are talking (…) I need you to face this way and listen thanks.' She gives a brief tactical pause and resumes the flow of the lesson. I've used this approach a number of times with large groups in assemblies. This is to be preferred over silly questions ('Are you talking?'), challenges ('Do you want to run the lesson, eh?'), negative directions ('Don't talk while I'm teaching'), or just reactive frustration ('You! Over there. Shut it!').

Incidental directions/questions

Lisa and Chantelle were into serious, heavy-weather chewing gum. Chewing gum is hardly a major issue in most schools—however, it is often mentioned in the school rules. As I was moving around the classroom I casually walked across to the duo. I had a brief chat about the work and added, 'By the way, the bin's over there. Thanks.' As I walked away (giving take-up time) they grumbled and walked over to the bin (one spat it, the other dropped it in). Mentioning the bin (incidentally) was a way of directing to the rule—least intrusively. I use this approach at upper primary and secondary levels.

Different class, same scenario.

'Daniel, you're probably looking for the bin—right?'

'Nah!' He looked briefly across to the bin, frowning. 'Well the bin's looking for you!' I remarked, as I walked away.

Restating or reminding via the rules

Refer the individual, or group, back to 'our rules'. 'Michael, you know our rule for lining up.' Sometimes just the reminder is enough. The use of inclusive language helps identify the individual's behaviour as it affects 'our' class. If several students are calling out, a general rule reminder will be appropriate. 'Remember our class rule for ...', or 'In our class it's hands up without calling out.' (Then look for a hand up.)

The rule reminder can also be expressed as a question. 'What's our rule for ...?' (Add in the specific rule area: communication, manners, safety ...)

If a student won't reply, the teacher can restate the rule. 'Our rule is ...' If the student says she doesn't care, the teacher can add, 'Even if you don't, we do. We care. Can you do it anyway?' If she chooses not to, point out the consequences.

If the child starts a discussion, repeat the rule and follow up later. Many low-frustration-tolerance children go into sulk mode when they have been disciplined firmly. If they do, give them a healthy dose of tactical ignoring until they choose to work productively. If they don't, follow up with consequences later (see pp. 96f).

'Simone and Maria, you know our rule for safety with the scissors.' Keep the reminder brief, just the rule, the voice, and firm eye contact. If necessary, show assertion by non-verbal emphasis (outstretched but open hand, making the point). Michael is calling out during the up-front part of a lesson. 'Michael, you know the rule for asking questions—use it thanks.' No more. Keep it brief and then refocus attention on others.

Rule reminders can be used with students of any age. They can be said quietly, humorously or assertively as the situation requires. If John, out of his seat, argues about it, we can reassert the movement rule. 'John, you know the rule for ... Use it thanks.'

Restating the class rules can also be effective with the whole group if noise levels are too high, although the effectiveness of this approach diminishes with frequency. If there is a regular problem with class noise, it is better discussed at a classroom meeting (see p. 185).

Reminders (the verb 'remember ...')

Several students were being silly with their art work, pushing and pulling their pictures (in Year 8 boy–girl hormonal bonding). I walked over and had a brief chat. 'Well, how's it going then? Let's have a look at some of your work.' Having refocused to the task, I walked away leaving them with a reminder. 'By the way (scanning all their eyes), remember to use your working space thoughtfully.' They knew what I meant. What I didn't need to say was, 'Don't be so stupid with your work, this is an art lesson not a fun park!' If necessary I could have asked the key 'bonders' back at the lesson close for a chat.

'Remember to ...' is more invitational to the ear than 'Don't forget ...'

If students are talking above 'working noise'—'Remember to use your partner voices at this table ...' At the close of a lesson—'Do the next class a favour folks. Remember to put chairs under ...' Sometimes we'll need to add in the 'reasoned reminder'. 'The felt-tip pens dry out quickly. Remember to put the lids back on when you're not using them. Thanks.'

Rule reminders and prep to Year 3 students

One way of giving rule reminders to younger, primary-age students is to use a word that briefly and concisely expresses the required action, or behaviour, implicit in the rule. For example, 'Don't run in the classroom Sandra' becomes 'Sandra (to gain attention, use the child's name), walking'. If two students are arguing, the teacher walks by and says, firmly, 'Scott, Paul, sharing thanks' or 'Helping' or 'Asking'. Rude behaviour receives a 'Manners Natalie' and a student who keeps interrupting is simply told, 'Waiting Anna'. The required action, expressed as a participle, reduces the likelihood of long discussion. Make the point clear, firm and non-threatening, and expect compliance. If the disruption is low-level forgetful behaviour, say it with a smile.

If two students are talking loudly while you are working close by with other students, it may be enough to turn, extend your hand, and say, 'Excuse me Maria, Michelle, partner voices, thanks', and turn back to the students you were working with. Establish eye contact, speak briefly, clearly, expectantly—so expectantly, you will turn away as soon as you have restated the (fair) rule. If the noise continues, then use more decisive steps. It is surprising, though, how effective brief rule reminders are. They are effective because the student is referred back to *our* rules. This puts the responsibility back where it belongs—with the child.

Prefacing

Rather than coming in with immediate correction it is possible (in some contexts) to preface the correction.

Brendon was abstractedly gazing at his motorbike magazine during a Year 10 English class. I'd finished the instructional phase of the lesson and I was moving around the room having a chat here and there, encouraging, refocusing, clarifying etc. I'd noticed Brendon was off-task but tactically ignored it, thinking he might get on with his work. The magazine was clearly a distracter so I walked over, approaching from the side, 'G'day Brendon (…) how's it going then?'

'S'allright, I suppose.' He pushed the magazine aside, covering it with his arm, but I caught a glimpse of the bikini-clad, nubile female form of the motorbike rider—helmetless.

'Interesting magazine Brendon' I said, glancing in its direction. He grinned. 'Yeah.'

'We're talking serious melanoma if she rides like that.'

'What?' (He seemed not to know that term.) I slipped in a brief bit of health ed. 'You know, skin cancer.' He raised his eyes to the ceiling. 'It's just a magazine.'

'I know Brendon—but it's the safety issue that bothers me you see; she's not wearing a helmet.' He sighed, but grinned. I added, 'What are you supposed to be doing at the moment?'

He told me, adding that he hated this subject. 'I remember the feeling. It can be annoying to do work you hate, eh? Can you do it?' (I knew he could.) 'Yeah, I can.' (sigh) 'Okay, give it your best shot. I'll come back and see how it's going later (leaving him with a task-related reminder). By the way, I'd like you to put the magazine in your bag or, if you like, on my table.' This was the discipline part (the corrective part) of our brief interaction.

'I wasn't reading it.' He sighed—must have been tired, poor chap. 'Even if you weren't (…)' I eyed his bag non-verbally and looked at the teacher's desk and moved off ('catch you later'), leaving him with the ownership of the task behaviour. A little later I saw out of the corner of my eye that he was putting the magazine away. I walked over later and had a chat about the work. It's important to re-establish working relationships reasonably quickly.

Prefacing is basically a way of addressing behaviour incidentally within a relational focus. It is not possible in all discipline contexts but it can be applied often during the on-task phase of a lesson and particularly in the playground.

The decisive negative

There is a time to say *no* to children on issues that count. The unambiguous 'not', 'no', or 'can't' is a full stop to pleadings of unfairness.

If children become argumentative about our unilateral 'no', we can add some partial agreement. 'Maybe you do want to go outside to play a game today, but we can't today.' (We will already have given the reason.) We could add, if the students are argumentative, 'What part of "no" don't you understand?'

It's the *overuse* of 'no', 'don't' or 'can't' that's the problem. It creates an unnecessarily negative corrective tone. 'No, you can't go to the toilet. I've just started reading the story.' 'No, you can't work on the computer yet, you haven't even started your first draft. How many times have I said to do the draft first?'

Conditional directions

By rephrasing the negatives we can make the direction more invitational in tone: '*When* you've finished the first draft *then* you can work on the computer.'

Jeff asked to go to the toilet within a few minutes of instructional time (a Year 8 class). I could see the grin on his face (I suspected he wasn't desperate). 'We'll organise the toilet breaks *after* this part of the lesson.'

Melissa wanted to work with the play dough but hadn't cleaned up from the previous activity. 'I wanna do play dough now.'

'*Yes*, you can do play dough *after* you've cleaned up the paper, scissors and pencils here.'

Two ways of saying something

Unconsidered	Considered
'Didn't I tell you to put a margin there—goodness, do I have to keep reminding you?'	'What's missing on the page Dave?' (said casually with a smile).
'Can't you walk? What do you have to run for? I've told you before.'	'Walking, Kylie'—a rule reminder said firmly, with a smile, if appropriate.

Unconsidered	Considered
'You spilt the paint! Can't you be careful? Look at all that mess. Go and wash your hands—you're not doing any more painting now.'	'How can we fix up this mess Paul? Okay, grab the cloth over there.' (Well-planned classrooms have cleaning materials handy.)
'You're not supposed to be playing with the MAB blocks! You're supposed to be grouping them. If you can't use them properly, don't use them at all!'	'That's an interesting shape Maria—now see if you can make them into two groups of ten, as well.'
'Don't grab those scissors! What are you—can't you see he's using them?'	'Lee, you can use the scissors *when* (ever a useful word with younger children) Paul's finished. Okay Paul?'
'Look, I've shown you how to cut out on the line before (sigh, sigh). C'mon Simon give it to me—I'll show you again!'	'You've started to cut out the shape. Show me how you can cut closer to the line.'
'Don't forget to ...'	'Remember to ...' (see pp. 290f)
'Oh, Richard, yes you! You know I mean you—get over here—now! Listen son, I don't care how you speak at home. In my class ...'	'Richard, I want to see you now! You know the rule about swearing.'
'Every time I walk past you two you're talking. I'm fed up with it, do you hear? Now get out, Danielle and move over there!' (She argues.) 'Don't you argue with me. I said go!'	'Keep the noise down thanks, I'm trying to work over here with Michelle and Angela.' The noise continues. 'Danielle and Simone, you know the rule for working noise—if you can't work quietly, I'll have to ask one of you to move.'
'Don't ...'	'Do ...'

Calling out

When children butt in or call out and say, 'I know the answer to that!', a teacher can effectively use a form of tactical ignoring by speaking around such students, making no direct eye or verbal contact. 'Some of you know the answer to this problem already but what I'd like you to do is hang off for a while because we'll be discussing these problems in small groups.' The teacher chooses not to be drawn by such attention-seeking and diverts potential disruption.

Jessica has her hand up and is vigorously clicking her fingers to get the teacher's attention. The teacher's first step is to try tactical ignoring. She becomes more insistent and calls out, 'Look, I'm asking a question, why don't you answer?' The teacher turns, makes direct eye contact, and with an outstretched hand, palm out, says, in a decisive voice, 'Jessica, you know the rule for communication—use it thanks.' She might preface it with 'when ... then ...' No more. She then turns back to the group and continues her discussion.

Some students will call out for attention, some from habit, some from excited anticipation. In the establishment phase of the year the teacher can remind the student that sometimes students are so keen to answer a question (or ask) they first blurt it out. They may not mean to; it might be excitement or habit. The teacher can then explain how it is important to wait rather than call out, as 'it gives everyone a fair go'.

If a student has a habit of calling out and has only a marginal response to public reminders or correction, it will be important to work on a one-to-one plan that can help him focus on the hands-up rule. In this one-to-one session, the teacher could mirror the old behaviour (with the student's permission—see p. 176), model the required behaviour and work on a behaviour agreement to increase the hands-up and waiting aspect of class questions (see pp. 177f).

When reminding older students about their calling out or butting in during a class discussion, a simple 'One at a time thanks' is enough.

Questions

One of the most common teacher questions is the open interrogative 'why?': 'Why are you talking while I'm trying to teach?', 'Why are you calling out?', 'Why haven't you started work?', 'Why can't you ...?', 'Why are you rolling on the floor?', 'Why are you leaning on your seat?'

Some teachers use the hidden interrogative: 'Oi, are you running in the corridor?' 'Are you being stupid?', 'Are you late?' (I'm sure students are tempted to reply 'Of course I'm late!')

Many students (especially at lower primary level) don't know why they're doing what they're doing. Even if they did know they're hardly likely to reply, 'Well I was into some low-grade and active attention-seeking, that's why.' Older children may bend the truth or lie to avoid facing the question. This is normal.

Direct questions

The direct form of a question ('what?', 'how?', 'when?') requires the student to make some value response. It also gives the student the opportunity to focus on what ought to be happening now and allows the teacher to avoid coming in too early with a consequence. ('If you don't ... then ...')

> Simon is out of his seat and has decided to sit and talk with Angie in the desk behind. The teacher walks up beside the desk, giving direct eye contact to Simon. 'Excuse me, Simon, what are you doing?'
>
> 'Nothing, just sitting here—not doing anything wrong!' 'Actually' says his teacher, 'you're out of your seat talking loudly to Angie.' Simon whinges, 'Gees, I'm just talking.' He grimaces and pouts (behaviour that the teacher tactically ignores). 'You're always picking on me!' The teacher asks another question, not taking this new bait for discussion. 'What should you be doing?'
>
> 'My work.'
>
> 'I want you to go back to your seat now, thanks.' (Simple direction.) If he argues, she will reassert the direction or give a simple, clear, choice.

What questions are more effective than *why* questions. They place the responsibility for some sort of feedback on to the student. 'Kerry, what's happening with these unifix blocks?' challenges the child to give feedback. Because most children say 'nothing' to the question, 'What are you doing?', it's more effective to briefly point out what they are, in fact, doing. Not a lecture, but clear feedback by the teacher. 'Actually, you're playing around with it. What should you be doing Kerry?' This asks Kerry for more feedback by directing her back to the task.

Teacher-baiting

Some children give smart answers as their response to *what* questions. 'What's it look like I'm doing?' Children who try this approach are often baiting the teacher. It is generally better to say, 'It looks like you're mucking around with the science equipment. What should you be doing?' If they say, 'Don't know, do I?', tell them (some students say it in a sulky, insouciant tone). If they say, 'Nothing', simply remind them of what they should be doing and redirect them. Be sure to follow these children up later (see p. 96) but at the time minimise unnecessary heat by keeping the dialogue task-focused. If the student's tone or comment is particularly offensive it will be enough to assert briefly, 'I don't speak to you like that and I don't expect you to speak to me like that.' She will then repeat the question, or direct the student to the task or required behaviour.

Giving in to the temptation to take the bait ('Listen smart alec, don't come the raw prawn with me!') is hardly worth it. Keep the transaction brief and focused on the rule and/or task. If the child's agenda is to contest, why give her an audience and a contestant?

Noises, gesturing and posturing

Students sometimes squawk like crows, bark like dogs, snort like pigs or blow raspberries. Certain children will gesture with fingers behind the teacher's back (the index finger sign is a common one), or throw their hands up in acted anger when asked to move away from desks they shouldn't be sitting in.

All children, in some way, seek attention; some children seek to get it in ways that are frustrating and annoying to their teachers. The provocative child gets attention by posturing at the teacher.

The teacher directs Sophia to move because she and her partner are too noisy. She procrastinates. The teacher has already given a choice to the student to work quietly or face the option of moving. 'Why?' says Sophia. 'She (turning to her friend) was talking as well. Why are you always picking on me?' The teacher doesn't get dragged into an interminable debate about justice. He redirects by reasserting, 'Take your books and work over there.' If the child wants to argue, the teacher merely reasserts the simple direction, 'I gave you a choice, take your books and work over there'—firm, non-argumentative and non-aggressive.

Sophia stands up, stamps the foot, snorts, goes over to the other desk, slumps down, glares and folds her arms. Dramatic posturing is another form of secondary behaviour (see p. 29). The teacher has finished this little discipline transaction and now tactically ignores the student's residual sulking. The teacher walks around the room (past the sulking student) working with the other (on-task) students, reinforcing, commenting, chatting briefly, marking, teaching. The sulker waits until the teacher's back is turned and blows a raspberry and then gives a 'two-up'. One smart alec calls out loudly, 'Sophia just stuck her fingers up at you' and then quickly sniggers. The class goes into quiet mode as the teacher quickly replies, without looking either at Sophia or the smart alec. 'Well, I'm glad I didn't see it' and moves on. Thus the teacher does not get drawn into a new debate.

If the sulker picks up her pen, the teacher, with his regular eye-sweep, will casually walk over and give her some respectful treatment by commenting on her work. 'How's it going?' Need some help?' Oh, I see you managed that part.' Many sulkers, when spoken to normally in this way, often speak back, or grunt back, as if to say, 'I don't like you at the moment.' It's emotional pay-back time. They are, in effect saying: 'Why don't you comment on my sulking and pouting and give me attention for it—others do!' Of course, if the teacher starts saying, 'Look don't speak to me in that tone of voice' or words to that effect, it only feeds the residual attention-seeking. The teacher just speaks normally, gives some respectful attention and moves on. He may keep Sophia back later to discuss her behaviour.

Some silly noises can be tactically ignored. If they continue, a teacher can try a firm, simple direction, rule restatement or defusion (humour—where appropriate). If the noise continues, give a choice or remind the child of the rules or perhaps even take the child aside and quickly discuss the behaviour. 'David, either the noise ends now or we'll have to discuss it later.' (Move off.) 'Cathy, you know our rules about class manners.' If the child is young, the teacher may need to withdraw him and explain firmly that crows make nests, they don't do cut and paste in Room 17.

With a student who habitually seeks attention in these ways the teacher is best served by checking with other colleagues to see how general this behaviour is, and making an individual management plan (see pp. 107f).

Persistent crowing or snorting or 'I'm going to get your attention one way if I can't get it another' routines cannot be ignored and are best handled with a clear, firm choice. That includes in-class (or out-of-class) time-out as an immediate consequence. Be sure to follow up later with the student and sort out what the problem is—that is the time to give right of reply. In some cases it may require a discussion with the home-group teacher or year-level coordinator. The issue of follow-up and follow-through is discussed later (see p. 96).

A specific problem

What to do with flatulators?

> Several boys down the back of Ms H's humanities class were abusing the olfactory organs of most of the class members. She wasn't exactly sure who the culprits were. After a couple of sessions of this, she decided on a rather novel approach. Armed with a spray deodorant, she went in the following Tuesday and both heard and smelt the attention-seeking behaviour. A decisive five-second spray and she walked off. There was laughter but it soon settled down. Before the end of the session she quietly said, 'I'll see you four at the close of class.' They protested; she tactically ignored. She directed them to

stay back and discussed their flatulence, future consequences and said, 'Okay, what are you going to do about it?' The problem diminished.

When you are confronted with a problem like this, consider this approach:

■ Give options within class rules.
■ Follow up with students later (see p. 96).
■ Minimise grandiloquence.
■ Remember that regular, respectful consistency will make dealing with such incidents much easier.

Arguing with students

Darren is eating a chocolate bar in class. A minor issue but it is against the classroom rules. It's on-task time, the teacher is moving around the room assisting. She walks over to Darren, gives a brief 'preface' (see p. 71) and directs him. 'Darren, nice chokky bar there (she frowns and winks) ... in your bag thanks.'

'Oh come on, I'm hungry aren't I?'

'So am I, Darren. You know the school rule. In your bag thanks.' She could have said, 'I don't care if you're hungry—put it away now!' What she has done is reassert without arguing.

She is about to walk away to leave Darren to 'own' this minor rule reminder when he adds, 'Gees, it's nearly lunchtime.' The teacher looks at her watch. 'You're right Darren, but it's still a school rule ... in your bag or on my desk.' She almost whispers the last 'choice' as she walks off. She is not upset by Darren's procrastination, nor has she let him argue. She has refocused the main issue and left him with the responsibility of choosing the consequences. He knows, if necessary, that this teacher will follow up with him after class, not just because of the 'eating in class'—but because of this 'choice' not to work within the fair rules.

Arguing with students in front of their peers:

■ wastes time
■ heats up conflict
■ often forces either side into a win–lose position.

By reasserting, giving a choice, taking the student aside, even apologising where necessary, we 'save maximum face'.

Answering back or defiance

When a student answers back or makes a smart or challenging comment, many teachers will say, 'How dare you answer me back! Apologise now!'

'No way ...!' is often the reply. Later, the teacher may say, 'He shouldn't have answered back', or universalise it as, 'No students should answer back to their teacher!' But he did! That's the reality, isn't it?

Of course we prefer students to be amenable but if they aren't, our demands will rarely make them more compliant. The demand, 'Things *must* be this way or I can't stand it!' will certainly cause us to be unnecessarily stressed. It will further decrease the possibility of effective, long-term resolution.

If a student continues to bait or speak aggressively, the teacher can:

- restate the clear rules briefly, or assertively address the student's behaviour
- call the student aside for a quieter one-to-one word
- give a clear choice to remain in the class and work by the fair rules or face time-out
- always follow up such behaviour (see p. 96).

Asserting

There are some comments and behaviours that call for the unambiguous expression of our feelings.

Personal comments

A Year 10 student comments on the female teacher's 'great gear' (her clothes). He says it in a provocative way. She gives direct eye contact. The whole class watches the non-verbal exchange. Speaking from the front of the room she says, 'I don't comment on your clothes and I don't expect you to comment on mine.'

He swivels his head to his mates either side and protests, 'Gees, I was just joking.' She adds, 'Maybe it's a joke to you. It's not to me. I don't expect comments like that. Now (…) let's get back to work.' She looks and sounds confident, convincing. She has judged that *this* comment, in this context, needed a degree of unambiguous assertion. In other contexts it may have been appropriate to use 'repartee'—not now.

Very young children sometimes make unthinking remarks about a teacher's appearance or clothes—they are not intended to hurt.

During the reading of a story to a Year 1 class, I remember a five-year-old boy sniffing my shoe and laughing. 'You got some poo on there, hee hee!' He pointed to my shoe. 'That's right.' I briefly acknowledged and distracted him (and the class) back to the flow of the story. It may be appropriate to point out to older students the unnecessary nature of the remark ('We know that remark is unnecessary right now') then refocus back to the flow of the lesson or dialogue.

The degree of assertion in language and non-verbal behaviour (such as tone of voice) depend on context and behaviour. A comment on a teacher's clothes said softly, in passing, might warrant a quiet drawing of the student aside for a brief one-to-one explanation of what is offensive (if anything) about the remark. The same comment made loudly, in front of a whole class, would occasion a firm, unambiguously assertive direction or command.

Put-downs

A student in one of my Year 8 classes called out to a student in the front of the room. 'Gees, you're a dog-face!' and started to laugh and quickly pulled in several of his coterie, who laughed with him.

I eyeballed him, without moving close, and said, 'Stephen (…) That's a put-down. That language is totally unacceptable here.' He started to argue. 'I was only joking.'

'That's not a joke in our room, ever. It's a put-down.' He started to butt in. I put up a blocking hand. 'I'll speak to you later.' My voice was angry but assertive. Put-downs, if used frequently in class, should be followed up on a one-to-one basis or form part of classroom-meeting discussion on the nature of positive and hurtful language (see p. 192).

An assertive comment refers to the right affected—briefly. 'That language is unacceptable here.' The tone needs to convey our anger but with assertive control. Address the behaviour without attacking the student.

When we're assertive (on issues that count) it is important for the individual or class to hear (and feel) the seriousness of the assertion without it becoming a haranguing session or lecture.

Overlapping

Mr O is sitting next to Paula trying to teach her how to calculate the long side of a right-angle triangle. He doesn't crowd or tower from behind but sits next to or alongside, or sometimes kneels to get to the student's level, to bring the power relationship down to a more 'human' level. While he is working with Paula, he hears Daniel and Dimi talking really loudly. He turns his head and firmly asks, not aggressively or with hostility, 'What are you doing Daniel?' Daniel replies, 'Nothing!'

'Actually, you're talking really loudly to Dimi. What should you be doing?'

'My work.'

'Okay, I want you to get back to work, thanks. Remember your partner voices.' He gives his attention back to Paula.

Mr O did two things while working with one student. He divided his attention briefly and decisively to discipline (question and direct) the two noisy students. This is preferable to running from one mini-crisis to another. Jacob Kounin (1977) called this teacher strategy 'overlapping'. Keeping a regular eye-sweep, a teacher is able to 'overlap' the discipline with the teaching.

Overlapping works when teachers are aware of what is happening in the room. I once worked with a teacher who, apparently, didn't hear the stomping under the desk during the off-task part of the lesson; another whose visual field missed the low-level play-fight on her left; another who completely missed the paper-spitters on his left. That is not tactical ignoring but blind ignorance.

Ms P is working with Mark (Year 1) at his desk. Jess comes up. Ms P notices Jess waiting for five seconds and then immediately turns and reinforces her. 'Thanks for waiting Jess, I'm nearly finished with Mark.' She gently calls over to George, who looks like he's about to muck around with the maths blocks and diverts a possible disruption by giving a simple direction. 'George, sit down, I'll be over in a minute.' She finishes with Mark and looks at Jess's work as she walks across the room. She marks it at Jess's desk then proceeds towards George, noticing two girls pushing and poking in the reading corner. She quietly walks over and gives them a choice. 'You can either both read quietly here, or I'll have to ask one of you to go back to your seat.' She uses brief eye contact. They stop. She moves off as if they will act responsibly. As she walks over to George she reinforces Simon and Con at their desks. 'You're working well on those maths problems. When you've finished you may go on with your spelling words. Okay?' They smile and nod.

She gives feedback; shows she is aware of what's going on. She doesn't let incidents get out of hand. It's pointless waiting until there's a fight in the reading corner, or until Mark gets over to his mate with the MAB. Timing is important in discipline.

When overlapping, keep the following in mind:

■ Correctly target disrupters by briefly focusing on the rule, or behaviour.

■ Discipline from where you are. When working with X, discipline Y and Z from that position.

■ Give simple reminders, or directions—even 'choices'. 'Excuse me Nikki, you can either work by our safety rule or I'll have to ask you to leave the experiment and sit over there.'

■ Be brief in the direction of the disruption, then overlap back to what you were doing. Expect compliance—act as if compliance is the most natural outcome.

■ When the disrupter has settled, go over (some minutes later) and give some specific encouragement. 'I see you've worked out how to do that problem there Dimi—well done. How will you do the next one?'

Choices

Directed choices

Children sometimes bring *objets d'art* to the classroom (footy cards, comics, toys etc.). These can interfere and distract from on-task learning. Rather than snatch up the baseball cards, the teacher asks Jade to put them in his bag or on her desk. (I've never had a student yet say, 'Oh thanks for giving me a "choice" within the fair rules— I'll put it on your desk. No worries!')

Some students will whinge, 'But I wasn't looking at the cards!' Rather than argue, the teacher refocuses the student (but partially agrees). 'Maybe you weren't. However, I want you to put the baseball cards in your work-tray or on my table. Thanks.'

Two students have been talking and restless for ten minutes or so. The teacher has reminded them. Twice. She walks across (she knows not to rush and thereby telegraph unnecessary emotional arousal). 'Danny and Ali, if you're finding it difficult to work here I'll have to ask you to work separately.'

She telegraphs the consequence as a 'choice' before applying the consequence. It is not a threat. It sounds as if she is putting the responsibility back on to them.

Residual sulking

I'd asked Bonnie and Rafa to settle down to their work. They continued in bursts of laughter, culminating in Rafa falling off her chair. I made the 'choice' and consequences clear (as above). A few minutes later Rafa fell back off her chair. 'Rafa (...) bring your books and work over here. Thanks.'

Rafa grumbled and groaned but eventually walked over to the only spare seat (it was fortunate there was one!) and slammed her books down. Sulking. Later in the lesson I went across for a brief chat to re-establish some working relationship.

It is important to communicate to children, especially older children (seven years and onwards), in the language of choice. Empty threats by teachers are quickly seen by children as meaningless.

'One more word, just one more word and it's a thousand lines for you, do you hear?' It is important to focus on their actions and the likely consequences. One way of doing this is to present them with a choice. If we have given a direction, or warning, or restated the rule, or used a question–feedback approach and the child is still behaving disruptively, then she needs to be given a clear 'choice' in the light of appropriate consequences and the fair rules.

Relocation in the room

If a child has been given a choice to work quietly or face moving to another desk and refuses to move when asked, saying, 'I'm not going to move, you can't make me!' (powerbroking time), there is little point in the teacher forcing a no-win battle, or sending the child out with a yell, 'Right, out! Get out of my class!' Agree with the child: 'That's right, I can't move you, but if you choose not to work over there, I'll have to ask you to stay back and we'll discuss the issues then ...', leaving them with a deferred consequence. If the student settles down at this point it is still important to follow up at some stage to address the argumentative behaviour in class.

It's also worth pointing out that few teachers can actually move a big, loud, tough Year 10 or even Year 6 boy or girl. By using the language of choice rather than threat, the teacher can save face on both sides. 'I'll have to ask you to move' is better than 'I'll make you sit down the back' or 'I'll send you out of my class'. If they continue to act disruptively in a way that cannot be tactically ignored, employ the exit and time-out procedures (see Chapter 5).

If a child is persistently calling out, and if tactical ignoring, rule reminder or simple directions are not working, the next step would be to give a choice via the rules. 'Corey, you know the rule for asking questions (or communication or whatever the stated class rule is). If you continue to call out we will have to ask you to leave our discussion.' With smaller children who are persistently rude, brash and aggressive, direct them to sit away from the group or to face exit and time-out procedures.

Most children will stop if the teacher decisively communicates the fair rule in a non-aggressive way. If persistent students do stop calling out through any corrective language a teacher uses, it may still be important to follow up later to remind them of the rule and discuss what they intend to do about persistent rude behaviour (see p. 96).

If relocation is used, it is important to distinguish, in the child's understanding, between isolation from the classroom itself (time-out) and isolation to work away from the group (logical consequence).

Reasserting: dealing with procrastination

Harry is out of his seat for the third time. His teacher ignored the first two excursions, but this time asks him a question. 'What are you doing?' Her voice tone is not hostile, just clear and firm. 'What are you doing, Harry?'

'Nothing.'

'Actually you're out of your seat. What should you be doing?' If he says, 'In my seat' then the teacher would simply respond with, 'Okay, would you get back now.' She would probably add a task-related reminder and then, later, when the child is on-task, go over and ask him how his work is going.

But not Harry, he is resolute. 'I was just getting a rubber from Sean!' He says it as if the teacher is an advance scout for the Inquisition. *If* she responds with 'But you know you should be in your seat' then Harry will drag her into a neat little argument. 'But it's not fair, you never pick on the others.' This teacher is too experienced for that. She knows that if she falls for his attention/avoidance behaviour she only accedes to it and gives him an audience to boot. Turning to face him, she reasserts, 'You know the fair rule for movement in our room.'

'But I was just …'

She calmly repeats, reasserts. 'You know the fair rule for movement. You can either work by the fair rule or we'll need to discuss it later in your time.' He stomps back to his seat and sulks. She leaves him quickly and attends to the other children. She knows sulking is another form of attention-seeking. Not drawn in by it, she waits until he's cooled off. When she notices Harry creep back to his work, she simply walks over and says, 'How's that problem there? Do you understand it?' In other words, she treats him respectfully when he's back on-task. She doesn't berate him with, 'About time! Sulking like a baby! Gee, you annoy me Harry!', or get into a discussion about his sulking and why she had to move him.

Verbal blocking

Verbal blocking is the repeating of the reminder or behavioural direction two or three times. It is the decisive action of a teacher not to get drawn. It may be a simple desist, such as when two whining students come across to a teacher on playground duty. She puts up a gently blocking hand, 'Stop (...), Nikki and Lisa, stop (...)—I'll listen when you're using reasonable voices.' She says this rather than 'don't whine' when students are chatting during instructional time. She names the students, 'Ali and Lee and Jono (...) facing this way and listening thanks.' If they procrastinate ('We were just talking about the work') the teacher will keep the focus on the primary issue and not get drawn. She verbally blocks the comment by *repeating* the direction. Take-up time is important here; having reasserted the direction she gives a brief pause and resumes the lesson flow as if to say 'I expect you to comply.' The lesson is more important *at this point.*

The more quickly we can enable the student to get back on-task, to get some success out of learning and social interaction, the better for all. Later, the teacher can have a quiet word with the students about their behaviour but in the group, at the point of disruption, she minimises audience-seeking by using decisive discipline that is non-hostile but decisive and respectful.

Reassertion is a useful stance to take when a student is plainly out to argue, procrastinate, confuse and confound you. It is simply the restatement of an eminently fair rule, process or decision.

I had asked Darren (Year 3) on two occasions to remember his bathers if he wanted to go swimming. If he forgot them again, he had been told he would not be allowed to go swimming. Despite this, the bathers were forgotten again. Thus, swimming was out. Ready to pit his obdurate little will against this grossly unfair adult, he started his whine, 'But I want to go swimming, it's not fair!' (even though he had been clearly and fairly warned). He got a brief, firm explanation and 'You'll have to miss swimming for this week because you forgot your bathers. You'll have a chance to remember your bathers next week.'

'It's not fair!'

I repeated the same words and then turned to give attention to other class members. I have not got time in a busy class to sit and discuss with a frustrated child. I have to decide what I will do in the best interests of Darren and the class. He tried once more with a well-articulated and acted 'sob'. 'But I like swimming and I want to go!' He stamped his foot. 'I know you like swimming but you won't be going swimming Darren because you forgot your bathers' (reassertion). He humped his way to his seat and sat with his arms folded. Later I gave him a chance to talk and we worked on a simple reminder plan he could use at home. Next week he brought his bathers.

Partial agreement

Sometimes it is appropriate (especially with older students) to extend the assertion by tuning in to the students' secondary behaviour before reasserting. We can do this by partially agreeing with what they say and refocusing back to the primary issue (the required behaviour) or back to the essential right or rule being affected by their behaviour.

Lisa is chewing gum. 'Lisa, you know our rule for gum—in the bin thanks.'

'Gee I'm not doing anything wrong!' (Sulk, pout, arms folded—secondary behaviour.)

'I'm asking you to put the gum in the bin, you know our rule.'

'It's a dumb rule!'

'Maybe you think it's a dumb rule, but I'm asking you to put the gum in the bin.' Here the teacher moves off to give the student some take-up time (see p. 57).

Lisa marches off and makes a scene by throwing it in the bin; a scene the teacher chooses to give no direct eye contact to. If Lisa had refused to put the chewing gum in the bin, the teacher would have left the choice with her: to put it in now or follow up with her later. The teacher would then move off to let Lisa 'own' her decision. It's only gum after all. It's hardly an 'issue'.

With extended reassertions, tune in quickly with an 'I' message, then refocus the student's attention to the appropriate direction, rule, or choice, for example:

■ 'I hate this class!'
'Maybe you do, but I'm asking you to ...'
■ 'You never listen to me!'
'Perhaps you think I don't listen to you, but I'm asking you to ...'

The most common response I get from students on issues like eating in class (or jewellery, or being out of uniform) is 'Other teachers don't hassle us about ...' I find it helpful to agree partially. 'I know it sounds like a hassle, but the rule is clear. In our class chewing gum goes in the bin.'

'I'm not going to get it on the carpet am I?'

'Probably not, it's still a school rule though. The bin's over there.'

Reasserting is our message to the child and the group that there is a time for discussion and that time is not now. Now is when you work by the fair rules of our group, and respond to the fair treatment of the teacher or face the fair consequences (be isolated, stay back and discuss it later or, in extreme cases, leave).

It is a waste of time arguing with children such as Darren. Act. Be firm without yelling or humiliating. Your verbal repertoire should state the case as it is. Normally two or three reassertions are enough. Most students comply even if sulkily or moodily. Repeat the same form of words. This gives the clear impression that you are decisive. 'Ali, you know the fair rule for ...' If they *still* argue, clarify the consequence and leave the 'choice' with them.

Challenging the work

'This work's boring, isn't it?' When a student dishes this one up many teachers see it as an affront to their status and a criticism of their effort when, in effect, the student may be quite right. It may well be boring or apparently irrelevant. The student may be exercising her right to question the curriculum. How this is handled is very important.

A reaction such as 'Listen, smart alec, just do it, okay?' and overly discursive approaches such as, 'Look, I spent a long time preparing this. It's an important part of the curriculum. Be fair!' only prolong hostility or procrastination. A teacher is better served by simply acknowledging the student's feelings and then refocusing to the task, or combining reassertion and simple direction.

Sometimes a student may really be angry about not only doing the work but the subject itself. In a language class a student said to me, 'Gees, I hate doing French. I hate it.' He was doing a worksheet prepared by a colleague. 'It can be annoying doing work you hate' I said, acknowledging how he might be feeling. It didn't take long (and I meant it). The harder part was refocusing him on the worksheet. 'Can you do it Con, the work on the sheet?'

'Yeah, I suppose.'

'I could find another student to give you a hand.'

'Nah, it doesn't matter really.' Sometimes peer assistance can help. If the student has genuine concerns about the work we can acknowledge that and point out that we can discuss the issue personally later—after class, or even raise the issue at a class meeting if necessary (see p. 185). Discussing issues like 'relevance in the curriculum' at a separate, designated time gives students' rights and obligations due weight.

By correcting in this way, we are trying to engage and invite the emerging adult in the child, a willingness to tolerate some frustrations and ambiguities in life (especially school; that place where we spend a third of our waking day). By tuning in briefly to how the student might be feeling we show we can empathise without making the issue a counselling session. It won't help, either, if we ask the student, 'Well, what work do you want to do then?' This has the student setting the agenda. A teacher's capacity to empathise is commonly rated as among the most valued teacher quality cited by pupils (Kyriacou, 1991).

Task refusal

Task refusal is any behaviour which indicates that the student is unwilling to understand or engage in a task or activity. Care must be taken to separate unwillingness from inability to undertake the task. Out of sheer humiliation at not being able to succeed, many students reject a task rather than expose their failure or weaknesses to the class and the teacher. Task refusal is often a mask for inadequacy and fear of failure. In some situations it may be a form of attention-seeking or even a power struggle.

Behaviour	*Setting and causes*
Avoiding the task	
Forgetting the necessary equipment: physical education gear, pens, books, locker keys.	Usually outside the class. The student's goal is to make it difficult to participate.
Lateness to class.	
Truancy or school refusal.	
Rejecting and demeaning the tasks	
Destroying instruction sheets or throwing away textbook.	Usually at the commencement of the activity. An avoidance strategy or indication of power-seeking. 'You can't make me or tell me.'
Verbally passing opinion on the usefulness of the task: 'This work sucks!', 'Bloody rubbish.'	
Procrastinating the commencement of the task	
Continually seeking further instructions about one task.	Inside the class. The student may be trying to remain as unobtrusive as possible. Sometimes it is used as a form of attention-seeking (keeping the teacher busy by constantly coming back to the student).
Taking excessive time in preparation: sharpening pencils, borrowing equipment from others.	

Passive resistance/withdrawal

Accepting instruction sheets and going through the motions but not actually doing the task.	Inside the class
Taking the whole class period to copy out the questions or task instructions.	

Remember to investigate contributing causes for task refusal (for example, the situation at home) as well as use consistent approaches in the classroom.

Strategies for dealing with task refusal

Stage one

The student has announced that she doesn't intend to do the work which has been set. The teacher points out that, 'If you won't do it now, we'll have to follow it up later. It's your choice.'

'You can't make me do it.'

'That's right. It's your choice, but we will be following that up later.' Teacher walks away.

Deflective statements using humour can be helpful for this type of behaviour also. 'Gees, this work's boring, sir.' Teacher picks up the work, has a look, puts on a studied expression and says, 'You're right!', winks or smiles and walks off. He'll come back later to see how things are, but at the point of 'heat', he uses repartee. The main thing is not to get into pointless arguments. If necessary reassert or give a choice (see p. 85).

Refocus on the task

It can also help to complete the discipline transaction by leaving the student with a task-related reminder, direction or question so that the parting words (as we move off) are focused on the learning not just the behaviour we are addressing. 'I'll come and see how things are going a little later.' 'What should you be doing?' (Here the student is asked to focus, for himself, on the required task or behaviour.) 'Carry on with ... and I'll come back later to see how your work is going.'

Task reminders (time)

It can help to remind the class how long a task is likely to take, so they'll be able to pace their work time. For students who are easily distracted and have trouble focusing and attending to a task it can help to draw up simple, negotiated task cards (Rogers, 1994). The work for that particular session or activity is set out on a task card and the student times herself on each phase of the task. With visual learners it can help to have the times written with a tick-box next to each task plus a personal timer so they can monitor the task themselves.

Stage two

When a disruption makes it impossible for you to teach and others to learn, give the disruptive student a choice—settle down or move to another desk. It needs to be clear to the student that when he makes it difficult for people to work he faces the immediate consequences of relocation in the room or time-out. There is a distinction between the blatant task refuser who tears up work, and the passive task refuser who doesn't do the work due to imagined or real inadequacy. One helpful method is to include the passive task refuser in group activities which are not task-oriented, such as self-esteem games or cooperative group activities. Introduce these activities on a monthly basis. Build up self-esteem by encouraging the small steps a child makes. Avoid concentrating on failure. Failure crushes every small effort in students with low self-esteem. Provide learning tasks in which the child can achieve some level of competence. Such children find it extremely difficult to build on failure so we need to enable them to build from failure to experience some success. Short work or task contracts are one way to cater for mixed-ability problems; another is to arrange for some learning tasks to be based on cooperative learning, whereby the student can share the learning task with others. This enables the student to learn with, and from, others.

Beyond classroom discipline

The management of disruptive behaviour by students cannot always be settled, in the short term, at the classroom level. Teachers (with colleague support) need to have a longer term supportive discipline policy in place. This should include:

▮ follow-up and follow-through by the teacher after class (see p. 96)
▮ conferencing and contracting approaches (see Chapter 5)
▮ notifying parents, although this depends on the circumstances. Teachers and senior staff need to think carefully when and how they will contact some parents. Normally the school will have a clear policy on this.

Jason's parents were told about his aggressive behaviour when they came to pick him up one Friday afternoon. The teacher thought it was about time they knew what was happening and had asked that they come to the school to pick him up and have a talk. Jason's father immediately yelled at the child in front of the teacher and carted him off to the car. As the teacher watched through the window she saw Jason get a belting as he was pushed into the back seat.

Giving students the right of reply

We all like to feel we've been given a chance to tell our side of the story. When a student claims, 'It's not fair, you never listen to me!', she may be right. Obviously we can't have lengthy discussions in the classroom; we rarely have the time. We can, however, accord right of reply in one of two ways.

Take the student aside

■ Take the student aside during the lesson and have a brief chat to find out what is going on (at this point, too, the teacher can briefly tune in to how the student might be feeling).

■ Refer the matter to a later time, after class or at recess.

Follow-up beyond the classroom

There are situations that require a teacher to follow up (and follow through) from a classroom or playground incident. Follow-up may:

■ address a concern the teacher has about work or behaviour (It is important to consider whether an after-class chat or a more formal one-to-one session is required. At primary level this is much easier to control. At secondary level we often need to make an appointment with the student to meet at lunch, recess, or use 'detention' time to follow up and work things out.)

■ address an issue of concern between students engaged in teasing or put-downs in class time (see p. 192)

■ engage a student's responsibility over an uncompleted task, when the student was actively engaged in time-wasting and procrastination, or has left a mess, or has not completed the pack-up routine.

Follow-up often acts as a deferred consequence as when a student has refused to clean up or complete a task.

Jamie (Year 1) had thrown some pencils and felt-tip pens on the floor in a fit of pique. I was conducting an art activity and I'd noticed Jamie's loud wailings. I walked over to try to calm things down. Apparently someone had wanted the felt-tip pen Jamie was using. After settling the group and refocusing them to the task, I directed Jamie to pick up what he'd thrown on the floor. 'Jamie, there are pencils and felt-tip pens on the floor. They need to go back into the containers.' I pointed to the containers. 'No!' He stood defiant. I clarified the situation adding the deferred consequence, '... if they aren't picked up, Jamie, you'll need to stay back at lunch play.'
'Humph! I don't care!'

'But I care Jamie. In our class we look after our equipment and clean up our work area.' The rest of his group looked at me as I left Jamie with the (in effect) directed 'choice' (see p. 85).

At the close of the lesson I dismissed the class and asked Jamie to stay back. He stood near the door sulking, arms folded as his peers walked off to lunch recess. I left the classroom door open (for ethical probity). He groaned, 'I wanna go to play now!'

'Jamie, I know you're upset, annoyed, you want to be out there.' (We looked out the window to the sunshine.) By now the whole class had gone. I beckoned him over to his work area. He reluctantly followed, a big frown on his face. 'Jamie (I motioned to the strewn pencils) there are the pencils on the floor. When you've picked them all up and put them in the containers you'll be ready to go to play.' I walked off, giving him take-up time. He sulkily stamped and made a flurry of noise as he cleaned up.

Students will often comply with a deferred consequence but exhibit residual secondary behaviours (pouting, groaning, stamping, overt loudness, tut-tutting …); would we expect less? Do we expect a cheerful child, singing 'Whistle while we work …' as he quietly cleans up? I find it helpful to tactically ignore such behaviour and give the student some take-up time (working abstractedly at the teacher table).

He came over to me. 'I finished.' His tone was a little more subdued but still sulky. I walked back across to his table. 'Yes, I can see all the pencils and felt-tip pens are off the floor, back in their containers. Chairs under the table. Looks tidy Jamie.' All Jamie needed was a little bit of supportive feedback. Not praise, no 'Well done!' (he should have done it in the first place), no 'Brilliant!' (what was brilliant?), no 'Good boy' (he's not good—he should have done it as the others did). 'You're ready for play now Jamie.' He walked off muttering, 'I going to play now!' When he got to the door, I called across the room, 'Jamie …?'

'Yes!' he whined back, shoulders drooping (I think he thought I was going to 'make' him do more cleaning up). 'Jamie, enjoy your play time.'

'All right' he smiled back weakly. I wanted to separate amicably.

Some basic considerations about follow-up beyond the classroom

1 Emphasise the certainty of the consequence (rather than intentional severity of consequences)

Some teachers use the follow-up time after class to get back at the student or give them a lecture about their behaviour. I've seen teachers harangue students, with pointing finger in the corridor, after the bell has gone. 'You could be outside now, couldn't you, playing with your mates, eh? But no, not you—you said you didn't care before when I said I'd keep you back if you didn't clean up! I bet you care now, don't you, eh? Well it serves you right.' I've seen teachers bail a student up against a wall and give a five-minute lecture that can be heard from one end of the corridor to the other. While this kind of emotional pay-back (revenge?) is tempting, it's unprofessional and poor modelling. Sharing how we feel about a student's behaviour is different from haranguing.

2 Briefly tune in to how the student may be feeling

I'd directed Jayson to stay back; he'd pushed Celia in the back a few minutes before the bell. She'd looked annoyed, but shrugged it off. At the close of the lesson I gave the goodbyes to the class and finished with, 'I need to see Jayson briefly after class.' (I looked across to his surprised, then immediately, frustrated eyes.) 'Sh——! What do I have to stay back for?'

'I'll explain later.'

He slumped in his seat, sulking. After the class had left (a few of his mates lounged in the corridor), I beckoned him over. 'Yeah, well what did I do then?' he grumbled.

'Look I can see you're annoyed that I've asked you to stay back. I won't keep you long (it is important to let students know how long the follow-up, or deferred consequence will be, especially for younger students) but I need to talk with you about what happened in class when ...'

3 Focus on the behaviour or issue of concern

While it may be tempting to lecture the student, it will be more effective to focus on the student's specific behaviour (or issue) and the effect it had on others. 'Jayson, I'm concerned about the way you pushed Celia in the back during pack-up time.' When students challenge, or argue, or minimise the effect of their behaviour it is important to keep the focus on the main concern or issue that has necessitated the follow-up (see also p. 87). Students will often shift blame on to others, or say that 'this class is boring ...' or 'I hate this subject.' It is important to acknowledge briefly where appropriate ('Yes, it can be annoying to do subjects you don't like but at the moment I'm talking about ...'), refocus the dialogue back to the right or rule and then work for reconciliation or appropriate restitution. 'Gees, I was just mucking around!' This is a common response from students, especially boys. 'Maybe you were, Jayson, but what's our class rule about fair treatment?'

I once kept two students back in a colleague's class (music) for pulling each other's headphones off while playing the electronic keyboard and then punching each other around the shoulders. When I described their behaviour, even mirroring it (see below), they both said, 'But we were just joking an' that!' It is important to refocus the students on the essential right affected by their behaviour. This often includes the teacher's right to teach and other students' rights to learn.

4 Mirror the student's behaviour

It can sometimes be helpful to 'mirror' students' behaviour back to them so they can see what it looked like to you. Mirroring is a way of helping a student to see and hear her voice tone, body language and visual presence, recreating, as it were, the disruption in class.

Obviously this technique is one that a teacher has to be comfortable with. For example, I never mirror swearing or violent behaviour, though I simulate some expressions of anger and the body language of swearing so students can see themselves and their behaviour. I have mirrored such behaviours as calling out, butting in, pushing in line, loud voice usage in class, rolling on the mat (lower primary) and other attention-seeking behaviours. Some behaviours obviously cannot be mirrored, such as climbing trees in the playground (although this can be mirrored with fingers describing tree and climbing). Also, if you are not fit it won't help to show a Year 1 how she rolls under the table during morning talk. A colleague of mine actually got stuck when she tried to demonstrate this to a five-year-old boy. He sat and laughed. 'You got stuck under the table Miss. Ha ha ha!'

Mirroring is a modelling technique that can:

■ illustrate and disclose the typical 'shape' (even goal) of a student's behaviour (see p. 181)
■ enable a focus for discussion with the student of the behaviour in question
■ let the student know that you know that he knows that you know what it looks and sounds like when he calls out, butts in, walks in an exaggerated fashion.

Mirroring is not a technique to be used to make the child feel small, or to give some emotional pay-back. It is purely illustrative.

When mirroring, always:

■ Consider if this approach will help in the clarification and discussion and remediation of behaviour.
■ Mirror one to one (although it can be productive to use *general* mirroring in a whole-class setting).
■ Ask permission from the student to mirror: 'I'd like to show you what it looks like when you ...', 'Do you mind if ...?', 'Can I give you a "demo", so you can see what it looked like when ...?' I said this to the two boys who had pulled each other's headphones off in music. They laughed when they watched me simulate their behaviour and said 'That's stupid!', with a mix of embarrassment and surprise. 'Well, that's what I saw you doing, when I looked in to your class before.' If a student says 'no' to your request to mirror, respect his right (I've never had a 'no' yet) and use descriptive and specific language instead. I've used mirroring approaches with students aged from five to seventeen.

It can also help to use simple and specific cartoon drawings to increase awareness of behaviour (Rogers, 1994).
■ Consider the ethical probity of any one-to-one situation, especially a male teacher following up an issue of concern with a female student.

Chelsea, Year 10, had been rude—even arrogant—in her body language and tone of voice in class. When I asked her to stay back for a chat I made sure that a female colleague was present in the background of the classroom while I had a chat and mirrored her tone of voice and body language. Her response was, 'Yeah, well I don't do that all the time do I?'

'I don't know Chelsea, but that's how you spoke to me several times earlier this morning.' We then chatted about basic respect being given and received and parted company amicably. 'You and I have got to work together for a fair while, Chelsea, that's why I wanted this chat, to make things clear. See you next time in English. Thanks for taking time to stay back.'

▌ Be brief, focusing only on the behaviour.

In order not to 'emotionally contaminate' the place where one has actually mirrored the student's behaviour it is helpful to step back a few paces and indicate with an open hand to the vacated space (as it were): 'That's how it sounds when ...', 'That's what it looked like earlier in class when ...'

The 'stepping back' reconfirms the adult role and leaves the mirrored behaviour in the student's immediate short-term memory.

A lot of students will laugh (naturally) as they see their teacher revisit their behaviour. This needs to be accepted for what it is— their behaviour (revisited) does look ridiculous, stupid, funny. Sometimes the student will laugh out of nervousness, anxiety or the incongruity of it all. The teacher can then use words like 'rude', 'hostile' (tone of voice or body language), or 'annoying' (relative to aspects of attention-seeking, especially frequency and intensity of behaviour).

It is important to keep the tone of the dialogue supportive. Give the student right of reply but be sure to focus on the primary issue. Emphasise a problem-solving focus not just a telling focus. Ask questions such as: 'Is there any problem I can help you with?', 'Is there a problem with me or my teaching?', 'In what way does this (your behaviour) affect the rights of others?' These questions can, if delivered genuinely, be quite disarming for the adolescent who is a show-off or smart alec: 'How often do you think you do that?', 'What do you think when you do that?', 'How do you think I feel when ...?', 'What can you do to change this ...?', 'Somewhere, sometime you learned to behave like this. Can you think of another way to behave in class that is helpful for you, to other students and to me—your teacher?'

These sorts of questions may need to be adapted and modified depending on the student's age.

Always finish any mirroring and discussion with an invitation to work on a verbal or written agreement on future behaviour in class. Make sure such an agreement is simple, specific and workable (see Chapter 5).

5 *Wherever appropriate, give the student a right of reply*
This is especially important with older students and in longer one-to-one sessions. It can be helpful to give the student a chance to use a written right of reply, or, for younger students, the teacher can use some focus questions to clarify the problem, invite student feedback and work towards a solution. Focus questions could include:

■ 'What happened?' (in terms of the behaviour that has caused the student to be in the position of having to stay back after class, or go to detention or time-out)
■ 'What is your side of the story?' or 'Why do you think it happened?'
■ And the key question, 'What can you do to fix things up?'

I sometimes add the question, 'How did it make you feel?'

Many schools have a proforma for usage across the school (see Appendix II). Very young children can be encouraged to illustrate their responses to key questions on a sheet of A3 paper. This written, consequential step is to be preferred over the writing of lines, or just copying out the rules as punishment. At least, using this approach, the child is writing with some purpose. If the written answers are non-specific, direct the student more specifically.

Michael (Year 7) wrote (in answer to the question 'What happened?'), 'I was bad.' I directed him to extend the answer: in what way and when. If a student struggles with writing it is more productive for the teacher to ask the questions and then write down the student's responses. The teacher can then add supplementary questions ('Are you saying then ...?', 'Let me get this clear ...', 'So how many times did you call out or ...?')

I was working with Troy, a 15-year-old student, during time-out. He'd sworn at his teacher in class (a relief teacher). I gave him a written proforma with several key questions. He wrote: 'I was having a bad morning and he (the teacher) made me do the work twice much neater. I mumbled a swear word, the f—— word, and I walked away.' His version of events was different from the teacher's, who later admitted he'd only heard the mumbled f—— word, and maybe it was a result of frustration rather than directed at him personally. In response to the question 'What can you do to fix things up?' Troy had written, 'Try not to do it again.' I asked him what he could do to fix things *today*. 'Yeah, well I don't even know his name. He's a relief teacher and that. But if I can see him again today I'll apologise.'

'Okay Troy. I'll tee it up for lunchtime, all right?' I met the colleague in the staff room and asked him if Troy could see him at lunchtime to explain how Troy had seen the 'incident' and also to apologise. The teacher agreed.

At lunchtime we all met at my colleague's classroom where he accepted Troy's explanation and apology, adding, 'It's not easy to apologise to a teacher, but you took the time to do it. I appreciate that.' They shook hands and separated amicably. The consequence had been completed with some repairing and rebuilding.

I'll often read the student's answers back, with the student adding clarifications and noting them down on the sheet. At secondary level a proforma can be a standard tracking procedure for any detention process; if a student has filled in three such forms in close succession then she may need to work with a senior teacher on an individual behaviour management plan (see Chapter 5).

6 *Work on an agreement about future behaviour in class*
Track the student's future behaviour in response to any follow-up to see if this kind of behaviour is the result of a bad day or characteristic in pattern. If there is a pattern of frequency and intensity of

disruptive behaviour as well as generality across the school (and subject areas) then the student will need to work with a teacher on an individual behaviour-management plan (see Chapter 5). The earlier this is developed (term 1), the more effective it will be.

If a teacher is hesitant or lacks confidence in following up a student, it can help to have a third party (a colleague) sitting in on the process.

Refusing to stay back

What if a student runs off at the end of a lesson, refusing to stay back? This is more common at secondary level than primary but if a student walks off muttering, 'Nah I'm not staying back, what'd I do?'—what do we do? (I've had a few students, secondary, just run off muttering or swearing under their breath). We could chase them but it looks a bit 'off' to see a teacher running down a corridor or across a playground in pursuit of a non-compliant student. It also over-services the student's need for attention (and anyway, who needs a coronary just to prove that we have to win right *now*!)

With younger students it is important to keep the child in sight (if they've climbed a tree, or the roof, or done a runner …) until we can direct the audience away from the student and get a third party on the scene (for example if we're trying to get all of our Year 1 class inside and one of the attention-seeking boys is hiding around the corner!).

At secondary level, if students do run off it is important to follow up at a later stage. I find it helpful to keep a notebook with me at all times when teaching and on playground supervision to record the names of students I need to follow up with or have a chat with after class or make an appointment with for a lunchtime meeting. Most do stay back—thankfully. The notebook is my *aide-mémoire*, plus when I read the name(s) out at the close of the lesson it accords a degree of 'public' seriousness to the behaviour, and the other students are (very briefly) aware that this teacher does follow up. If the student chooses to run off, the reminder is in my notebook. I'll track the student in another class when I've got a free timetable slot. Knock on the door and ask to see Adam, or Lucas, or Craig, or Ali (it's mostly boys) and they get quite a shock. They wouldn't have thought I'd make that kind of effort to follow through. I've never had a teacher yet refuse me the option of withdrawing a student from their class for a teacher–student dialogue! It lets the student (and their peers) know that this teacher cares enough to follow up. If they still refuse then a special consequential meeting between the class teacher, the student and a senior teacher will need to be arranged.

Physical restraint

The whole issue of physical touch, holding or restraint is an issue that has become significant in the last ten years or so, especially for male teachers. Yet if a student is a significant danger to himself, or others, then partial physical restraint may be a necessary short-term option. The school will need to have discussed if and how, and under what circumstances this might operate and what alternatives are available if a teacher is not comfortable about physical intervention (as, for example, when two Year 1 children are punching each other and locked in 'mortal combat', or two Year 9 boys are 'punching each other's lights out' with an audience cheering them on). At secondary level—with adolescents—there are many teachers who are not willing ever to engage in physical intervention of any kind. Although physical intervention as a teacher action might be rare at secondary level, it needs to be discussed within the school's management plan. No teacher should be left in the unenviable position of having to intervene in dangerous student conflict without appropriate back-up, specified in a well-thought out behaviour plan.

Accountability dialogue

When students are engaged in put-downs publicly in class it can help to direct the students to stay back after class to work through the issue with the teacher. If the issue is particularly serious then a special appointment can be made to sort out the issue and highlight accountability on the one hand and some form of restitution (where appropriate) on the other hand.

> Jono told Louisa to 'Shut your face' in class. He said it loudly. The teacher faced him and said, with some assertion, 'Jono, that language is not acceptable in our classroom.' He butted in, 'Yeah, well

she called me a pervert!' (Apparently Louisa and Carly had called him this in the gym before they had come into the class.) 'Jono, stop (...) (the teacher blocked the student's protestation with his hand), we'll talk about this at the end of the lesson.' Turning to the rest of the class he said, 'Right, the show's over. Let's get back to work.'

Loud put-downs should never be ignored or tolerated, in my view. We need to make fundamental rights and values clear, briefly and persuasively. Later we'll need to follow up with the students in question.

At the close of the lesson the teacher directed Jono and Louisa to stay back. He briefly acknowledged that it was recess and they probably wanted to be out with their mates.

'I'm concerned about what you said to Louisa, Jono.' Jono started his well-worn theme. 'But she said ...' Holding up a blocking hand, the teacher said, 'Hold on a moment, you'll have your chance to explain. Louisa, I'm concerned about what Jono said in class earlier.' He noticed Louisa was looking annoyed. 'Yeah, well he said ...' Before she could continue the teacher offered a suggestion:

'Louisa, if you're comfortable, could you look at Jono and tell him what he said and how it made you feel.' Louisa turned to Jono, who stood uncomfortably, kicking the carpet and giving Louisa skewed eye-contact. She explained how what he'd said had made her feel.

'What do you want to happen Louisa ...?'

'Well, just not hassle me in class, that's all.'

'Could you tell Jono?' She faced Jono, repeating it.

'Well Jono, you've heard what Louisa has said. How do you account for what you said and the way you said it in front of the class?'

'Yeah, well ...' He looked at the teacher. 'Could you face Louisa and explain it to her?'

Jono found that difficult (it was easier to connect to the concrete through the carpet with his shoe). He turned to explain that he was angry that she'd said he was a pervert. She added that she and her friends felt uncomfortable that he had been staring at her in the gym.

The teacher concluded by reaffirming the basic right to be treated and spoken to with respect. 'We solve issues here without yelling at each other in class, or putting each other down.'

This approach is often used by teachers where there is a fairly clear victim–perpetrator situation. It is often used in harassment cases. It gives the victim the opportunity to:

▋ explain what it was that concerned or upset them about the perpetrator's behaviour
▋ explain how they felt and still feel about such behaviour
▋ say what they want to happen now—most victims want acknowledgement by the perpetrator that what happened did happen, and that it wasn't the victim's fault
▋ an apology, and an assurance that this kind of behaviour (or any harassment) won't happen again.

It gives the perpetrator an opportunity to explain and apologise or offer appropriate restitution. The teacher can then briefly remind the perpetrator of the rights and responsibilities related to his behaviour.

If the precipitating incident is particularly serious, the teacher will direct the students to have another meeting in a week's time to see how things are going. This lets the perpetrator know there will be a review of his stated assurance that 'it won't happen again'.

When a student has faced such behaviours as teasing, friendship exclusion, having notes written about them, put-downs or swearing, this process gives the victim a chance to tell the story and seek appropriate acknowledgement and apology. No victim should be forced into an accountability dialogue—if she is too upset, or traumatised, or lacking in confidence the teacher will have to act on her behalf and go through the accountability process without the victim present. This approach, however, does empower the victim to face the perpetrator and get the story straight with the perpetrator in front of a teacher. If the dynamics of perpetrator–victim role are ambiguous then both parties go through the key issues noted earlier and the teacher encourages mediation by the students where possible, suggests a solution or arbitrates.

How assertive?

Assertion is best seen in contrast with aggression. When a teacher is acting aggressively, he is only concerned with his needs and beliefs ('I *must* win; she must do as she's told, the little b——!'). Behaviour is hostile, often demeaning and embarrassing for the student. Voice and gestures often portray aggressive power.

When a teacher is acting submissively or non-assertively, he often allows the other party to dominate the transaction. The non-assertion may be a result of fear of rejection or of having to face conflict and 'losing'. Indecisive, non-assertive management results in the student deciding the agenda. Non-assertive teachers often start off trying to be fair, nice and reasonable, but when pushed to the limit by trying children, will resort to pleading and shouting.

Acting assertively means that we act from a position of our rights without riding roughshod over the other person's rights (tempting as that may be!). We speak decisively, firmly, clearly, expressing the requirements at hand or, when angry, our own feelings, and we take care to separate the child from his action. 'Kim, I am angry about the way you're speaking to Lee. Stop it now. You know our rule.' The teacher follows up later. If communicating to the whole class, eye-sweep the whole class and speak firmly and clearly about that which upsets us. Avoid angry yelling and humiliating 'you' messages. 'You make me sick 8D, it's always the same isn't it? You're like a pack of animals. I've had it with you.'

If we're too angry to speak rationally, explain that we're too uptight now, and follow up later. When children are too angry or uptight, use time-out as a means to cool off and follow up at a later time (see pp. 279f).

Speak within a rules–rights–responsibility framework rather than from a status perspective. The issue at stake is generally one relating to basic rights. It is often helpful to speak from a rules focus because rules focus on due rights. With older students (Years 10–12) it is often helpful to use language that conveys where our rights are infringed.

A rude student continues to butt in. 'Excuse me, John (this is said more firmly than what follows). You can see I'm trying to speak. I can't with that noise level. I expect your cooperation. Thank you.'

'Excuse me, Simone. You want to talk to Melissa, I need to teach. You know our class agreement. Thanks.' While such an approach gives significant attention to the student we at least assert our due rights without attacking the student.

Remember:

■ Be aware of the student's feelings. Sometimes it may be appropriate to take a child aside (lateness, crying, worry, no equipment, etc.).

■ Observe the protocols of positive discipline noted earlier (see pp. 14f).

■ Work hard at building a positive class climate. The essence of positive discipline is creating a social learning environment where correction is seen for what it is—a clear reminder to act responsibly and respect rights. Even the recidivist will be more likely to take the hard work of behaviour ownership on board and the necessary consequences when the class tone and teacher behaviour are positive.

Planning discipline steps and negotiating disruptions

Levels of teacher action should become increasingly more decisive according to the level of disruption and the context of the disruption (see Figure 3.1). In the course of any lesson there are three general phases that establish the context:

■ the establishment and instructional phase
■ the on-task phase
■ the relinquishing phase–lesson closure.

It is worth noting these, as our discipline plan needs to be modified depending whether we are up-front (instructional time) or moving around the room when students are on-task.

The establishment and instructional phase

This is the beginning of the lesson, when students are filing in, settling down and we need to establish initial attention and engage students in the instructional phase. Primary school teachers, at least in elementary grades, use all sorts of listening games to get children seated and attentive. The older children get, the less they respond to novelty. We do, however, need to establish, and sustain, initial attention quickly so that we can focus in on the learning activities (see especially Chapter 6).

It is very important to greet students when they are settled, have a brief chat and clearly focus where the lesson will be going for that session. If we are indecisive and uncertain here, it will affect all that happens from then on.

The sorts of disruptions that occur at the beginning of the lesson are:

■ shuffling, whispering, private conversation
■ general noise level
■ calling out and/or butting in
■ silly noises
■ clowning
■ late arrivals.

When disciplining 'up-front', when we are the primary (although perhaps not the only) focus of attention, it is better to use:

■ tactical ignoring, where possible, or non-verbal cues
■ brief, simple directions
■ clear rule reminders
■ diversions and distractions
■ light humour.

When giving a direction as corrective discipline up-front, it is important not to over-attend by walking across to a student and getting into a long discussion. This only gives more attention than is due. Keep it brief and redirect attention quickly to the lesson. Brevity, expectation, positive language, take-up time and lesson flow are important in the instructional phase. Matched with enthusiasm for the subject and the ability to communicate that enthusiasm, classroom management becomes a means to an end rather than an end in itself.

The on-task phase

At this stage, the teacher is moving around the room while the students are supposed to be on-task. During this time there is an initial settling down during which some students will:

■ not have pens, pencils, books or equipment (see p. 205)
■ say, 'What do we have to do again?' or say that they have not understood what you meant when you said ...
■ stare idly out of the window
■ be out of their seat for reasons best known to them.

As the on-task phase continues some students will:

■ call out across the room
■ wander
■ change their seating or leave without permission
■ refuse or avoid tasks
■ clown around.

During this phase of the lesson, a teacher can use a much wider repertoire of discipline approaches as she divides her attention across the group; from least intrusive approaches like tactical ignoring and non-verbal messages, simple directions, rule restatements and reminders or casual statements, to the more decisive questioning approaches. Where students are upset, angry or quarrelsome she may take them aside or give a clear choice. Where appropriate, she will use humour (if it's an approach she's comfortable with). At all times she will be prepared to reassert a rule or direction in a fair way. She will avoid arguing, blaming or preaching, but look for ways to put the responsibility back on to the student. This is the essence of a plan, using appropriate discipline steps with a decisive manner.

The relinquishing phase

This is the winding down of activity: packing up, giving any final instruction (for example homework), cleaning up mess, putting chairs away, a final cheerio. The sorts of disruptions occurring here are:

■ slow finishers
■ uncompleted tasks

■ early finishers (Have some activity they can do so they are not disturbing others: worksheets, extension activities, reading a book, library corner.)
■ students who attempt to 'beat the bell' (see p. 216)
■ calling out.

Because the teacher is resuming a focus up-front again, it is important to keep any discipline brief. Keep the instructions clear, establish positive pack-up routines. Leave the classroom tidy, put chairs under desks (or on them), and encourage an orderly exit. Insist on this from day one by making the expectations clear. It is something that can be discussed during the rule-making phase (see Chapter 4).

The context of disruption

In all discipline transactions, the teacher's behaviour is affected by the context in which disruption occurs. If the disruption is low-level, merely walking close to the student's desk or even tactical ignoring may be sufficient. If a student hasn't got the correct uniform on, for example, the teacher would probably be best served by calling the student aside quietly (preferably near the close of the lesson) and reminding her or simply asking for an explanation. If a student is late, instead of a big discussion at the door, it is better to merely direct the student to his seat, letting him know you'll talk with him later. If a student hasn't started work, if two students are merely off-task with their talking, or if a student is daydreaming, it is entirely appropriate to simply walk up and casually ask, 'How's it going?', 'Where are you up to?', or 'Can I see your work?' Casually asking a question says to the student, without a big debate, 'I'm here, you're here, you know I'm here to remind you to get back to work, or to help, or to correct.' All this can be communicated by a casual statement or question. If we sense the student is disturbed or upset, we can call the student aside, away from the others to minimise embarrassment or audience-seeking or the possibility of hostile one-upmanship. If we're speaking from the front to a student who is persistently calling out, then our voices will need to be more assertive than if we're speaking to two talkers while we're doing 'the rounds' (when students are supposed to be on-task at their desks or tables).

A sense of humour

'The attempt to develop a sense of humour and to see things in a humorous light is some kind of trick learned while mastering the art of living.' Victor Frankl (1963) was a Viennese psychiatrist interned in the concentration camps of Dachau and Auschwitz. He wrote in his book *Man's Search for Meaning* that 'one could (even) find a sense of humour there as well; of course only the faint trace of one, and then only for a few seconds or minutes. Humour was one of the soul's weapons in the fight for self-preservation. It is well known that humour, more than anything else in the human make-up, can provide an aloofness and an ability to rise above any situation, even if only for a few seconds or minutes ...'

In the classroom or playground, humour can defuse tension and help people feel a little less stressed; and when we feel better we tend to act better. Humour can help put things into perspective or even just emphasise the funny side of life. Sarcasm, by contrast, intends to hurt the receiver or bignote the one handing out the cutting comment, the smart remark or the put-down. It is only fun for the giver. Humour can range from the quirky or funny faces we pull and the slightly off-beat non-verbal behaviour we use to the verbal repertoire we employ, including irony, repartee or the *bon mot*. Of course humour has a lot to do with our personality and temperament, but it is something students clearly enjoy seeing in their teachers.

One of my students was blatantly passing a note in class to his *amore* in the front row. I walked over and put my hand out and asked for the note. At first he declined ('No!'). I persisted. As he handed it over I quickly glanced at the love missive. He said 'Don't read it!'—a kind of wild panic in his eyes. Walking to the front of the room I readied myself to read his note. 'Don't read it!' he whined. Of course several students chorused, 'Read it, read it!'

I started to 'read' aloud it as he cringed in his seat.

'One of the things I really enjoy about being in Mr Rogers' class is that he'd never embarrass me publicly by reading private correspondence. Signed Brett.' I folded it in half and handed it back. 'Interesting note Brett, put it away now. Ta.' He gave a sigh of relief and a wry grin. I never had any note-passing from then on.

Teachers often hear muttered swearing in the classroom these days. While a simple rule reminder and an after-class chat are the norm, humour can be an appropriate response. When I hear the muttered sh—— word, I often walk across and sniff a few times.

'What are you doing?' asks a confused student.

'Just checking—you've got to watch that stuff; it smells and attracts flies.' There's often a raised eyebrow and grin in return. Sometimes I add the interrogative 'Where?'

'Where what?'

'The thing you just said.' Then the penny drops. Tension is defused and I have a brief chat about the sh—— word and help them refocus. Most students make an effort after that to curtail the easily dropped sh——.

One of my colleagues, a science teacher, was handing out some worksheets. A class wag let out a moan, 'Gees, not this sh——.' Following the inevitable laughter the teacher looked at him and said, 'Adam—we're doing organic solids next week, not this week.'

I remember a student qualifying his frustrated expression with a religious word, 'Holy sh——!' I asked him what denomination. 'Eh?'—he finally got it. I laughed and we looked at his work (the source of his frustration). I asked if he'd like to work with another student to give some assistance. He did, he settled down and after class we had a chat about better ways to express frustration and seek help.

Of course the use of humour is most effective when one has a positive working relationship with the student in particular and the class in general. The incidents noted above do not occur in isolation. As in any behaviour transaction, the teacher needs to read the situation quickly and decide what to address and what to tactically ignore. This is the impressive skill required of teachers in a setting where a number of things are often happening simultaneously.

Summary

How we combine the approaches detailed in this chapter and our use of language constitute our discipline plan. The more conscious we are of what we say and do when disruptions occur, the more effective that plan will be. The more consistent we are in the practice of the plan the more likely it is that on-task learning is enhanced. Knowing what we can do and developing the skills, especially the language skills, also minimises the degree to which frustration affects our ability to cope. It is difficult to decide what to say in the heat of the moment. A plan gives us confidence that we have chosen the better options.

The approaches outlined in this chapter have sought to clarify an approach to teacher language and behaviour that consciously observes the protocols discussed earlier (see Chapter 1); they form a basis for a general discipline plan that any teacher could use with confidence. Specific discipline plans (for individual children or problem classes) or contingency plans are discussed later in this book (see Chapter 5) but even those plans will employ many of the approaches discussed in this chapter. Many teachers have shared with me the difference that a positive approach to discipline has made in their classrooms, especially the rephrasing of language. Simple things such as focusing on desired, rather than undesired, behaviour, for example 'Walking thanks' rather than 'Don't run', 'Facing this way and listening thanks' rather than 'Don't talk while I'm talking.' As many colleagues have said, it takes *reflective* practice and an initial conscious awareness of what we are saying (and doing). Initially such language may not be within our natural 'comfort zone'. Practice helps; frequent usage normalises and makes new language approaches comfortable, makes them our own. Partial agreement (see p. 189), for example, is quite difficult if we are used to confronting every piece of student procrastination, answering back, or last-word syndrome (see pp. 80f).

Is it worth it? The answer depends on what we value in our teaching role. The ability to have a plan and a conscious awareness that in the heat of the moment we are saying one thing rather than another will affect the teacher–student dynamic. The willingness to consider how teacher behaviour (verbal and non-verbal) can assist in keeping a positive flow in discipline transactions is part of our planning—most of all it emphasises the importance of the relationship aspect of discipline.

In the end, when a disruption occurs in our room, we have to do or say *something*. Planning that something, ahead of time, is what being professional is all about. When we make a good fist of that, the odds are we'll not get as upset, as often, for as long.

Questions to consider

Developing a classroom behaviour management plan

■ What are the essential elements of your classroom behaviour management plan?

■ How did you establish your classroom rules? Do you have a framework for the application of behavioural consequences (for common situations such as lateness, uniform breaches, homework problems, task avoidance/refusal, not having appropriate equipment)?

■ What are the essential establishment procedures, routines, and activities relevant to your grade/faculty (for entry/exit, settling, initiation, and sustaining of group attention, dealing with 'early' disruptions to lessons, transitions, noise-level, etc.)? Is there a time-out plan in the school? How does it operate (at classroom, team and playground levels)? If you need to exit a student who is persistently disruptive; who is threatening, hostile or aggressive (to person or property)—how do you direct him from your classroom to some formal cool-off-time place? What is the back-up plan if he clearly refuses to leave/go? (See Chapter 5.)

■ How aware are you of having a least-to-most-intervention approach to corrective discipline?

■ Are you aware, particularly, of your characteristic corrective language?

■ When engaged in corrective discipline how focused are you on the student's behaviour (avoiding unnecessary confrontation, focusing on primary issues, keeping the language positive where possible, being assertive but not aggressive where necessary)?

■ In what ways could you improve your current behaviour management plan?

■ What support, from colleagues, would you need?

Following up and following through with students beyond classroom correction

■ Do you normally follow up students yourself, or do you pass that task on to someone else in the team (year-level coordinator/grade leader, head of department)? If you do refer the student what procedures do you go through? Are they normally effective? At what stage do you follow through and engage the student in conflict resolution? (Remember, she will be back!)

■ What do you do if a student refuses to stay back after class or doesn't turn up for a teacher–student interview?

■ Are there any guidelines for follow-up of students in your school? What are they? In what way do such guidelines assist your one-to-one interaction with the student (for example in an after-class-time follow-up session)?

■ What detention system do you have in the school? Who runs it (class teacher, faculty, year-level)? How effective is it in terms of helping students take some ownership of their behaviour or following through with some restitution?

CHAPTER 4

Rights and rules in the classroom

> *In giving rights to others which belong to them, we give rights to ourselves.*
>
> **John F. Kennedy**

Whenever the issue of student rights, or democracy in the classroom, is canvassed, there are those who express the opinion that it will mean reduction in teacher authority, the 'thin end of the wedge', uncontrollable student behaviour or 'that airy-fairy rubbish'. 'We've got enough problems with students without teaching them about their rights! They won't be able to handle it.' Since the 1980s onwards there has been a resurgence of interest in discipline policy based on rights. What does this mean?

The notion of rights is not a new, post-60s idea. Neither is it anarchistic or anti-authoritarian. It is the basis for the United Nations declaration on human rights: the fundamental application of justice and dignity to human treatment. One of the classical definitions of rights is: the expression of aspects of human behaviour, in value, attitude or action, as fundamentally right or proper about being together and working together, as humans.

In exploring rights with all members of the school community we begin with the fundamental values we agree on as a school community. These values need to be brought out into the open by discussion and teaching. Most often the assumed values are: a fair go, cooperation, the fundamental dignity of a person (regardless of gender, race, culture, religion or even taste in music!), honesty, mutual respect and so on. They are the basis of what we deem right or proper about social relations and groups.

Of course there will be a clash of values at times between teachers from dominant middle-class backgrounds and students from low socioeconomic backgrounds. Teachers who struggle with this clash of values often concentrate on issues like perceived disrespect, student manners, dress, standards of work and language. Teachers who work successfully with such student populations have learned to earn rather than demand respect; expect and invite rather than demand compliance; model fair treatment; and look beyond the window-dressing of 'culture'. Many philosophic 'liberals' have changed their practice when forced to interact with students whose ethnicity or social background clashes markedly with theirs.

Teaching rights in the classroom

Under the aegis of rights a teacher will seek to weld a group of disparate individuals into some sort of community. In the course of that process, she will bring to the surface fundamental values by teaching, discussion and expectations which will focus on such questions as:

- ■ 'What do we value about others in our school community and the wider community, of which I am a member?'
- ■ Is it right to put other people down just because they are a different colour, have a different religion, speak differently, stutter, are disabled, look 'ugly', are 'not as bright as us,' live in poverty, etc.?
- ■ How do rights *and* responsibilities work together?

A different social climate

There is no question that significant numbers of teachers disenfranchised students of their due rights in the past through intimidation, dunce's caps for 'dummies', pushing, shoving, pulling hair, poking, even belting. The power balance was certainly in favour of the teacher.

Students today develop early the notion that they have rights. They may not articulate that notion well or clearly but their behaviour indicates that no longer will they be treated as inferior because of their status as a child or minor. The days are long gone when a teacher can call on role authority to demand respect. These days, teachers have to earn respect by the nature of their treatment and the manner in which fundamental rights are respected.

No automatic rights

In establishing rights, the degree of student discussion and involvement will depend upon age, situation and how confident teachers are in approaching this topic. In teaching rights to elementary-age students, teachers can use drama, storybooks, role-play or games to illustrate how we help or hurt others by how we think of and consequently treat them. Older students can easily fill a blackboard with what they believe their rights to be. When working with students on the issue of rights it will be important to focus on the non-negotiable rights in a school community:

■ The right to feel safe. This includes physical safety as well as emotional safety. Issues such as bullying and harassment are related to this fundamental and essential right.
■ The right to be treated with respect and dignity. This goes for *all* members of the community in their relationships with each other.
■ The right to learn. This includes the right to teach.

These rights are based on fundamental human rights. Often students have the language of rights ('I've got my rights') as a list of things demanded or expected. When directing classroom discussion, teachers need to guide the discussion towards responsibility. Our discipline, our treatment of students will be directed towards them taking responsibility for their behaviour *as it affects the rights of others.* We will treat them as persons who can and should account for their actions and face up to the consequences of their actions.

No one enjoys rights automatically. The right to learn, for example, implies a responsibility on the part of both teacher and students. When discussing rights with students, we will often explore responsibility by asking, 'Well, if you have a right to learn how can you enjoy that right? How is that right protected?' Just saying, 'We have a right' explains nothing about its exercise or enjoyment. Teachers can easily remove a student's right to fair treatment by put-downs; hostile, demeaning or sarcastic comments; intimidation and the like. Students can easily take away other students' rights to learn and be safe by fooling around, butting in, put-downs, and so on, just as a teacher's right can be affected by student rudeness and irresponsible and confrontational behaviour.

Defining what a right is helps students to see that the fundamental nature of rights is concerned with relationships, justice and fair treatment, not just with personal demands. Female teachers, for example, have a right to the same basic respect as male teachers, even if some students' ethnic or cultural heritage predisposes them to see females as non-authority figures. Fundamental human rights transcend cultural differences. No one in our classroom will be put down simply because they are female, or 'different' by virtue of ethnicity or cultural background. Sexist, jingoistic, cultural baggage is no defence against the moral law.

As C. S. Lewis pointed out in 1943 (Lewis, 1978), behind all laws we make there is a natural 'moral law', a fundamental concept basic to all civilisations. Your right, is, in a very real sense, my responsibility. I don't actually enjoy my right (as a due) until, and unless, other members of the group allow me such enjoyment. The teacher's managerial role then is to protect rights, encourage responsibility and enforce rules not as an end in themselves but because of the inherent values implicit in the rules.

However, a teacher is unwise, even foolish, to simply demand respect because it is a stated right in the school behaviour code. If, as a teacher, I don't act and speak respectfully to my students, how can I demand respect in return? There are still teachers who treat students with discourtesies that would be regarded as rank incivility or at least bad manners in any other social context. Teacher modelling has a powerful effect on the developing social climate of a classroom and how mutual rights and responsibilities are perceived.

In pursuing the issue of rights with older students a process of listing priorities usually ends up with several rights which follow from those essentials noted earlier (see p. 120):

▌ A right to express myself.

- A right to be an individual.
- A right to learn (and at a fair, individual pace and from teachers who act in a professional manner and who prepare adequate curriculum with some attention to mixed abilities).
- A right to teacher assistance.
- A right to move around the classroom. (This will need to be addressed contextually, for example compare the more academic focus of a maths class with the freer movement of a home economics class.)
- A right to safety. (This might address psychological safety such as safety from intimidation and harassment, as well as physical safety.)
- A right to participate in the schooling process.
- A right of reply.

In one sense, the rights of teacher and student are shared. Even the right to teach can be shared by students, where appropriate, though the responsibility to teach and lead the group is fundamentally the teacher's.

Values
What is a value?

- A value is something we consider to be very important.
- A value is something we hold as desirable.
- A value is something that lies behind what we actually do.
- A value is something we believe is worthwhile and significant about how we relate to each other.

We hold our values as a whole community of parents, teachers and children. If we value respect, then we express that as a right. So a right is something we ought to respect within the community, and from the community, because the community values it. In this way, because the community values these things, it also expects them and holds them as rights.

These are the fundamental values, which are often encouraged, taught and promoted within the school community.

Values	Expressions of the values we hold
Self-discipline Self-control Self-responsibility	Rather than merely controlling the child by using adult authority, we are seeking to promote an environment where we help children to control themselves. Obviously this will relate to the child's age and development, but at every opportunity we seek to teach children that they are responsible for their own behaviour.
Self-esteem Self-respect	Self-esteem means the value we place on ourselves. It means that we distinguish between a person and that person's behaviour. We can value, esteem and respect the person yet still call their behaviour to account.
Equality of treatment Dignity Worth Fairness Justice	Regardless of sex, colour, background or nationality, children are treated equally and have equal access to educational opportunity within the school community. Justice in the school community depends on having clearly agreed rules—rules that uphold our values and protect our rights. Justice is the fair treatment of children within these rules, rights and relationships.
Consideration for others Respect Courtesy Tolerance Teamwork Trust Honesty	The spirit and practice of democracy is encouraged and promoted in the social as well as learning environment. Civility and manners are an expression of courtesy, consideration and respect for others in the community.
Pride Effort	We have pride in the school, in work, in effort as well as achievement. There is willingness to try rather than give up just because a task is hard.

Human fallibility

Any discussion of human rights in any context, let alone a school, has to live in creative tension with human fallibility. We all get tired, cranky, annoyed, frustrated and angry—especially teachers. Students too, experience the restrictions that community living and learning place on them. This is perfectly natural.

We have to distinguish between the accidental and the intentional. While it is important to have some conceptual and practical flexibility in our management we need the framework of rights, responsibilities, rules and consequences to educate, enforce and support the values we hold.

Whenever I read a school policy outlining rights I'm tempted to add 'bad day notwithstanding!'

Developing rules with students

'I think that the rules should be made by the kids and the teacher. It would be fairer and then the kids couldn't complain about the rules.'

I was discussing the need for classroom rules with a robust Year 7 class. As a visitor to their room I thought it pertinent to ask the basic question, 'What are the rules in your classroom?' One wag down in the back row yelled out, 'We're not supposed to call out, we put our hands up!' I imagine he thought that because he had his hand up *while* he called out, his behaviour was okay. I ignored him (tactically) and asked the question again until somebody put a hand up. Obviously, having a rule and enforcing it are two different things. Rules (like rights) can't guarantee responsible or civil behaviour. They set the framework for the behaviours we aim for. It is the teacher's duty to develop, make clear and positively enforce such rules and encourage responsibility.

For rules to be effective, they need to be linked to a process of discussion with students during the establishment phase of the year. This is when we need to make clear our leadership style and establish our credibility to teach, guide and direct the group. Good rules are the preventative side of discipline. It will be quite normal that the rules, even when made by the students, will require some testing to establish their viability and credibility.

The rights–responsibilities–rules focus: a basis for positive student–teacher interaction

The *values* held by the school community

Fundamental values about dignity and the worth of persons; values of honesty, cooperation, caring, tolerance, 'a fair go', personal responsibility.

The expression of fundamental values as *rights*

Rights of self-expression, safety, learning; rights to religious, cultural identity; rights to fair treatment.

***Responsibilities*: ownership of behaviour**

The enjoyment of rights by the exercise of responsible social action.

***Rules*: Classroom rules**
      School-wide rules

A positive expression of what ought to be accepted (fair, right, proper) behaviour.
Rules clearly outline due responsibility and provide a fair basis for discipline.

***Consequences*: ownership of behaviour**

Children taking the consequences of their actions.
Being taught to 'foresee' the outcome of one's behaviour.
Making consequences 'fit' the particular behaviour.

Repair/rebuild

Beyond consequences and punishment there needs to be support for reconciliation and change.

Figure 4.1

For younger students, teachers need to concentrate on the rules side of rights ('When someone is speaking we don't speak, we wait our turn'); for older students we would include rights as a feature of rule-making ('We will respect the right of everyone to speak without interruption'). Behind the rule for communication, for example, is the right to have our say, share our opinions, talk (at times) while we work. The rule side of the right enshrines the responsibility for speaking respectfully in ways which don't hurt, demean or put others down or limit them having a fair go. It teaches that freedoms for oneself are only reasonable when they do not deny others their freedoms. In general, rules should be:

1 Positive in intent (where possible).

'In our classroom we put up our hands to ask a question' is obviously more behaviourally focused and positive than 'Don't call out'. 'Walk quietly' is better than 'Don't run', in that it focuses on the required behaviour. Try to maintain a balance of positive language in the formation of the rules rather than only emphasising the negative expressions ('Don't call out', 'Don't run', 'Don't speak while the teacher is speaking', 'No eating in class', 'No

OUR RULES
we make em!

THOU SHALT NOT PLAY IN
THE AISLES DURING LESSONS

THOU SHALT NOT COVET
THY NEIGHBOUR'S PENCILCASE
IN A LOUD AND UNSEEMLY
MANNER

THOU SHALT NOT MAIM IN

CLASS

running in corridors'). It can help to write the rules using inclusive language ('In our classroom we ...'). This also helps when giving rule reminders (see p. 69). 'In our room we put our hands up to ask questions, without calling out', or 'We've got a rule for asking questions.'

2 Simple, workable and achievable.

3 Related to the non-negotiable rights of safety, treatment, learning. This emphasis on fundamental rights should be common across the school.

4 Congruent with school-wide rules to avoid students playing one teacher off against another (for example no chewing gum, hats and sunglasses off in class).

5 Few in number.
We need to avoid the farcical situation of a long list of rules that even the teacher cannot remember. (No running; no throwing blocks; no fighting; no jumping on anyone's back; no shouting; no scissor fights; no climbing on tables; no hitting were only a few of a list of twelve I saw in a Year 2 class!)

6 Clear and specific.
A rule should outline what is and is not acceptable. 'We walk quietly in the classroom; we do not run.' 'In our classroom we put up our hands to ask a question without calling out.' 'At our desks we talk quietly so others can work well.' Rules ought to specify what is and isn't the accepted behaviour. Simply saying we should all be cooperative is not very helpful as a rule (although a desirable aim). 'Do unto others ...' is an excellent (perhaps even the best) philosophy but it hardly clarifies the 'what' and 'when'. Make the rule clear and specific, make the general consequences clear as well (see p. 154). Keep away from tacit assumptions.

7 Taught and enforced.
Rules should be regularly referred to and enforced. A good deal of discipline will often include quiet rule reminders. Obviously, if such rules have been made with the students, compliance is more

likely. The fair rules, rather than merely teacher authority, become the basis for mediation and arbitration.

8 Published wherever appropriate.
This is especially important at primary level. The children can also illustrate them and display them in a key (usually accessible) area in the classroom. My colleagues and I have also done this at middle-school level and found it a helpful adjunct in the establishment phase of the year.

It will also be helpful (at primary level) to send a copy home to parents as part of the grade teacher's establishment phase. It clarifies how this class will operate with *this* teacher *this* year. If all grade (and specialist) teachers use a common framework with common language this will further assist reasonable consistency and clarify the home–school partnership.

Ownership of the rules

It is important to discuss the reasons for rules with the students. With younger students, the rules can be discussed through stories, acted out in role-plays and portrayed in picture rule cards. With older students (Years 3–6), the rules can be discussed through small groups and even written up by the children on cards to be displayed around the classroom. When setting down the final form of a rule, it is generally better to have a key descriptor such as 'Talking rule', 'Our communication rule', 'Our safety rule', 'Our movement rule', or 'Moving around the room rule'. With post-primary students, it is important that rules not be seen as mere teacher imposition ('These are my rules!') Students are more likely to 'own' rules if they feel they have had some part to play in their formation.

Exploring rules through the notion of rights is also important. Children these days are aware of their rights though they often communicate such awareness without a due respect for responsibilities. This aspect of rule-making is essential for older students in Years 5–12.

Specialist teachers at primary school (phys. ed., library, relieving teachers, art, etc.) will not have the luxury of time to negotiate their rules but are well served, nonetheless, by discussing the rules up-front: why they are needed, what purpose they serve, and what the general consequences will be for outright disruptive behaviour. With young students the discussion can be aided by having the rules written up on cards, briefly and positively stated. Another way of presenting them is to use overhead transparencies and a hand-out sheet. The main point is to facilitate the discussion process.

Discussion groups (primary level)

One way to develop rules is through a whole-class discussion on the meaning of rights. Focus on a right as a privilege or an entitlement which we enjoy in relation to others whose responsibility enables our entitlement. Emphasise that rights in the classroom, on the roads, in sporting clubs, in a family, in society are not merely automatic expectations.

Where do we see rules? Who is responsible for making rules? Who is responsible for enforcing rules? What are some of the places you go to that have rules (clubs, shops, libraries, the beach)? How are rules made known? Who is responsible when rules are broken? Brainstorming helps children to see the fundamental and necessary place of rules in society. Our classrooms, too, are part of society; we too need to make our rules.

We all have a right to our say, providing that we have our say fairly, speak at appropriate times, and give the same courtesy to others as we expect for ourselves. Students quickly see the logic in this and benefit from seeing rules as 'mechanisms' that seek to protect individual rights (my right as teacher to teach; students' rights to learn, be safe, settle conflicts peacefully, ask questions, get help with their learning, learn without interruption, etc.).

Forming the rules

In making the rules, teachers can wind up the classroom discussion and move on to one of the following approaches:

1 'Well we can see from our discussion, as always, we need rules. I've set up the rules we'll be using together in 8D this year. Let me share them with you and get your responses.'
2 'What I'm going to ask you to do is split up into four or five groups and come up with several rules essential for our class.'

After 20–25 minutes get the feedback and draw out the common, essential rules.

3 A variation of this is the 2, 4, 6 discussion groups approach. The class is divided into pairs for ten minutes and asked to come up with several rules we'll need if we are to work well as a class. After ten minutes, the pairs join up with another pair to share and reach common agreement. After another ten minutes, three pairs join for a final sharing. In this way, there are several clarifications, with each pair testing out their ideas and beliefs. The teacher will then receive feedback from the groups of six on their common, agreed rules. These become the class rules. (Generally they come up with much the same as what a teacher would want or expect.) The final stage is to write up the rules in some way, either to be displayed on cards on the wall, or written up as the 'Rules for our room', or 'Our classroom agreements'. At secondary level it is important that the essential class-based rules be discussed across the year level or within tutor groups so there is a common understanding of rules.

Some secondary schools prefer the term 'behaviour agreements' rather than rules. It can help to have the *common rights and responsibilities* that form the basis of any rules published in every classroom as well as corridors and school foyer.

The language of rules

It is important that teachers develop with the students their own language for expressing the classroom rules. Students from Years 3–4 upwards can be encouraged to write the rules in their own words. Generally speaking, there are several rules that can be culled from classroom discussions. These need to be expressed appropriately for the particular age level.

Communication (for younger students the term 'talking rule' is sufficient)
This rule would cover: hands up for questions and discussion; working noise at desks; use of positive language (to be contrasted with hurtful language, such as swearing, put-downs, racist language,

teasing). Another way to cover the use of language is to make a 'positive language rule'. 'Positive language is language that helps us to feel good about ourselves and each other.'

Of course, working noise, or work talk, in an art room or trade area will be different (in degree) from that in a maths class. Working noise may also be different when working in small groups or during set times. This needs to be made clear with the students (see especially p. 206).

Problem-solving (for younger students, problem-fixing rule)

There are any number of disputes occurring in the life of a class. 'He's got my rubber!' 'She's nicked my pen!' 'He hit me again!' 'She's not my friend any more. I hate her.' It is important to have a basic rule governing peaceful dispute-settling because we don't have time to sit and negotiate each problem in the space of a lesson. Settling of disputes should stress negotiation, with the teacher's help if necessary. 'We solve problems in our class without hurtful language or fighting. If we can't sort things out by talking we will need to ask for teacher assistance.' (This will often occur later, after class or at another time if necessary.)

Movement

This rule is difficult to specify because of teachers' different views regarding acceptable movement. The rule, however, should specify the amount and kind of movement acceptable in our room. If you believe children should only get out of their seats with permission, say so in your rule. Added to the movement rule may be the 'coming in' and 'going out' movement rule, to be applied when lining up, sitting on the mat or moving seats. Appropriate permission for leaving the class can also be covered by this rule.

Safety–security

This covers use of equipment, protection of property, safe behaviour in certain classes (art, trades, science, home economics, etc.) as well as in the non-specialist classroom. The safety rule may also note the wearing of unsafe clothing and jewellery or possession of any toys which are unacceptable and/or inappropriate for school.

Learning

This rule covers the student's learning climate. It should cover at-seat learning, procedures to get teacher assistance during on-task time, routines for work stations and early finishing, and bringing of appropriate equipment to classes.

As part of the learning rule in one primary school, students are reminded that when moving around corridors they should recognise that lessons are going on in classrooms and when entering a class (for example, to deliver a message) they use their START approach:

S **S**top ... is it necessary/appropriate to go in now?

T **T**wo firm knocks, and enter.

A **A**pproach teacher and **A**ddress by name.

R **R**equest is made. **R**eply **R**eceived.

T **T**hank you is said before leaving.

This simple routine is a way of teaching and encouraging basic civility.

Treatment (the way we treat one another)

It is important that everyone in the classroom is treated respectfully and fairly. This means not putting people down because they look different from us, have different backgrounds or come from different countries. It will also address issues like protecting the right to personal space and property. Like the right to safety, this right is also related to issues like sexism and racism.

Consequences

The fundamental point about consequences is to make the 'if ... then ...' nature of the rules clear to the students. One way of doing this is to ask the students what consequences ought apply for X behaviours. Often they will be quite Draconian and we will need to push their thinking back to the issue. 'How does that (stated consequence) help to fix up the behaviour?' Some consequences need to be clear in advance. Here are some 'if ... then ...' examples.

The framework of our behaviour policy

The three strands of discipline—rights, responsibilities, rules—should work together to create a caring community atmosphere and are linked together by relationships within the school.

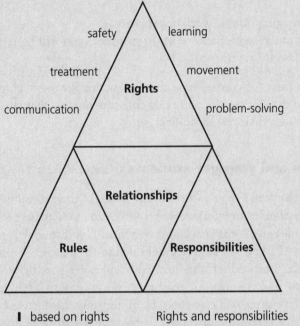

safety learning

treatment movement

Rights

communication problem-solving

Relationships

Rules **Responsibilities**

▮ based on rights	Rights and responsibilities
▮ positive wherever	work together.
possible	
▮ negotiated	Responsibilities require
▮ fair	that we are accountable
▮ certain	for our behaviour.
▮ published	

Adapted from Barnes and Daniels, 1996.

Figure 4.2

1 Calling out

If you continue to call out you will be reminded of the class rule for communication.

You may be asked to stay back and explain your behaviour.

You may be excluded from class discussions for a time.

2 Fighting in the classroom (this will include inappropriate horse-play or 'testosteronic bonding').
There will be immediate consequences (sit apart).
You will work separately until you've calmed down.
You will stay back to work things out.

3 Damaging others' work or property.
If you damage others' work or property, you will be required to replace it in some way.

We can't, of course, have a consequence for every contingency but we can discuss the nature of consequences so that students are clear about their responsibility.

Rules and younger students (Kinder to Year 1)

Small children live in a world where much of their social movement and play begins to interface with rules by the time they reach school age. Rules give some shape, dimension and limit to social and moral activity (Piaget, 1932). They help define the acceptable and unacceptable. For smaller children, clear rules are part of the general teaching and training for reasonable socialisation. They assist the smooth running of a classroom by minimising the need to be overly discursive each time disruptive behaviour has to be addressed and corrected. 'But I didn't know' should not be an easy excuse.

Rules help define 'the good' and, of course, small children need appropriate limits; it gives them security on the one hand and confidence (if the rules are fairly enforced) in classroom leadership on the other. Rules assist the process of self-discipline, so the means of enforcement are as important as the rules themselves. When we enforce the rules (bring moral force to bear) we will do it in a way that draws attention to the students' responsibilities in regard to the behaviour focused upon by the rule(s).

On day one, Mrs D has set up the Prep class for maximum involvement, comfort and learning. The room is bright, tables are well grouped, cupboards are clearly labelled with bright signs for scissors, clag etc. She has name tags for everyone. Later she will help them illustrate the big name tags for the 'lockers'—the plastic bins holding all their gear.

She knows the importance of rules for young children and has already illustrated five cards that depict aspects of desirable social behaviour in the classroom. (If the teacher is not a wonderful artist, she can employ a Year 5 or 6 student, who can also assist in sharing the rule ideas.) She holds up each card and discusses the behaviours depicted as 'our rules'. She discusses why rules are important. 'Ever tried to play a game without rules?' 'What sort of rules do you have at home?' 'Why are rules important? How do they help us?' 'What do these cards say about our rules here in our class?'

The pictures (see Appendix XII) illustrate the main aspects of the rules:

- the fair limits to talking and asking questions
- movement around the room
- safety (use of equipment such as scissors)
- manners and cooperation.

When discussing the 'helping rule' (manners, treatment, respect, cooperation—words she will emphasise in the language/literature program), Mrs D discusses and role-plays helpful words for asking and borrowing. Calling up two students she asks, 'How can I borrow a rubber from Michelle? Show me.'

'Sometimes people will snatch.' (She will model.) 'What is a better way and why?' She discusses words and expressions such as 'please', 'thank you', 'Can I help you?', 'Can I borrow?', 'Will you help me?', even phrases like 'Excuse me' when moving around another's personal space. Mrs D will regularly and firmly appeal to these rules by reminder or restatement. If two students are arguing over a rubber, she will gently direct their attention to the 'problem-fixing' rule or the 'helping rule' pinned up on the wall.

Knowing full well that children will test the rules, she will be prepared to enforce them by firm direction. 'Amy, you know the rule for asking questions. Hands up, thanks.' She will rely on a firm rule-reminder (or restatement to all if necessary) to establish social harmony and teach responsibility. Much of the discipline in the Year 4–7 age range is 'training'; rules are a useful vehicle for such training. If students argue ('I was in the library corner first'), the teacher will resist counter-argument and reassert the rule, several times if necessary. 'But, Amy, you know the rule for the library corner.'

As part of the discipline plan, rules form the fundamental focus backed up by positive teacher direction and use of consequences for ongoing disruptive behaviour. The class will know that the time-out area is there for students who persistently refuse to work (in effect choose not to work) by the fair class rules. It is the cool-off or settle-down place where they go until they have calmed down and are ready to work by the fair rules (see p. 166).

Some examples of visually represented rules

Our Talking Rule	**The card symbolises:** hands up talking noise level
Our Moving Rule	**The card symbolises:** lining up walk don't run sitting on the mat
Our Manners Rule	**The card symbolises:** helping please and thank you cooperation
Our Safety Rule	**The card symbolises:** care for the classroom using equipment properly
Our Problem-fixing Rule	**The card symbolises:** arguments and problems should be talked about asking for the teacher's help

Developing rules for school assemblies

At the primary-age level it can help to develop a school-wide approach to rules governing whole-school assemblies. Collaboration with students is a crucial part of such rules and would need to address why we have assemblies, the different purposes for whole-school gathering times and what special considerations about behaviour need addressing (see Appendix VIII).

Duty-of-care management outside the classroom

The bell goes, you leave your classroom and head down the corridor—the noisy corridor as 200-odd adolescent bodies jostle their way to the exit door—and to partial freedom. All you're thinking of (probably) is having your well-earned cuppa. You notice a couple of boys 'testosteronically bonding' (Ali jumps on to Mustapah's back and calls him a 'poofter'. Craig and Kim laugh at this free entertainment. Mustapah whips round, in mock anger, and says 'P—— off yer dickhead!') Should you address this fracas? How?

Blind-eye syndrome

You hear some loud swearing, you see a couple of girls eating as they 'cruise' the corridor (the principal has made a point about messy corridors and eating, a few weeks back). You notice all this as you head for the staff room but you're not on corridor duty; you're tired. Should you address these small issues of behaviour? Also you suspect that if you address the swearing, the running in the corridor, the eating, the 'testosteronic bonding' they'll probably argue or hassle or whinge. Is it worth the effort?

The answer is yes. We're always in duty-of-care mode even if we're not on a roster. If we simply walk past such behaviour we tacitly say 'it's okay' or that we don't really care.

On my way to the staff room of a large metropolitan high school recently, I passed through the doors bearing the 'no student thoroughfare' sign. I saw three boys enter the admin area, past the sign. As they saw me, one said, 'Sh——! It's him!' and walked the other way. I'm not a martinet but they knew I'd remind them of the rule and they probably couldn't be bothered with the hassle. A female student walked through the doors past the 'no student thoroughfare' sign. I knew her. 'Natalie, morning, have you got a pass to come through here?' I was pleasant. 'I don't need a pass. Mr D said I could see him in the staff room.'

'You still need a pass to come this way to the staff room.'

'Gees, I told yer …' she started to argue. 'Even if you're going to see him, Lisa, you need a pass to come through this part of the school.' She walked off. One of my colleagues saw this exchange (of bluff-the-teacher-for-a-shortcut) and said, wearily, 'I wouldn't waste your breath.' I joined her for a cuppa and tried to point out that there was (and is) a basic 'duty of care' principle at stake here. If we, as teachers, have established some fair basic rules and routines for reasonable social behaviour about movement in corridors, then we need to fairly and consistently enforce those rules—all of us.

Edward Glynn (in Wheldhall, 1992) has noted correlational studies in primary schools that indicate that the number of fights in playgrounds vary according to which teams of teachers are on playground duty at the time. I suspect there is a similar correlation when it comes to corridor supervision, wet-day supervision, bus duty, even the 'relaxed supervision' of Year 11 and 12 canteen areas. I've been in some canteens that look like a rubbish tip! Even with students of this age, staff can develop basic behaviour expectations (published in a user-friendly form), and encourage and enforce such rules, as well as apply fair consequences where appropriate and follow up with challenging students who are rude or abusive when fairly reminded by teachers about litter, or feet up, or …

Some basic areas and issues worth addressing are:

■ Walking, not running, inside buildings (except gym/hall when engaged in games etc.). Call the student over if necessary, although positive reminders are generally enough, for example 'Walking thanks' rather than 'Don't run!'

■ Exit from classrooms, especially in schools with long (potentially noisy) corridors. Each class/subject teacher can briefly discuss this with the class and go over the reasons for an orderly exit from class. It can help, at secondary level, to address this issue briefly at a year-level assembly on day one. The exit-from-class routine will be age-related and based on basic considerations of others, not a Darwinian survival of the fittest!

■ Eating in corridors. Often a quiet word, or rule-reminder, is enough. Have bins strategically located at least at exit doors and corridor intersections. Use first names of students, whenever known, when giving a brief (and least intrusive) reminder to a student. Take students quietly aside from their peers, if possible, rather than make it a big issue.

If students argue over rules, or fairness, or claim that 'other teachers don't care if we …' (the most common challenge), re-direct them to the rule. If they are rude or abusive about any issue, use the follow-up and follow-through procedures of the school. These will often include some school-wide reporting and tracking procedures.

When the teacher makes the effort of tracking a student for follow-up and speaking to them, with the support of a senior teacher, she conveys a powerful message about fundamental civility in the school.

■ Hats on when there's hot weather outside; hats off inside. The hats-off-inside rule sounds like small beer, as an *issue*. It is enough to point out it is not necessary to wear hats inside—full stop. A non-verbal signal is enough for 'hats off inside'. If students argue about taking off hats, point out that this is the rule and you'll follow it up later. Never snatch a student's hat off as a quick way to make the point. Avoid getting into an argument over minor issues like 'hats off in class'. If a student is frequently arguing, the issue is not the rule—it is normally a power struggle and will need to be addressed on a one-to-one basis. Point out publicly, 'If you choose not to take it off them I'll have to follow up with you after class.' Make this deferred consequence as relaxed and expectant as possible. Leave it at that for the moment.

■ Bags neatly stowed in passage (outside class—normally primary level) to allow maximum unencumbered corridor movement.

■ Students do not come into administration area buildings unless directed by a teacher or for genuine first-aid concerns. Basic rule for students is check with duty teacher first.

■ Corridor voices. Some of my primary colleagues have been able to encourage their students to use two-metre voices instead of ten-metre voices in corridors.

Discuss with colleagues what routines for duty of care are essential, helpful and desirable. The issue of duty of care outside a classroom setting needs a school-wide focus, whether it is corridor supervision (even the indirect 'supervision' of a teacher going from A to B), bus duty, wet-day duty or primary playground supervision. Some schools involve other staff, such as canteen staff, caretaker, bus drivers and school-crossing supervisors in an annual management planning session.

At the annual management planning session:

■ Review behaviour in non-classroom settings, inviting students also to review positive and negative aspects of their behaviour in the corridor, playground etc.

■ Analyse observations in terms of their frequency and seriousness, typical age group and physical areas of concern.

■ Address current managerial practice, especially rules, routines, any published plans.

■ Analyse such plans in the light of meeting aims such as student ownership of behaviour and basic rights of health and safety and fair treatment of one another.

■ Review managerial practice in terms of common protocols (see Chapter 1) and positive corrective practices (see Chapter 3), emphasising to students and teachers alike that simple routines can help habituate positive behaviours that consider mutual rights. These expectations can be encouraged (and enforced where necessary) in a relaxed, positive way. We don't need to be martinets or naggers, just consistent.

When we need to raise our voice outside a class, we'll do it on issues that count. Mostly the point of a raised voice is to gain attention from a distance or to stop a cycle of perceived aggression or harassment. Lift the voice initially, firmly call the name—where known—of the student or use a general attention-getting cue such as 'Excuse me' or 'Oi', *then* call the student(s) quietly aside in a more controlled but assertive voice.

A relaxed managerial consistency across the school will convey the message that:

■ the rules are here (at our school) for a good reason
■ the teachers (here) take the purpose for the rules (basic rights) seriously
■ there is a whole school ethos about behaviour expectations
■ there is fair enforcement (including follow-through).

Playground management

As teachers, the bane of our week is often the 'patrol' time. The older the age group of children, the more difficult the time spent outside. Many secondary school teachers will report the 'blind-eye syndrome'—they don't want to see what is happening out there. They just want to finish 'the rounds' as quickly as possible. When students answer back or refuse to pick up litter or argue defiantly or come up with the 101 issues they want resolved, many teachers feel the effort of playground discipline is just not worth it.

Children spend up to 20 per cent of their school day in the playground. It is natural there will be interpersonal conflicts over property, space and friendships. Teachers know what sorts of behaviours they are likely to encounter in a playground setting. It is imperative then that teachers work collaboratively in developing a whole-school playground management plan.

The plan should be reviewed each year and address the frequency and seriousness of common behaviours observed by teachers (and students) as affecting rights of safety, fair play and fair treatment. Ask students where they feel safe (or unsafe) to play and *why* (a map on which students can mark out safe areas can be a helpful visual *aide-memoir*). It can help for staff to correlate their accident and reporting records with the students' perceptions of safe play areas. Most bullying occurs in playground environments. It will be important to survey this aspect of playground behaviour.

Solving the problem of playground behaviour is threefold:

1 There must be adequate, reasonable, enforceable rules.
2 Those rules must be clearly understood by students, teachers and parents.

3 Such rules must be enforced, and relevant consequences must be consistently applied.

The playground problems basically revolve around:

■ unsafe areas, out-of-bounds areas, non-ball-play areas, designated areas such as small children's play areas
■ swearing (including defiance directed at teachers)
■ unsafe play or fighting, over-aggressive play
■ smoking
■ 'dobbing', dispute-settling and teasing
■ litter.

What often creates problems for supervising teachers is that rules for these behaviours are often unclear, uncertain or inconsistently enforced.

Miss P sees a Year 6 boy kicking his footy in a no-ball area. She asks him what he's doing and he replies rudely (the territory of the playground is very different for some students regarding respect, basic courtesy, etc.), 'I'm not doing anything wrong!'

'This is a no-ball area. Take your footy and play down there (gestures to the ball area) please.' He replies with the standard procrastinating line, 'But Miss Davies says I can play here', and so it goes on. Playing one teacher off against another. I've heard some older children (at primary level) say, 'You can't tell us what to do. You're just a Year 1 teacher' and walk off.

Making the rules clear

The focus of a better playground behaviour policy is reasonable, just rules that protect the rights of all members of the school community. Discuss playground rules with the students; make them a focus across the whole school. It may be possible with older students to negotiate some of the rules, although some will be non-negotiable (leaving the playground area, smoking, aggressive behaviour, bullying). One totally non-negotiable rule for safety in the playground regarding throwing (for example stones) is 'Never throw anything *at* anybody—*even in fun*'. Students will often protest that they only threw the stick, or small piece of tanbark, or ball at so-and-so 'in fun'. Tag ball games will need to be carefully assessed in light of safety.

It is important to make sure playground rules and their purpose are clearly understood by all students at assemblies, in the classroom and at home-group level. A clear rule is one that specifies expected and acceptable behaviour, boundaries for such behaviour and consequences for flagrant rule-breaking.

Once the rules and consequences are agreed it is important that they are published and that each class teacher has a copy. It will also help (at primary level) to have large copies posted on the inside glass of the building, looking out, at key sites in the school.

Agreed plans for enforcement

Rules are one thing; the certainty of them being tested, resisted and broken is another. One way of better enforcing the rules is for all teachers to have a consistent plan for dealing with common disruptions.

We know we are daily going to face behaviours within the range from littering to fighting. It makes sense then to work together on a more uniform approach that enables us to answer these questions:

■ Faced with X behaviour, what is the best, or most appropriate approach to take first, second, third and so on?

■ What back-up can we organise if we meet flagrant defiance or hostility? (Staff support, time-out areas in the playground with primary-age students, follow-through procedures and consequences)

Some common examples of playground management

All the skills discussed in Chapter 3 are relevant to playground settings. Several common examples of playground behaviours have been noted here with examples of management language. The key in developing a more consistent management approach is to discuss with staff common issues in our own school. We know we'll have to address these issues, on a frequent basis, and it will help to have a common staff management plan that can even include some common examples of language we might use.

Litter

This is a common issue in most schools. Apart from preventative measures, teachers can encourage students to pick up litter by picking it up with them, even at secondary level.

The teacher approaches several Year 8 students. 'How's it going?' Their faces suggest (non-verbally) that 'It was better before you came.' Students at secondary level do not always expect their teachers to interact with them in playground settings as they do at primary level. 'There's a fair bit of litter here, folks.'

'It's not ours' they chorus. Not arguing, the teacher adds, 'Even if it's not (after all she didn't see them drop it), I'd like you to give me a hand to pick it up. Ta.' Most students will (if grudgingly) give a hand. 'Thanks, every little bit helps.'

They might continue to protest, 'Yeah, but other students were sitting there before.'

'Maybe they were (the teacher tactically avoids an argument) but you're all here now, so let's do the cleaner a favour.' At lower primary level it's so much easier. Ask any group of Year 1 children, 'There's a fair bit of litter around here. How's about you give a hand and we'll pick up ten bits each?' and their earnest reply is likely to be 'We'll pick up a million bits of litter!'

If we see a student dropping litter it's a different story. A simple reminder or direction delivered non-confrontationally is likely to be more effective than a lecture on laziness (tempting as it may be to tell them they are 'unthinking, uncaring, irresponsible').

If they argue and challenge then the issue is clearly not the litter but a power game. In this case the teacher is best served by making the consequences clear. 'I saw you drop it, I'm simply reminding you to put it in the bin. If you choose not to I'll have to follow it up later with …'

I've met adolescents who then add, 'I don't care.' Instead of giving the student the power play she's seeking it's probably more 'effective' to add, 'But I care—I'll follow this up later.' Even if the student does (then) decide to put the rubbish in the bin it will be important to follow up with this student to address her rudeness and incivility (see p. 96).

During a recent playground supervision, I noticed several 'lads' standing, talking, and saw one screw up his chocolate bar wrapper and flick it on to the asphalt. I walked over casually and greeted them. 'You a new teacher here?' They showed some 'checking out' kind of interest so I had a brief chat. As I walked off I casually called the student who'd dropped the litter aside. 'Yeah?' His face showed surprise.

'The bin's over there.' Our eyes quickly scanned the litter, 'Oh yeah—right!'

'Catch you later.' I gave the goodbye and as I walked off I noticed him pick it up. This 'approach' hadn't taken much longer than a straight direction and directing the student quietly 'aside' had kept the discipline least intrusive (see p. 16).

Unsafe play

Sean and Damien (Year 4) are karate kicking in the playground. Several students are watching. While this is basically 'testosteronic bonding', it can get out of hand quickly, plus it sets an unhealthy precedent for younger students who have even less self-control. The teacher calls the boys, by name, across from their attendant peer-group. He does this to minimise the 'grandstanding' that sometimes occurs when teachers correct children in front of their peers. As he calls them across to him he turns aside to chat abstractedly with other students. By dropping his direct eye contact and turning away after the direction he is, in effect, giving the students take-up time (see p. 57) and face-saving time. We'll often need to beckon the students a few times to compensate for social deafness. While these teacher behaviours may sound inconsequential, taken together they telegraph a teacher's confidence and expectation.

When the students walk over, they stand frowning, nonplussed. 'Yeah, what's up?' The teacher uses the question and feedback approach noted earlier (see p. 76). 'What are you doing fellas?'

'Nothing' (more frowning). The teacher gives some feedback.

'Fellas, I saw you karate kicking for several minutes. High kicks too.'

'Yeah, well, we were just mucking around.' The teacher gives some partial agreement. 'Maybe you were, fellas—but what's our rule for safe play?' By refocusing on the fair (known) rule for safe play, the responsibility is now put back on the students. 'But we were just …'

'I know, fellas, but what's our fair rule for …?' The boys sigh, 'We keep our hands and feet to ourselves.' The teacher adds, as the boys walk away, 'Skilful kicking guys but save it for the karate club.' They grin wryly.

On playground duty recently, my colleague and I noticed an agile student hanging upside down by her legs, practising gym, on a steel bar above the concrete path. My colleague walked over and quietly called the girl down. 'Tracey, touch the concrete. How does it feel? Hard, right? Now touch your head and face. How do they feel? Soft? Who's going to win?' While it is appropriate to direct students to play gymnastics elsewhere, I was impressed with the way Toby had used a brief, reflective questioning to enable the student to think through her behaviour.

Playground altercations

When children come up to duty teachers in the playground and complain that they have 'no one to play with', or 'no one likes me', or so and so 'swore at me' or 'took our ball' or 'won't let us play in the sandpit', you can see teachers raise their eyes to the heavens. ('Oh well, here we go again—how many days till the end of term?') It is important that teachers discuss this common management issue to avoid the easy responses of telling the students not to 'hassle me' or to 'grow up' (I've seen teachers do this), or over-servicing the students' possible attention-seeking, or, more commonly, becoming 'judge and jury'. Whatever approaches we take it will be helpful to enable the students to take responsibility wherever appropriate. It can help, for example, to use focused questioning to the individual, or group. 'What can you do if no one will play with you?' 'Okay, they took your ball, what can you say to them to get it back?' We can offer suggestions and invite solutions and even stand nearby to encourage the students as they go back to the sandpit or ball game and try out our suggestions on asserting due rights to property! On other occasions it will be necessary to draw all participants in the conflict aside and run through some basic mediation. Sometimes a rule-reminder to fair play, or a direct question about the fair rule, is enough. If the issue is serious the teacher will need to make the consequences for safe, fair play clear (thus giving the students a directed choice—see p. 85) or even direct some students to time-out areas to cool down and think about their behaviour. Where conflicts between students appear potentially serious, cool-off time and follow-up mediation will be necessary.

Many primary schools now train older students in mediation skills, enabling them to interact with their peers to work through the typical low-level disputes that occur in many playgrounds. This school-wide approach benefits both the mediators and those they work with as they model non-aggressive approaches to mediating and resolving conflict.

Playground environment

It is important to enhance the playground environment so that it contributes to positive behaviour and reduces thoughtless inactivity and boredom:

■ Ensure that there are plenty of decent rubbish bins with small openings so the paper cannot fly out!

■ Beautify the grounds where possible; even asphalt playgrounds can be attractively set out with potted shrubs and trees.

■ Provide ample and reasonable seating for students, preferably with some shaded areas for hot days.

■ Have some well-marked areas for ball games.

■ Improve the play equipment (ask students for ideas within reason, and budget!). I've worked in many inner-city schools where staff have worked with the children on developing playground activities, for example creating quiet areas where children can play board games on outside tables. Games and activities can be taken outside by rostered monitors (in large tubs) and re-stored for the next lunchtime play recess. Games such as bat-tennis, Newcombe, no-touch football, etc. can be rostered on in warmer weather. In playground areas with limited space it can help to nominate specific areas for skipping, running games, quiet games, etc. This plan can be published for students and supervising teachers alike.

▮ Join in student activities. Teachers enjoying games or activities with the students at recess can really enhance the tone of play time.

▮ Stagger play times in larger schools.

▮ Stagger canteen times to avoid the rush when the bell goes.

Enforcement

As with all enforcement, if the consequences are not consistently applied, the students see little point in making the effort to work within the rules. A positive playground discipline plan needs to be:

▮ discussed with students where appropriate

▮ communicated to students and parents

▮ the subject of consistent enforcement.

It will help if staff have a monitoring book to record all significant behaviour concerns that may have been difficult to address in the immediate moment, particularly rudeness or insolence on the part of the student, or any harassment or bullying.

Follow-up of playground incidents is always difficult in terms of time management. It will be important to have an agreed means of following up and following through by senior staff in consultation with duty staff. The monitoring book will help that process. The certainty of consequential follow-up is important for all students. Reinforce positive playground behaviour where observed and make sure the playground management plan has strong support from staff and parents. A playground plan needs to be tailored to the age of the students, the school setting and resources. Its ultimate success will depend on the degree to which staff and students have decided upon the best possible actions they can take and the follow-up they can employ (Rogers, 1995).

Summary

▮ All ages of students in groups need rules to guide and govern the way they work together; to protect the due rights of all.

▮ Rules ought at least to be discussed with the class and where appropriate worked out together with the teacher.

▪ Rights as a feature of rule-making guide children towards collaborative democracy. There is no guarantee they'll follow such a process but the 3Rs focus (rights, rules, responsibilities) gives a just and reasonable basis for membership of, participation in and enjoyment of the benefits of a social group.

▪ Rules should be clear and as situation-specific as possible, with understood consequences for significant infringement of rights.

▪ Clear rules (up to Year 7 or 8) can be displayed around the room, or inserted in students' books as a reminder.

▪ It is easier to discipline when rules are fair and clear. A teacher can more easily discipline by referring back to *our* rules for 'safety', or 'settling problems' or 'movement' ...

▪ It is expected that the basic rules would be fundamentally the same for all teachers across the school.

▪ Rules need to be taught. Part of positive rule enforcement is the establishment–training–enforcement cycle: regularly, quietly reminding the students when they are off-task and reinforcing when they are on-task with the rules.

▪ It is important that staff work together on common management plans for all duty-of-care management outside of the classroom setting.

Questions to consider

Duty of care beyond the classroom

▪ Is there a general duty of care plan covering corridor/wet-day supervision and playground supervision? How does it operate? Is it published or known-by-experience? What are the essential elements of the duty-of-care plan? Does it, for example, address the follow-up and follow-through of students who refuse reasonable teacher requests about behaviour?

▪ How does the duty-of-care plan fit in with the concept of preferred management practice as applied in classrooms (for example a least-intrusive-to-most-intrusive approach to correcting, acknowledging and encouraging positive/cooperative student behaviours; avoiding a confrontative and argumentative situation; using positive corrective practice where possible)?

▪ Do staff and students have the opportunity to do a needs analysis each year on playground issues, bus-duty provision, wet-day options and procedures, etc.? How are those opportunities realised? (See Appendix IX.)

■ Is there a policy and due process for dealing with harassment/ bullying in the school? Is it published? Are key stakeholders (teachers, students, parents) aware of the due process?

■ Is there a time-out plan for the playground setting? How does it operate? How are students 'tracked'?

■ What is the follow-up procedure beyond time-out? For example, if a student has been in time-out for unsafe play, or damaging school property, is there normally a secondary consequence (beyond the primary consequence of time-out)? If so, how is that procedure normally carried through (by the initiating teacher, an internal incident-report sheet, a senior teacher acting on behalf of the teacher reporting the incident)?

■ What is the procedure for developing individual behaviour plans for repeatedly disruptive/aggressive behaviour in the playground?

■ What consideration is given to environment and behaviour: seating? shade areas?

■ Are there recreation/play opportunities, play areas and litter bins? Are there enough? Are they strategically placed? Is there enough play equipment (balls, ropes, bats etc.)?

■ Are there any areas in which we need to improve duty-of-care management (for example playground environment, playground management, bus duty, wet-day management, excursions, canteen)?

■ List the areas of concern (and why) and suggest ways we can fine-tune, adapt, modify or change our current duty-of-care plans.

Supports to behaviour management

Everybody's talking at me ... they don't hear a word I'm saying.

H. Nelson

Behavioural consequences

Andrew sports a crewcut and has a pinched, drawn expression; he seems perpetually sullen and annoyed with the world. Although only in Year 3 he already has a well-developed battery of task-avoidance and attention-seeking strategies. The late Rudolf Dreikurs (1982) would argue that by these strategies (frustrating to teacher and students alike), he is seeking to belong. No doubt that is true. It is also true that Andrew's home environment includes bashings and emotional harangues. Do we blame society for his behaviour? Do we blame Andrew? Do we blame the parents? Do we avoid blame altogether?

During process writing Andrew spits on Frousoula's work. She calls out to the teacher, 'Miss, Miss.' She waves her hand in the air and finally the teacher comes over. 'He spat on my writing Miss!' Andrew immediately says, 'Well she ... anyway she said I couldn't have a rubber!' The teacher is faced with the question, 'What will I do—both immediately and in the long term?' She doesn't waste time in sorting out who started it—she'll do that later. She says to Andrew, 'Get a Kleenex and wipe the spit up now thank you.' She is firm but not aggressive. He refuses. She thought he might say that so she doesn't waste time arguing. She directs Frousoula to a spare desk or to work with a friend away from Andrew. She ignores the sullen Andrew—she'll follow him up later. She gently tears off the spat-upon page and leaves it on her desk. Andrew has some formal time-out in the class room (see p. 166).

After ten minutes, she gives Andrew a choice. 'You can either rewrite that page now or I'll have to ask you to stay back and write it during your playtime.' No comment. She moves off. He sulks. She tactically ignores.

Just before recess bell she reminds him. 'Andrew, stay back. I want to talk to you.' When the class has gone she acknowledges he's probably not feeling the best about having to stay back (see p. 96). She asks him what he can do to fix up the spat-upon work. After a brief discussion of possibilities for restitution, he agrees that the work is damaged. The teacher encourages him to rewrite the work (and later, apologise), not because Frousoula wants Andrew's copy but because Andrew needs to see some form of logical outcome to his anti-social behaviour. She did the same when he used the scissors to scratch the desk. He stayed back and sanded it. His teacher, rather than just punish him, used logical or behavioural consequences.

Andrew, despite his home background, is responsible for *his* present behaviour. While the teacher is sympathetic to Andrew's plight she doesn't blame that chimera, society. She believes that the child should be held accountable in some way in the short term, and assisted with behaviour-change strategies in the longer term.

Behavioural consequences are essentially the connecting of a responsible outcome to the social disruption. They can be decided by the adult, with the child, or with the class group. The whole class will have discussed the nature of consequences and responsibility along with the fair class rules (see Chapter 4). The teacher will have discussed the general nature of consequences with the class during the establishment phase of the year. We will not be able to supply a list of *logical* behavioural consequences for every situation, but we can discuss the nature of 'if ... then ...' relationships in social behaviour. We can also distinguish between non-negotiable and negotiable consequences, where the student(s) and teacher can work out the consequence together. With negotiable consequences the student contributes to the process and outcome of behavioural ownership.

Non-negotiable consequences are used with serious behaviours such as verbal or physical aggression; smoking; drug-taking; violence; possession of weapons; psychological, racial, sexual or physical bullying. The consequences for these behaviours are known in advance, published and applied without negotiation but will involve due processes such as appropriate restitution, behavioural contracts, accountability conferencing with those they have hurt (see p. 106). Non-negotiable consequences often involve detentionable outcomes, exclusion from privileges such as play times with others (see p. 158), or suspension. Behavioural consequences are based on the fundamental notion of respect for others' rights, and ownership of and accountability for one's own behaviour.

In whatever form they are used, however, the child needs to understand that behaviour is related to outcome. Desirable/ undesirable consequences ought to be seen as an outcome of choice. By 'logical' we mean there is a connection between behaviour and outcome that is as fair and sensible as natural justice can make it. By 'consequence' we mean that one thing ought to follow another. Students have to learn to accept that they are responsible for their behaviour and its effect on others and the classroom environment.

To make consequences work, a teacher needs a positive relationship with the class; a climate built on cooperation, respect, clear rights–rules understanding and one where the teacher seeks to model reasonable and fair behaviour. Because consistency is important to an ongoing relationship in a class, a teacher will uniformly apply the consequences, not giving up or in because of mood or circumstance. Try not to be distracted by excuses or special pleading or the 'It's not my fault' argument. While it is not advisable to be inflexible, it is important to consistently apply the consequence. We will need to apply consequences uniformly to the 'nice' student who leaves a mess as well as the 'not so nice' student. There are rare children who will refuse all responsibility and accountability. With these children we still treat them respectfully and follow through with contracting or problem-solving strategies. In extreme cases there will be students who will continually challenge teacher and school authority; their parents will effectively bully the school. In these rare cases a school will need to utilise suspension and expulsion options.

It is also advisable to decide, beforehand, the sort of behaviours to which you will seek to apply consequences. If Nicky hands in dirty work because she is a characteristically 'messy hands' child, will we decide that she needs to do it again? Are we going to correct it or discuss how she can improve on the general presentation of her work and that we will expect better next time?

It is also important to discuss with students the general use of consequences in class. If students make it difficult for others to learn, be safe, or be treated with respect they:

■ will be reminded of our rules
■ may be asked to work away from others
■ may have to take some cool-off time
■ may even be asked to leave our class for formal time-out
■ will always have to stay back to work through with the teacher ways in which they can improve their behaviour.

This discussion is not conducted in a challenging, threatening way but as the natural outcome of rights and responsibilities.

Degree of seriousness

Many schools have developed a levels system of discipline which includes consequential outcomes. Each level (say one through four or five levels) indicates the seriousness of the students' typical behaviour patterns and the sorts of consequences (including behaviours that require suspension) and support processes available. Each level requires increasing (and labour-intensive!) involvement by school administration, parents and support personnel.

The illusion of choice

In a normal verbal direction to a child, a teacher will better develop a sense of self-control by giving the child an appropriate choice. (I could say 'illusion' of choice because 'totally free' choices are not really possible.)

'Tim, you may do the process writing now, as we all are, or you will be asked to stay back and do it at play time.' 'Your mess can be cleaned up now Franca, before recess, or during recess.' 'You know the fair rule for communication in our room Simone.' (As a warning this throws up a choice to the child.) 'Adrian, if you choose not to work quietly here, I'll have to ask you to work over there.' This choice could be expressed as a question. 'Adrian if you're having problems working here, with Paul, would you prefer to work separately?' Even a knowing glance or firm, brief eye contact is a message to the child about choice. A short tactical ignoring of low-level attention-seeking can be a 'chance to choose' for the attention-seeking child (see pp. 59–63).

When to enforce?

Consequences should not been forced where there is high-level antagonism or safety concerns. To force or demand Con to apologise on the spot for calling the teacher a 'f—— bitch' is fruitless when Con is clearly being provocative or teacher-baiting. While it is important to address such swearing assertively (see pp. 295f) and use immediate (supported) time-out, any apologies are best worked through after both parties have cooled down. Even if the student is suspended for such swearing, it will still be important for the teacher, with a facilitator, to do some repairing and rebuilding later. Time-out and suspension are never ends in themselves; they need to be linked to some repairing and rebuilding to enable workable reconciliation. Positive discipline techniques use defusing/deflecting, rule restatements or choices as processes for handling high-level conflict, leaving a choice with the student, wherever possible. Later, the teacher will follow through with consequences such as 'fix up', 'replace', 'work for', 'apologise', 'write out', 'redo'. At the time of the disruption, the teacher acts in a way that minimises attention by the teacher and the student audience.

With low-level disruptions such as leaving a mess, throwing things, ripping a page, scribbling on another's work or low-level attention-seeking, the teacher can make the issue clear but indicate that the student will be asked to stay back and fix things up later (or at a specified time). A *deferred* consequence is one applied later in time; this acknowledges that students often want to 'save face' but keeps the certainty of the consequence in place. 'That language is unacceptable and against our rule—we'll discuss that later.' When

HOW A CHILD IS HELD ACCOUNTABLE

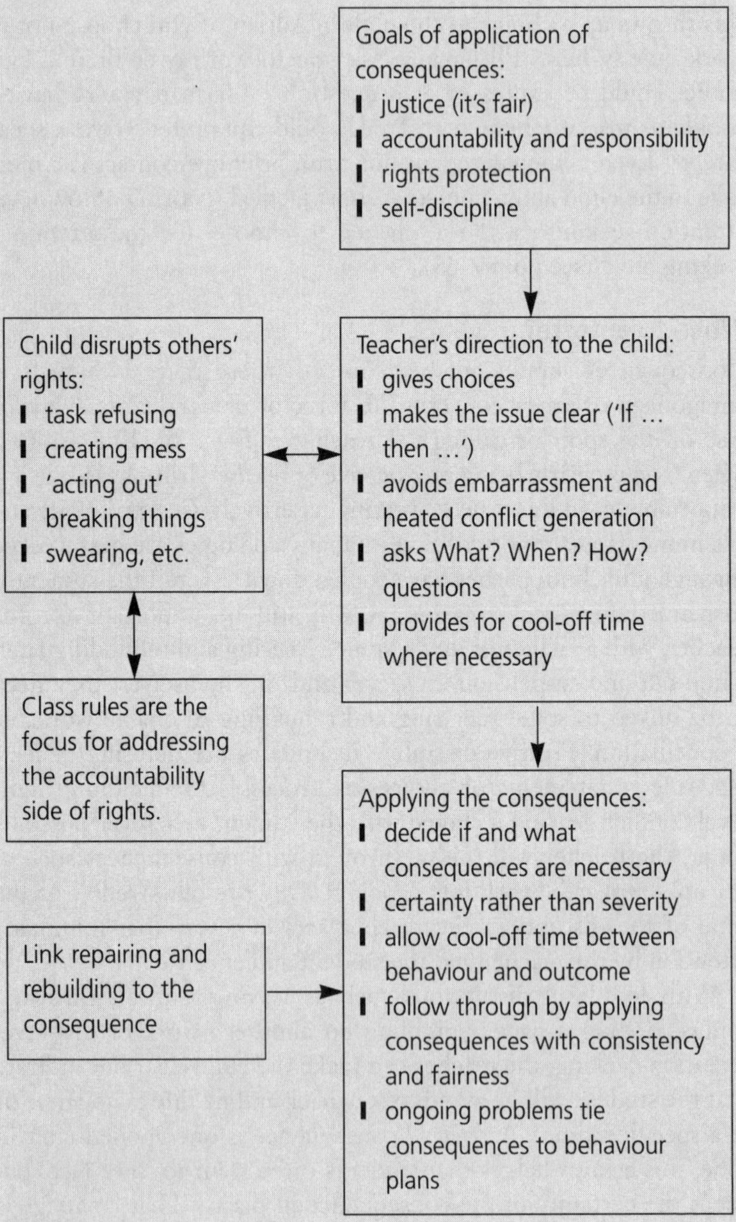

Goals of application of consequences:
- justice (it's fair)
- accountability and responsibility
- rights protection
- self-discipline

Child disrupts others' rights:
- task refusing
- creating mess
- 'acting out'
- breaking things
- swearing, etc.

Teacher's direction to the child:
- gives choices
- makes the issue clear ('If … then …')
- avoids embarrassment and heated conflict generation
- asks What? When? How? questions
- provides for cool-off time where necessary

Class rules are the focus for addressing the accountability side of rights.

Applying the consequences:
- decide if and what consequences are necessary
- certainty rather than severity
- allow cool-off time between behaviour and outcome
- follow through by applying consequences with consistency and fairness
- ongoing problems tie consequences to behaviour plans

Link repairing and rebuilding to the consequence

Figure 5.1

following up, ask the questions, 'What were you doing that was against our class rules? How are you going to fix it up?'

The climate of application of consequences is important. Consequences are not mere punishment; they are fair accountability.

What sort of consequences?

When I speak to children about fixing up certain behaviour, they often suggest: 'Give some lines', 'Pick up papers', 'Stay back', 'Tell his mum.' The question the teacher needs to respond with is, 'How will *that* fix up the broken desk, the busted racquet, the writing on the wall, the hurt child, the spit on the floor, the clay balls on the cupboard?'

Providing the teacher is not sarcastic, cruel, authoritarian or revengeful, most children respond with an understanding of accountability and a sense of justice. It is useful to ask them, 'What will you do about X?' It is an attempt to foster some connection in their thinking and future action. Behavioural consequences can start as early as four years of age. With most children, behavioural consequences are not applied to accidents or forgetfulness. In these cases, we simply encourage the student to clean up, repair or fix things up with an apology as necessary.

Ibrahim, aged nine, had gained a sense of belonging in the playground by belting others. Some teachers had nagged, some had yelled, some had pleaded. Worst of all, some had been dismissive— 'boys will be boys'. After some staff discussion, it was decided to use logical behavioural consequences. His teacher, with the principal, explained: 'Ibrahim, because you have chosen to hurt other children in the playground, you will have to play by yourself.' He whined that it wasn't fair. The teacher didn't engage Ibrahim in a discussion but repeated the consequence. 'Because you keep hurting others in the playground you'll have to play by yourself and not with other students at normal play time.'

At lunch, Ibrahim was kept in and he looked through the window at the other children enjoying their freedom. He had his play time later with a minder (rotated staff member). No one to punch, hit or strike, except the trees and asphalt! In this case it was important that he 'feel' the consequences of his behaviour.

Ibrahim—all by himself

After one week he was craving to be 'given another go'. 'Sure Ibrahim—as long as you play by the fair rules for play time.' A simple behaviour plan was drawn up with a few targeted behaviours for fair play. Each duty teacher received a copy of the plan (with suggestions on how to speak to Ibrahim when they met him on playground duty). The plan was monitored daily, then weekly. This approach was applied calmly, fairly, consistently and expectantly.

Rachel, in a fit of anger, busted a school tennis racquet on the school fence. What was the class teacher to do? Her mum was virtually impossible to contact and the third male live-in partner at the caravan park where she lived couldn't care at all. Was it worth contacting the guardians? Not really. We didn't want to see Rachel belted up. (There is a time and process for parental contact; it was not now.) When her high-level expression of anger had cooled down, her teacher said, 'Rachel, you've busted the school racquet. It cost forty dollars. It needs to be fixed up. What are you going to do?' He didn't waste time asking Rachel why she broke the class racquet. Neither was it worth getting into over-pitying because of her life at the caravan park.

'What are you going to do to fix it up, Rachel?'

'Dunno.'

'Well, you think about what you've done—it's your responsibility to fix it up. You've got a choice, you can pay for it in the next week, or we'll give you jobs to pay for it.'

'I ain't gonna buy one!'

'See this card, Rachel. I'm going to write two weeks down on it. You will be asked to do jobs each day to help pay for the racquet. This is the way you can earn the money' (or, really, learn about logical accountability).

She swept, washed, tidied and so on at set times. The teacher signed the card each day. She was not demeaned, or screamed at—just held accountable. Firmly, determinedly, supportively.

JOB SHEET

When a child has broken or damaged something the related consequence is that it is paid for in some way.

We believe that the child should take responsibility for their 'choice' of action.

Children pay for broken equipment by completing a job sheet to 'earn' the money to replace it.

The jobs they do are community jobs which will benefit the school and they are completed during play times. This is a form of restitution—a way of putting things right.

Job sheet to pay for broken car	
▮ sharpen pencils	20¢
▮ teach people to skip	20¢
▮ sort out games boxes	20¢
▮ tidy book boxes	20¢
▮ share books with children	20¢
TOTAL	$1.00

Adapted from the Behaviour Policy, Hare St Infant School, Harlow, UK.

Three boys let down the tyres on Mr S's car (a 'joke'). The VP firmly employed logical consequences. The boys pumped them up in their own time. Tom smashed a window in room 17 ('fit of anger' during art). His mother didn't smash the window so the principal used a logical consequences approach and the child cleaned out the glass, swept it up and prepared the window for the glazier. He was then 'on contract' for two weeks doing jobs around the school to link his restitution behaviour with 'payment' for the new glass. The contract was written up to give it an air of authority.

Many teachers let torn books, mess, unacceptable social behaviours, etc. go unaccounted for, yet resort to yelling, giving lines or dictionary copying. All these are understandable when a teacher is frustrated but they model poor frustration tolerance and create an illogical (mere punishment) perspective on disruptive behaviours in the thinking of children.

Staying back

While it is appropriate to keep students back after class, to follow up and follow through (see p. 196), detention that requires the student to just sit still—doing nothing—for 20–30 minutes is a totally unrelated consequence, like the giving of lines. There is no link to the behaviour except the power of the adult to coerce the child. There is often no attempt to repair and rebuild. In a sense it actually denies rational, social accountability. Mere detention or an instruction to 'write 100 lines on ...' is arbitrary and does not provide a logical or behavioural connection between behaviour and outcome. In a study on rewards and punishments in British secondary schools (Merrett and Tang, 1994) students rated 'being given lines' as the least effective (4 per cent), and only 17 per cent of teachers rated it as effective, yet it is still widely used as a punishment. I've heard colleagues say things like, 'Well, it's quick and gets some pain in!'

If a child is asked to stay back, there should be some directions such as explaining X behaviour, fixing X properly, tidying or cleaning X, apologising to X, or writing about X. The 4W form is useful in this situation:

■ What I did (against our class rules).
■ What rule or right I broke or infringed.

▌ Why I did it (my explanation).

▌ What I think I should do to fix it up.

· A copy of this form can be found in Appendix II.

Consequences can teach responsibility

Logical behavioural consequences are also very useful training *and* teaching processes for all children. A teacher will, from time to time engage the class in a general discussion about consequences and responsibility. This can also be a focus of, or theme in, a piece of literature or drama or self-esteem game.

Logical consequences enable students to think through the consequences of their own actions. Consequential and causal thinking (cause and effect) are important learnings for children, enabling a more responsible approach to social relationships.

When a child is being questioned about what consequences ought to apply, this too is a learning situation. Skilful teachers can do this with individuals (or groups) to encourage students to see things from another's perspective ('How would X feel if ...?', 'How would you feel if you had that problem?') and to see alternative solutions ('What else could you have done when you got angry?'). The attention, through such teacher–student interaction, is on how a person is thinking out her problem and the consequences. The teacher facilitates and guides that process, which is one reason why effective teachers use discursive approaches even when dealing with disruptive students.

Paul threw a piece of wood in a fit of pique during class and nearly hit his textile teacher. Evidently she'd called the Year 7s 'a pack of animals'. Acting as the advance scout for the Year 7 social justice unit, Paul threw the bit of wood in anger and (fortunately) missed! Quite apart from the teacher's behaviour and Paul's low-frustration tolerance, what consequences for his wrong action were to be applied? Deprive him of textile lessons? Get him to produce a written and verbal apology? Contact his parents? Deprive him of sport?

He said he had not intended actually to hit his teacher but he agreed his action was wrong. He was asked, 'What else could you have done?'

'Counted to ten?' was his reply. 'Sure, that's often helpful' replied the senior teacher. 'Or I could have spoken to her after ... or I could have stood up and said I don't agree.' (She wouldn't have listened!) After exploring other alternatives, he agreed his action was wrong. He wrote an apology, and verbally apologised. He took responsibility for his action. Because the behaviour was dangerous, he was also deprived of art for two sessions (it was felt this would be a salutary lesson to the others). What will affect long-term relations between Paul and his teacher, though, is how much she is prepared to establish a positive working relationship.

Logical behavioural consequences are most effective when teachers have good working relations with their students. At one school where the staff had carefully explained and discussed logical conse-quences with their children, and begun to apply them, the children began to even pick up the language. One little chap presented him-self at the principal's door. 'Yes, what do you want Mario?' he asked. Looking at the principal, with a dour and serious face, he said, 'I'm here for my logical consequences, sir!'

I'm here for my logical consequences

Behavioural consequences summary

▪ Behavioural consequences are part of group socialisation: consequences follow actions.

▪ Behavioural consequences are part of the rights, rules and responsibilities framework of a classroom and school.

▪ Behavioural consequences concentrate on *present* behaviour.

▪ Behavioural consequences can enable a positive working relationship with students.

▪ Behavioural consequences emphasise:
  – self-control
  – responsibility and accountability
  – choice.

▪ Behavioural consequences are a labour-intensive feature of classroom management but they are worth it.

Questions to consider

▪ What does the consequence teach the child?

▪ Is there a connection between the behaviour and the consequence applied?

▪ Is the consequence reasonable; is there a 'degree of seriousness' scale applied to the consequences we use? For example, bullying is significantly more serious than a uniform breach and yet some teachers will apply the same consequence (for example, detention)!

▪ Do we emphasise the certainty of the consequence or the severity of the consequence? Do we keep the respect intact when applying the consequence?

▪ Do we keep the focus on the present and the future—to encourage the student to repair and rebuild? Do we model a repairing-and-rebuilding focus or a punitive focus?

▪ What are the typical sorts of consequences we use for, say, repeated calling out, forgetting homework, lateness to class, not having appropriate materials, putting others down, avoiding or refusing to do a task?

It can help to discuss with colleagues the typical behaviour for classroom and playground that we all face and develop some common consequences we can 'negotiate' with our students.

Time-out

Shane is a testy little seven-year-old. The term 'spoiled rotten' would not be unfairly applied; his parents' break-up hasn't helped either.

In class Shane displays low tolerance to frustration in both learning tasks and social behaviour. A grand attention-seeker of the 'notice-me' variety; most primary teachers have experienced a 'Shane' at some stage in their career. He seems worse on Mondays (probably the father's access over Sunday). He arrives late, already making a scene as he enters the room. During morning talk he interrupts, makes silly noises and moves out of his place several times. Not only is his behaviour frustrating to the teacher, it annoys the other members of the class. Does the child need to be removed from his peers to cool off and rethink his behaviour?

Using time-out

The notion and use of time-out has been a phenomenon of Australian schools for over a decade, especially so since the abolition of corporal punishment in government schools. However, time-out means different things to different people. As a practice it can be open to abuse and it certainly is no panacea in the discipline context. Like any management practice it needs a clear philosophy of practice before and after its use to be effective. As a process, it should never stand by itself—it needs well-thought-out back-up and support.

What do we mean by time-out?

For some teachers time-out might mean sending the student to stand in a corner (in the old days some teachers made students stand in the corner facing the wall, sometimes with a dunce's hat on); it might mean isolating the student at a desk, away from other students; it might mean sitting him outside the principal's office or in a special time-out room. Though there are legal problems with supervision, some teachers remove a student to stand outside the class. However, when a teacher sends an attention-seeker outside the room, the student will most often use the window to get more attention. With small children, the notion of time-out might simply mean, 'hands on head' or 'all pencils down and hands flat on desks'. The most persuasive advocate of time-out as part of a well-developed discipline program is William Glasser (1969). He stresses that time-out is not a punishment but a time for a student to reflect on his behaviour and to come up with some solution, or at least renegotiate entry back into the social group.

Why time-out may be necessary

Time-out is very simply time *out*, or *away* from the group. It is, essentially, cool-off time, when a child is 'isolated' from his peers. All children want to belong to the group. With time-out what is essentially being communicated is that the student's behaviour is so disturbing to the teacher and her peers that she cannot any longer be accepted as part of the group *at that time*. The student is thus directed away from her immediate peers in the room, or in a place out of the room. Time-out, then, has a logical basis as well as a basis in utility. It's all very well for non-teaching people to overplay the case of the exit-student's rights; the rights of all members of the classroom (including the teacher's right to teach), need to be taken into account when disruptive behaviour is persistent or unsafe.

What prompts time-out?

Whenever a student significantly disrupts another student's rights, or significantly disrupts the teacher's right to teach and to manage the group, then the disruptive student should be 'timed-out' from the group. Examples of such behaviour would be:

▮ refusing to stop fighting
▮ racing around the room going 'bananas'
▮ constantly interrupting and refusing to settle down
▮ verbally abusing a teacher or student
▮ persistently refusing to obey the fair rules of the room and thus infringing the teacher's or students' rights to safety, movement, learning and positive social interaction.

Time-out is based on the following assumptions:

1 The teacher has fair, just rules that protect the rights of all class members. Such rules need to be clear, discussed with the students and reinforced with consequences where necessary.

2 The teacher has thought out the room organisation and procedures. For example, a time-out area in the room is helpful at primary level for those times when children need to be isolated for their own sake as well as their peers (for example if they are overly angry or uptight). Many primary schools (at infant level) have a cool-off time, or take-five, area. This is an area where the child can sit for five minutes to cool off. Some teachers even have a five-minute egg-timer there so the child can monitor his own time-out. It is important not to call this area the 'naughty corner', or 'naughty seat', or 'sin bin' (that's poor psychology, let alone poor theology!).

3 The teacher has a preventative management and discipline plan in place (see Chapter 3). But where positive correction does not resolve the issue, or more correctly, encourage the student to control his own behaviour, then time-out may be necessary.

As Glasser (1969) pointed out, time-out is not merely another punishment, it is *time* away from the group, *time* to reflect on behaviours, the broken rule, and how to fix things up so the problem is not repeated. Its goal is to give both the group and the persistent disrupter a 'breather'. It is important to recognise that time out *as a consequence* is not an end in itself. It is a *primary* consequence that will often necessitate a secondary consequence such as cleaning up mess, or completing unfinished work, or working through some restitution, *after* the time-out period. For time-out to work, whether in the classroom, time-out area, or in a room away from the class, several conditions need to be observed:

1 The student has physical isolation.

2 The time-out area or room is non-reinforcing. If a student goes to a place where there are toys or books, or the seat outside the office where she can 'preen' or watch the parade of people, then the time-out situation may become reinforcing and the process

will lose its effectiveness. A time-out area is not a jail (it is not solitary confinement), but neither should it be a place where the disrupter can chat with a counsellor, the school secretary, students who pass by, the principal. Counselling best occurs at other times. Students may associate time-out with unhelpfully reinforcing experiences. If a student goes to a senior staff member for time-out it is unhelpful to give the child special privileges. 'Would you like to do some gardening for a while?' This associates the time-out *with* the special privilege. Also ineffective is sending the student to the principal to get 'howled out', or humiliated. Some teachers believe it is the principal's (or coordinator's) job to 'fix' the student, as if by sending the student for the stern talks he will come back promising to be good for ever! The teacher who initiates the time-out process is responsible (with appropriate support) for follow-up and follow-through. If a student has been in time-out several times in close succession, then obviously an individual behaviour plan will need to be developed with that student (see pp. 170f).

3 The student knows why he was sent there; why he was isolated from *our* class. It is important the teacher communicates that it is the particular behaviour (rather than 'You make me sick with your calling out, now get out!') that is wrong and against the rules and that is why we are asking him to leave *our* class. We are trying to communicate separation from the group because he is too upset, too angry or refuses to cooperate.

4 Time-out is normally the last option when our classroom discipline plan doesn't work or when the student blatantly refuses to choose to follow the fair class rules. This is the way it would be communicated to older students. It ought never to be used as the easy way out for the teacher when a child is calling out, refuses a task, does not have equipment, comes to class late, is indulging in low-level clowning, etc.

5 Exiting of the students for time-out is clearly established as school policy. Should it be left to the teacher to send the student to the time-out area? Should a third party come and exit the student? A clear, school-wide policy needs to be worked out. This

policy will have a least-to-most degree of intrusiveness from five minutes cool-off time in the room, to the use of colleagues' classrooms for a time-out area.

It is especially important to consider how we address students who refuse to leave the classroom (or if time-out is used in the playground, how we deal with students who refuse to be directed to time-out in the school building). In the case where a student refuses to leave with a support teacher it will often be more effective for the support colleague to stay and supervise the acting-out student while the regular teacher calmly directs the class outside (to 'remove' the audience) to another area.

While the law basically allows some physical restraint of children who are a danger to themselves, or others, dragging or 'manhandling' older children out of a classroom can be very stressful for the teacher and the rest of the class. The basic rule needs to be, if we can't reasonably 'remove' a child from her audience, when she is significantly acting out, then we remove the audience from the child. No teacher should be left in the invidious position of having to scream and yell and threaten.

It is preferable in these cases that the student is 'escorted' to time-out by a third party, especially with post-primary students who are aggressive, hostile and abusive in their behaviour. I've seen some very ugly scenes where teachers have tried physically to force aggressive students from their classes. The exit process is best carried out as calmly and with as much dignity as is possible so that it doesn't become reinforcing to the disrupter.

In some cases, colleague-exit may be the only option (in small schools with limited staff, for instance). Teachers working in classrooms close to each other can use the exit-card system. A card with *exit* and the room number written on it is taken to a colleague's classroom by a trusted student. When the colleague receives the card, he leaves his door wide open, walks across or down the passage to the relevant classroom and directs the disruptive student to his own classroom for time-out. He gives minimum attention to the student and sends her back when he believes she is ready, or keeps her in his room until that timetable period is over. It is the responsibility of the initiating teacher to follow up and follow through.

6 A decision is made on how long the student spends away from the class. The student is there because of his disruptive-to-rights behaviour. He needs time to settle down and think about his behaviour. It will be someone's job (year-level coordinator, senior teacher, vice-principal, principal) to enable the student to renegotiate entry to the classroom. A student needs time to cool down, think and state his intention. Five minutes for *in-class* time-out is normally enough. Fifteen to twenty minutes is an average time for out-of-class time-out, unless the student, for some reason, is excessively angry or hostile. If the school has a time-out room then the student will normally stay there only for the duration of that timetable period. If a student refuses to cooperate then parents would normally be notified.

7 Where possible, the student has been made aware that if she continues (in her present behaviour) to affect others' rights then she will have to face time-out. 'Jess, I've asked you to settle down several times. If you're not willing to work by our fair rules I'll have to ask you to leave.' Avoid arguing. State, restate—leave the 'choice' with the student.

If a specific room is used for time-out, then it is preferable that all teachers are rostered to staff the room. A clear policy of teacher action should be established, for example:

- Ensure that there is minimal discussion with the child (at the time of 'cooling off').
- Record the details of time, child's name, class, etc. (see the 4W form, Appendix II).
- When the child seems to have settled down, direct her back to her class (if appropriate).
- Establish a clear policy of student movement to and from the time-out room.
- Establish a clear understanding of, and framework for, teacher follow-up. A time-out room is never an end in itself.

8 All students know the purpose of the time-out corner, time-out desk area (older children), or time-out area away from the classroom. They need to know it is part of the fair treatment in our room, and our school.

When a student is overly angry, throwing a tantrum, or very upset, he needs to be isolated to settle down before he can rejoin the group. The emphasis with all time-out is isolation from the group until the student can renegotiate his return. Where any student needs physical control, a teacher should talk firmly to him (while the physical removing takes place), explaining that he is being removed because of his behaviour. 'David, you cannot stay in our room when you keep hurting people. You can come back to our room when you agree to work by our fair rules.' Small children can be firmly held by the hand and led off to the time-out corner. Older students should always be directed verbally. 'Your behaviour is unacceptable, we cannot allow your fighting (or whatever).' Then direct a 'safe' student to get an exit-teacher to come and effect the exit. It is essential that the school has a well-planned procedure for this.

Time-out is a necessary part of the process of teaching students responsibility for their behaviour. Time-out, therefore, needs to seek a verbal or, in some cases, written 'contract' about future behaviour. Time-out, then, is backed up by all the other relationship-building steps that teaching staff engage in to enable and encourage a student to behave appropriately as a member of a social group.

Behaviour plans

Behaviour plans are an aid to a well-developed discipline plan. Essentially they are an agreement between the teacher and the individual or the teacher and the class group about desirable social behaviours or task goals. They are the result of negotiation and discussion between teacher and student or a teacher and the whole class. On some occasions, behaviour planning will involve senior administration and parents.

Behaviour plans may be verbal or written and may contain short-term or long-term goals. They can be modelled or rehearsed (with younger students) as a means of reinforcing the target behaviour and ought to be evaluated by all parties as part of the process of achieving behaviour change.

The rationale

Teacher and student(s) must be able to negotiate if they are to use a behaviour plan. If the relationship climate doesn't lend itself to this, the teacher may need to call in a support teacher to mediate and enable the process.

A behaviour plan is built on the belief and expectation that children can be helped towards better problem-solving, exploration of alternatives, making of choices, making of commitments and following through. The teacher's task is to enable, encourage and support students to take responsibility for their behaviour and learning. Students also need to understand that there are consequences of their choices or their non-fulfilment of the 'contracted' plan.

Students, therefore, need plans they can cope with; not too much too soon. The fact that an individual behaviour plan is being used often indicates that normal classroom approaches have not secured appropriate social or task behaviours. The plan should, therefore, not try to change everything overnight. Start with small, achievable areas.

Types of behaviour plans

If a behaviour plan (often called a 'contract') is written, it's better that the student participates in the writing, perhaps even signing (see Appendix III). Small children can be helped to draw a picture of the desirable behaviour, or have a chart for on-task work. If the plan involves behaviour modification, then task records or goal charts can be used. Little Boris wanders from class teacher to art to library with his little behaviour book. When he reaches ten stars in any day he gets a special stamp. He has a picture for his target behaviour, he has rehearsed it and his teachers expect, encourage and reinforce his behaviour plan.

Plans may be verbal. Essentially a plan is a commitment to do a certain task or follow a set of behaviours. The target behaviour is set. It may be rehearsed. The task can be modelled and rehearsed with small children, particularly angry, hitting children. 'When you get angry, I want you to come over here and tell me. Then I will suggest you go and sit in the time-out corner.' The modelling helps to specify the plan behaviour. This rehearsal approach can be

applied to tasks as well as behaviour, but should be practised at behaviour-neutral times and only one-to-one with the student.

Starting a plan

It's best to think through, with a helpful colleague, the problem behaviour and the desirable target behaviour/s. Remember, it is better to define the target behaviour clearly and in small steps. Here are some examples:

▪ sitting at the desk for five minutes during work sessions (then a follow-through to next step)
▪ writing half a page during diary-writing time
▪ putting up a hand and waiting, instead of calling or yelling out
▪ reading X pages of the reader with a friend
▪ doing a jigsaw puzzle, without upsetting the game
▪ asking for help from a designated person (teacher or aide).

The teacher starts the process at a neutral time by clarifying what the behaviour problem is. The best way to do this is by discussion with the student using a problem-solving approach involving a definition of the problems, an exploration of solutions, and selection and modelling of a target behaviour for the plan. The student needs to know and be treated (relative to age) as if she is a part of the process. Find an emotionally neutral time and start the process. 'Sonia, we need to discuss your behaviour in class. You know the rule for asking questions—we need to talk about ways to remember our class rule here ...'

Verbal plans

Huan is playing with his car on his desk during diary-writing time. (The teacher had explained to the class that no toys should be on the desks in the Year 4 room.) She gives him a choice to give her the toy, put it on her desk and get back to work or stay back at play time and explain his behaviour. This is it! This is Huan's cue to throw one of his anger fits.

He throws the car at the blackboard, then picks up his book and throws it at the board. He runs up and dances on it, tearing some of the pages, then slumps down on the floor folding his hands. He has his audience; what next? The teacher could yell, scream, demand, but none of these will work with this low-frustration-tolerance child. The teacher already has a plan. She sends a trusted student to the class across the passage to call in Mr B, thus initiating her exit-policy plan. Past experience has taught her that Huan is too strong to carry or drag out when he's wild (see p. 168).

Mr B calmly walks up to Huan while the other teacher is walking around working with the rest of the class and thanking them for not getting upset. In this way she distracts their attention. Mr B gives Huan a firm, calm choice. Huan does his 'slumped sack' routine and kicks the wall for some last-minute grandstanding. Mr B calmly directs him from the group. He says briefly, 'Because you are breaking the fair rules of our room I'm taking you from your class for time-out.' Huan protests but is ignored. Mr B thanks the class (thus not giving attention to Huan) for settling down while he is escorting Huan out. Even at the last, little Huan gets minimal attention. They go to the time-out room, which is off the library.

One of the senior teachers takes Mr B's class for ten minutes while he 'time-outs' Huan. (It's about fifteen minutes to play time.) Mr B tells Huan he can sit and come up with a plan to fix up what he did—when he's settled down. He asks, 'What were you doing against the class rules, Huan?' No answer. 'Okay, I'll give you a couple of minutes to settle down and think, then I want you to tell me.'

'Suppose I shouldn't chuck stuff!' Huan eventually says.

'What did you do that was against our class rules?' (Mr B's voice tone is clear and controlled but firm, though inside he's annoyed with Huan.)

'Yelling.'

'Yes—what else Huan?'

'Tearing the book.'

'And ...?'

'Chucking my car!'

'Yes, I know ... now what are you going to do to fix up this situation?'

'Dunno.'

'Well, you think Huan. I want you to come up with some ideas to fix up the wrong things you did.'

'You tell me', says Huan.

'It's your job. What are you going to do, Huan?'

Huan decides to say 'Sorry', fix the book and finish his work during play. This is his contract. Mr B will see he follows this up with his teacher. As they leave Huan puts up his chair on the table. He taps the teacher and says, 'Mr B you forgot to put your chair up!' and smiles. 'So I did. Let's go, Huan.'

Mr B has been firm, clear and accepted no excuses. They go back to the classroom. Huan says 'Sorry', sits down huffily and begins to tape up his book (logical consequences). His class teacher ignores his huffiness. She goes up, just before the bell, and says, 'I'm pleased to see you've fixed your book. Let's see what work you need to catch up on.'

This behaviour has happened several times before. Each time the plan and the verbal contract is carried out, as calmly as possible. It's working. Neither teacher excuses Huan's behaviour on the grounds that his father walked out on the family, or that he has low-frustration tolerance, or that he's a latch-key kid. Sometimes they will explain their feelings about his behaviour while directing him to do something about his actions. This approach has:

■ reduced his acting-out behaviour
■ kept class stress levels and teacher stress levels down (because both teachers have a *plan* and stick to it)
■ shown Huan that he is accountable for his behaviour and he will not meet with reactive teacher behaviour (which only tends to reinforce the child's inappropriate way of 'belonging').

Written plans

Tory was a 'problem' according to her Year 8 teacher, and was constantly being referred to the year-level coordinator for behaviour problems. She was rude in class, kept calling out, and was regularly late to classes, sometimes missing them completely. Quite apart from the need to firm up some of the discipline approaches used by her teacher, it was suggested that a behaviour plan be formed. A problem-solving group was organised; it included Tory, her parents, her year-level coordinator and a regional consultant. The process involved several stages:

■ making the problem clear (everybody is asked to contribute)
■ brainstorming possible solutions (the chairperson guides the process by reflective listening, probing, clarifying questions, restating. All 'solutions' are noted down at this stage.)
■ working through the solutions and deciding on the most appropriate
■ making a plan for implementation and meeting again to evaluate whether the plan is working.

It was hard work, but with careful guiding by the group's chairperson, all sides were considered and Tory came up with a tentative plan to deal with her behaviour. A timetable was drawn up to clarify her class times. It was decided that Tory should write the behaviour agreement herself, covering calling out and handling her frustrations in class (the cause of her rudeness). The year-level coordinator agreed to support her effort and make available copies of the 'agreement' to Tory's subject teachers. They decided to meet again in a

week. There was a significant improvement over that time, which was acknowledged and affirmed. The plan was reassessed and a few changes were made. Three weeks later they had the last meeting and agreed that Tory had handled her plan well.

This problem-solving approach requires that all parties have an opportunity to contribute and work through the process. This approach calls for careful guidance by the chairperson to work through each stage leading to the final expressed commitment. In the case of Tory, one of the by-products of this plan process was a more positive effort by the teacher to assist Tory. The teacher noted how she had begun to look for positive behaviours from Tory, expecting them, and commenting on them. The process had enabled all parties to acknowledge the problem and commit themselves to support for change. One of the important considerations of any behaviour plan is that all the teachers who work with the student agree to common discipline, encouragement and feedback approaches.

Behaviour rehearsals

With primary-age children and even some secondary-age children, it can help to rehearse the behaviour plan with the student:

1 Gently mirror the student's behaviour (with their permission—see pp. 99f).

Mirror the calling out, or rolling on the mat, or butting in, or pushing in line.

2 Clearly explain and describe target behaviour.
Make clear the target behaviour, explaining why X behaviour needs to happen in the group. Focus on the rules as a 'hanger' for why X behaviour needs to happen. Be firm, clear, fair and avoid embarrassment. 'We need to make a plan because ...'

3 Demonstrate target behaviour.
Demonstrate the appropriate behaviour concretely. Role-play it. While demonstrating this, talk with the student about the key points in the target behaviour. Hinge the behaviour on two or three specific reference points, for example 'When you notice yourself getting angry your plan is to:
a tell yourself what's happening
b calm yourself by counting back from ten to one, and rethink what you need to be doing
c ask to take five minutes self-imposed time-out if necessary.'

4 Encourage the student to demonstrate and rehearse.
Now ask the student to demonstrate (role-play) the appropriate behaviour. 'Nick, I want you to show me what you will do if you are starting to feel angry.' The teacher can add self-coping or affirmation statements such as 'I am getting angry but I know what to do. I can handle this.' The student is asked to verbalise the affirmation aloud a few times, then sub-vocalise. The teacher says, 'Show me now. What are you saying inside your head Nick?' Nick might reply, 'I am angry, but I am doing my plan', or 'I made a mistake but I know how to fix it', or 'I can stop getting angry when I use my plan. I can use it now.'

5 Check if the student understands.
Ask questions: 'Do you understand what you have to do?' 'Say it to me please. Show me again.' 'Well done, I can see you know your plan.'

6 Reinforce the student when he uses the plan.
In the class, when the student is acting out the plan (see example), encourage by giving feedback. 'I can see you have remembered your plan Kate. It's not easy to manage frustration but you did it.'

In the process of negotiating a plan we are trying to enable the student to take some charge of her learning and behaviour. The goals for the plan should be as brief as possible, clear and achievable. If they're not achievable, the child may give up too quickly, too easily. It is also important to emphasise to the student that it is *her* effort that makes the difference (see Figure 5.2).

Modelling target behaviour

The student will often need help to identify the circumstances that trigger off-task behaviour. Then the student can be instructed on how to use the same circumstance to develop self-control skills. It doesn't take long to 'act out' the contracted behaviour; it is another way of affirming the contract, for example:

1 'When you feel frustrated—you know, when you feel really upset about your work—I want you to sit still, put your hands on your lap and count slowly to five.' The teacher can model what is meant. 'Do it while you close your eyes. Let's practise it now. Well done, you remembered to ...' (Be specific.)

2 Then, 'Go back to your work and slowly start again. Say to yourself, "I am able to do my work when I try." Let's practise it now. Say it aloud. Now say it to yourself inside your head. Show me.'
Self-coping statements are useful tools to build in to the student's repertoire, for example:
  ▌ 'Shaun, what could you say to yourself that would help you to feel better when you are angry?'
  ▌ 'Shaun, I want you to try saying to yourself ... when you feel ...'

3 'Try these steps every time you get upset about your work time. Let's practise it again.'

Behaviour plans

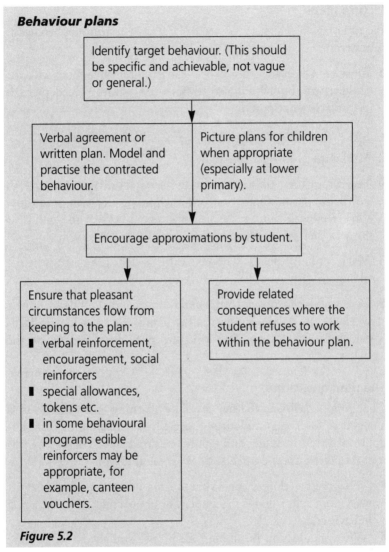

Identify target behaviour. (This should be specific and achievable, not vague or general.)

Verbal agreement or written plan. Model and practise the contracted behaviour.

Picture plans for children when appropriate (especially at lower primary).

Encourage approximations by student.

Ensure that pleasant circumstances flow from keeping to the plan:
∎ verbal reinforcement, encouragement, social reinforcers
∎ special allowances, tokens etc.
∎ in some behavioural programs edible reinforcers may be appropriate, for example, canteen vouchers.

Provide related consequences where the student refuses to work within the behaviour plan.

Figure 5.2

In the on-task time, the teacher would observe the student's behaviour and give a brief social reinforcer ('I can see you are practising your plan'), or just a slight pat on the shoulder. The point is to make the behaviour plan with the student, at their level of understanding, need and ability, have a rehearsal, then reinforce at on-task time. Renegotiate if the program is struggling. Short steps towards the longer term goal are better than trying too much too soon.

Picture plans

Picture plans (Rogers, 1994) provide a way of continuing behaviour reinforcement with primary-age children.

1 Illustrate target behaviours on a card and rehearse them with the child. It can be helpful also to have the picture plan depict the disruptive behaviour.

2 Use a mirroring approach to reinforce off-task behaviour.

3 Model the required behaviour.

4 Encourage the child to practise the behaviour. Point out that we get better at anything (football, swimming etc.) by practising. Give feedback during the practice session. Give the child his copy of the picture plan.

5 Make sure all teachers who teach the student have a copy of the plan.

6 Give regular feedback to the child (and parent). At least once a week ask the child what part of the plan is easiest, which is hardest, and why. Refine, fine-tune the plan and fade out as the behaviour generalises.

The plan questions

Changing behaviour, whether social or 'learning task' behaviour, is a big task for some students—especially when emotions of self-doubt, frustration, anger and failure are dominant. This is why it is useful to often use the *what, how, when* etc. questions:

■ 'What are you doing?' or 'What are you doing that is against our classroom rules?' helps the student to be specific about the actual behaviour.

■ 'What should you be doing?' helps the student to be specific about acceptable behaviour.

■ 'What can you do to change?' helps the student to be specific about solutions for future behaviour. It is important to point out to older children that behaviour is learned and able to be changed and that they can change things for the better with a plan. 'What can you do that is different?' helps the student to be specific about what should (and can) be possible.

▮ 'How can I help?' helps the student to think of solutions and assures her of support.

▮ 'Let's make a plan' helps the student to be confident about future support.

▮ 'When will you start?' encourages the student to be committed about the plan.

▮ 'Which of these things are you going to choose?' helps the student to be responsible and move towards self-control.

At all times the teacher is helping students to take responsibility for their own behaviour. We ought not get distracted or accept excuses. 'Yes, I can see you were angry, but what are you going to do now?'

Mirroring and disclosure of behaviour goals

I often use mirroring with students to help give them an insight into their possible behavioural goal. Rudolf Dreikurs (1982) has said that a student's fundamental social need is to belong. If the student feels (or believes) that he cannot belong in productive ways he will often choose to belong by drawing significant attention to himself or draw the teacher into power struggles (see pp. 81, 293f). Mirroring (in one-to-one sessions) can often highlight the non-verbal aspects of 'attention' or 'power' so the teacher can then use focus questions about the 'cause' of such behaviour, for example:

1 'Do you know why you ...?' (Here the teacher makes reference to the behaviour *specifically*—calling out, clowning, persistent seat-leaving.) By mirroring the behaviour first then asking the question, the teacher is increasing the attentional focus of the student.

Most students will shrug their shoulders at this question. The teacher can then *suggest* 'why' the student might be attention-seeking or engaging in power struggles (for example 'You can't make me!').

2 'I think you ... because ...'
    ▮ 'Could it be that when you call out frequently you want me or the group to notice you more or to look at you and laugh?'
    ▮ 'Could it be that when you refuse to do the work (I know you can do it) that you are saying that you want to be the boss? You want to show me that you can do what you want, that I cannot stop you or make you?'

Josh had been sent to the time-out room (for the tenth time). He had filled in a 4W form (see Appendix II) and we were discussing his behaviour in class. He said, 'Yeah, well she (the teacher) thinks I'm a smart-arse just cos of the way I walk.' I asked him if I could mirror what I'd seen a couple of times. I mirrored his annoyingly smart-alecky walk, body language and the tone of voice he used with some teachers. He grinned. I then asked 'Do you know why you walk and talk like that?' He gave me a wry grin—but no answer. I waited a little while and added, 'Could it be, Josh, that when you do that (gesturing back to the now-vacant spot where I'd just "become" Josh for 20 seconds) you're trying to show that you want to be the boss? You want to show your teachers that they can't stop you doing what you want, when you want?'

He quickly blurted out 'No!' (too quickly—his body language was saying 'yes'), 'Well, maybe, *sometimes*.' He dropped his head and gave an annoying grin that he thought could ameliorate his behaviour.

If the student is adamant that he doesn't do what he's doing for the reason you suggest (the key word is 'suggest'—at no point do we say, 'I *know* you do it for this reason'), re-ask the question: 'Well, if that's not the reason, do you know why?' Some students will deny they behave in the ways noted or for the goal suggested, but at least the suggested 'disclosure' has said, 'I know that you know that I know ...'

I find it helpful to finish such conversations by pointing out that the student is 'in charge' of his own behaviour and that no one *makes* him do what he does; and that I need his cooperation to work on a plan to help him with his behaviour in class.

The principles of goal disclosure are set out in the book *Maintaining Sanity in the Classroom* (Dreikurs, Grunwald and Pepper, 1982).

Behaviour plans summary

Behaviour plans can be drawn up through:

1 Brief verbal assurances that encompass a 'special' plan for student X.

2 Behaviour rehearsals (especially with primary-age students).

3 Formal written and picture contracts in which student and teacher address needs, rules, behaviour and responsibility. Keep the behaviour plan simple and situation-specific: 'The behaviours I need to change and agree on with my teacher', 'How I will do it', 'How my teacher will help me to keep my contract', 'These are the behaviours I want to stop', 'These are the behaviours I want to start' (see Appendix III).

Such behaviour plans can be designed on a one-to-one level, in a support group, or with parents.

So, the focus for the target behaviour is the current dysfunctional behaviour, not the historical antecedents over which we, as teachers, often have little or no control. We are aware of the student's emotional baggage, but contract with the student about her *current* behaviour. We do this by stating clearly objective tasks or behaviours. In this way, both the student and teacher can measure change. Behaviour plans consist of 'steps' which are small enough for students to focus on, and achievable enough for them to experience some success. Success is part of the reinforcing process. Struggling children find it very hard to build on failure; it's much easier to build on success.

Persistence and commitment characterise successful behaviour plans. The teacher best achieves outcomes by not giving up but by encouraging, giving feedback, using consequences and allowing the working through of failure. It is often the one-to-one attention given to the student in such plans that enables their success.

Experience and research shows that developing individual behaviour plans can be a productive adjunct to a teacher's characteristic discipline plan. It works best when the teacher has colleague support in the process: at the planning stage, in monitoring the plan, in implementing time-out procedures when students are disruptive, in 'tracking' the students' behaviour in other classes and in providing regular feedback on how the plan is going.

At secondary level it can help to have a key teacher act as 'plan supervisor' or 'case manager' to liaise with the subject teacher, the counsellor, the parent(s) and the student (Rogers, 1997).

Counselling

We have to deal with many difficult and challenging children in our role as teachers; children whose emotional, even physical deprivation may cause us to get frustrated, angry and greatly saddened about their home environment. If only we could step into the child's home history—but we can't. There are many factors which are outside our control.

Begin from the useful belief that a child is not simply a product of her past or present. It is not inevitable that she will end up 'at risk' because of social, economic, or psychological deprivation. Treat the child, therefore, as if each day has within it the opportunity for change for that child and for us.

There will be times when we counsel to provide appropriate comfort, such as when a child is clearly distressed (home break-ups; discord at home; being bashed at home; being sent to different care-givers at the weekend): 'Do you want to talk about it?'

Ciara (aged eight) comes in late. Her teacher says, 'Good morning, Ciara.' She mutters some words with head down, plus 'Sh——!' The other children say, 'Oooh, did you hear what she said?' The teacher quickly moves to Ciara and says, 'Okay, I can see you're upset, sit over there, I'll be with you soon' (distraction and diversion), then walks back to the children she was working with before Ciara came in. 'Ciara's upset. Right. Now back to work. How's your writing getting on Maria?' She continues to move around the room, leaving Ciara until she has settled down.

Later, when the children are all back on-task, she goes over to Ciara. 'Ciara, what's up?'

'My mum got me up in the night to go to my nan's place because my dad's fighting with mum!'

'Okay, Ciara, I can see you're upset. Let's do some writing now (distraction). We can talk later if you want.'

All the teacher needs to do is assure Ciara that she understands. She doesn't need, in front of the class, to get into involved discussion. Later she might follow up by saying, 'How do you feel now, Ciara?' She doesn't push Ciara or demand she perform at the same level as the others. It is nearly always best to assure students that we will give them time to settle.

When you sit down with a student to counsel for any length of time (listen, direct, clarify, guide) you need to observe the following conditions:

■ Make sure you're not alone. Sit near or in an office area with a door open, for ethical probity.
■ If it's a sensitive issue, invite a colleague in (especially for male–female counselling).
■ Keep a record for yourself.
■ Don't over-pity; show appropriate concern.
■ Help the student to sort out options by getting her story first.
■ Add options, action and solutions to her input: 'What do you think you need to do?', 'How can I help?', 'When will you start?', 'Who else is needed to help?'

Classroom meetings

It is the beginning of the school year and the teacher wants to discuss rights, rules and responsibilities with her students. She has used classroom meetings before, with other groups, so she decides to try it with the Year 9 English class.

As they file in and sit down, she writes 'Classroom meetings' on the board and draws, underneath, four quarter circles (the seating plan). As the students settle down, she introduces herself and explains that to start off the year she wants to discuss rights and rules with them. Handing out name tags (already written out from the class roll) she calls the roll. It is important to learn students' names quickly during the first few weeks of the year (establishment phase of the group).

Before she directs the class to move into a circle of seats she explains what a classroom meeting is, why it is happening, what the rules for the meeting are and what outcomes are expected. She directs the class to move their desks against the wall, bring out the chairs and stand behind them, a quarter of the class at a time.

Once the circle (amid normal chatter) is formed the teacher draws up a seat to join in. 'To start, let's try a simple little exercise.' She begins with a word game or ice-breaker. A student starts play-punching his mate. How will she discipline? She could ask a question or direct him but she distracts and diverts. Calling across the circle to the grandiloquent, attention-seeking Jack she says, 'Jack, can I see you for a sec?' Jack swaggers over (he is the centre of attention now). She draws him down by whispering, 'Jack (she rises up out of her seat), I'm swapping places.' Before he has a chance to think, she takes his place and distracts the group's attention by beginning the ice-breaker. She could have used a simple rule-reminder, 'Jack, hands and feet to yourself.' She chose that action because she knows the student from last year and thinks that distraction will probably work. Effective teachers have a wide, least-intrusive repertoire of discipline skills to enable workable and positive relationships with students. There will be several disruptions during the discussion; she will have prepared for these, at all times bringing the focus of attention back to the purpose of the discussion—*rights*.

'We haven't got any rights anyway', says Michelle, and so it goes. Bobbing and weaving her way through a lively discussion, the teacher gradually draws out some recommendations which are recorded by a volunteer student recorder. The class establishes, under her direction, some basic understanding of rights and what rules are needed to protect those rights. It is not easy, but it is worth the effort.

Setting up a classroom meeting

A classroom meeting involves setting aside a time for the whole class to discuss and think through issues of concern. The classroom, after all, is a social system. One child's behaviour both influences and is influenced by the other members of the class group. Behaviour concerns and problems can be addressed at a group level as well as the individual level. The group can learn to make decisions about curriculum, room organisation, procedures and even socially disruptive behaviours that affect the whole group, such as put-downs, swearing, off-task behaviour, attention-seeking, lateness, messy work and high noise levels.

Classroom meetings can also have an educational focus, for maths, science and humanities, as well as for issues affecting the social life of the classroom. The broad goals are always the same: cooperating, exploring issues, learning to take risks in expression of ideas.

According to Stanford (1980), Dreikurs, Grunwald and Pepper (1982) and Glasser (1969), teachers who implement group approaches in their classes often find the incidence of misbehaviour and disruption receding. Reason? Both the teacher and the group go through changes because a group approach forces, by its very nature, a different way of focusing on concerns and problems. A group meeting is a way of saying, 'This issue *affects us all*, we need to share responsibility and this is a forum for such sharing.'

This activity is not one where a teacher merely stands in the traditional up-front position to field questions (valid as such a stance is); it is, rather, a structured meeting where teacher and students have clear behaviour norms for the group; where cooperation is taught, expected and encouraged; where problems are confronted; and, it is hoped, where democratic decision-making is the outcome! I have worked with many teachers who have recalled failure in 'discussions' with classes. However, this failure was usually due to:

■ lack of careful planning
■ poor understanding of group dynamics
■ expectation of failure or a fear of losing control
■ lack of persistence during the first few meetings—it's easy to give in when a discussion ends up in mayhem and silliness
■ scheduling classroom meetings too early in the establishment phase of the group's life together.

Children need to be taught how to behave in a group. The 'lateral tyranny' of the peer group has sent many a discussion goal to an early grave. Like all learning, for cooperative discussion to occur there needs to be clear guidance from a democratic leader. Students need to experience the nature of democracy through clarifying their views, gaining feedback from peers, learning to participate in decisions and shouldering the responsibility flowing from decision-making processes.

The benefits

There are many positive outcomes for students from class meetings:

■ active student involvement, interaction and cooperation
■ development of a sense of openness to the needs of others
■ learning to listen to others
■ development of a classroom climate in which people's views and ideas are taken seriously and students can be more comfortable with one another's ideas and opinions and, consequently, less defensive.
■ confrontation of mutual problems such as social behaviours, problems in learning, problems in social organisation.

Of course there are benefits for the teacher as well: taking risks, getting to know what and how the class thinks about X, providing a forum for decision-making (even about an individual's behaviour). Group meetings can be organised at any age level, with appropriate modifications. I've worked with teachers who have run class meetings with children as young as five or six. One of my colleagues recently ran a classroom meeting with a Year 1 class to invite their assistance in helping a behaviourally disordered child with his behaviour plan. The plan involved a daily goal presented as a ladder; each ladder would help the child reach the top of a mountain. The mountain symbolised his weekly 'climb' of behaviour. The teacher found the process very useful.

> After this initial meeting the children were so supportive. They helped Adam enormously, which in turn helped me. Another idea we came up with was a message board where we could write positive messages for Adam about the things he did. We drew a picture of him and, at different times in the day, children went there to write their personal messages. 'Adam smiled at me.' 'Adam sat quietly in assembly.' 'Adam used the carpet rules.'

Running a classroom meeting

1 Inform the class.

'We will be having a special class discussion on Thursday and will be discussing ...' Plan for the meeting to be about 20 minutes (built up to 30 later), at a set time in the lesson, preferably towards the end. Friday afternoons are often a good time.

2 Organise seating arrangements.
   Seats are best organised in a circle or semi-circle. By arranging the chairs in a circle, the members of the group, including the teacher, are more 'open' to each other. The sense of territory changes when people are facing each other. When people start communicating, they can see each other, hear and focus on each other more easily. Members of the group (especially the teacher) can observe the non-verbal language that plays a very important part in feedback and communication. Tuning into non-verbal signals aids a teacher's insight, sense of timing, and control.

3 Establish clear rules and norms.
   Share what the expectations of the members of the group should be. For example:
   ▌ to share concerns and problems as we feel comfortable
   ▌ to act responsibly to, and cooperate with, others
   ▌ to give each member of the group a fair go
   Some colleagues at primary level use talk-tokens to restrain the more garrulous members of the group. Each participant is given three tokens. After each contribution is made, the speaker puts down one talk-token in front of where she is sitting. After the three tokens are 'used up' she can no longer contribute in that 20-minute session.
   ▌ to share our concerns, ideas and opinions without putting others down
   ▌ to take a turn to speak (raising hands may be appropriate)
   One school I worked in had a 'speaking pillow'! The Year 4 students could only speak when holding the speaking pillow. Students would not interrupt the speaker, unless the pillow was passed to a new speaker.
   ▌ to listen to each other.
   ▌ to stay on the subject
   The rules for the meeting are there to protect each member's right to contribute and be part of the group.

The teacher's job is to make these rules clear and enforce them. This requires firmness, warmth, sensitivity, determination and some judicious humour. My first few class meetings tested all these qualities to the limit, especially the warmth and sensitivity. As with all growth, there are stages of development, the most important being risk-taking and willingness to grow. I learned that leadership of such meetings only gets better and the process only gets easier with practice.

4 Reinforce the rules.

This is an important part of the group process. If one or two members of the group call out instead of using the fair rules, the teacher can tactically ignore them (not even look in their direction but give firm eye contact and verbal reinforcement to on-task members. 'Thanks for putting up your hand Frousoula. It makes our group work so much better.' 'What's your question, Nick? Thanks for putting up your hand, by the way.'

If certain members continue to call out, the teacher can use a rule restatement: brief, firm eye contact and restate the rule. 'Jane, you know the fair rule for making a point or asking a question. Use it thanks.' That's all, then give attention back to the on-task members. This can be applied to other behaviours such as put-downs and annoying, pestering behaviour. The teacher could use a brief question like 'What are you doing, Jane?' (being firm, not sarcastic or hostile). 'Asking a question!' may come the reply. 'You were calling out. Use our rule thanks.' Alternatively, the teacher could follow with a secondary question (especially with students up to Year 7). 'What should you be doing?' Don't add anything else. Make the assumption that Jane will respond on-task next time the question is asked. If the student continues to call out, put-down, tap her feet or disrupt in some other way, give her a choice to remain in the group, or sit out, or stay back and explain her behaviour at recess. When maintaining discipline, be as natural as possible in speech. Even when speaking assertively with hostile students, use a firm, calm tone. If they resist, remind them that they can either work with our fair rules or we'll have to ask them to sit out and explain later why they can't work by the fair rules. Shift attention quickly back to the on-task members of the group. Even in a group setting, the normal protocols and practice of discipline are observed (see Chapter 3).

5 Be a democratic leader.
   In running a class meeting, it is important that the teacher take the role of democratic leader:
   I Keep the students on the subject or question. Watch the issue doesn't wander.
   I Protect the weaker members of the group.
   I Encourage quieter members, without forcing them to contribute: 'Kim, would you like to say something?', 'Does anybody want to add anything more to that?', 'It looks like there are several possibilities here. Which of these should we follow?'
   I Watch the louder, overly assertive members of the group.
   I Keep to the fair, clear rules for the meeting.
   I Model and invite cooperation and listening using firm eye contact and reflective listening, and providing feedback to the individual student and the group.
   I Draw the threads of opinion and ideas together. 'It seems that the group is saying ...', or 'From what you've said, the group seems to agree that ...'
   I Enable the group to move towards a conclusion through maximum contribution, being fair to all sides, sticking to the point of the discussion/meeting, checking with the group and summing up towards a solution.

Our own modelling and reinforcing of others gives a lead and provides a training ground for their discussion skills:

'What's wrong Paul, you seem annoyed about something.'
'What do you think Dimitra? How do you feel when ...?'
'Jodie, have you anything to say? What if someone said that to you, how would you feel?'
'Natasha has suggested X. Does anyone else want to add to that?'
'Well, would that fix the problem? What do you think?'
'I see that you think we should punish Jo. How will that fix the broken chair?'

'You sound angry. I can understand we can feel angry about this, but what can we suggest to fix it up?'

'We're talking about put-downs, teasing and swearing today. We can discuss stealing property at another time.'

'David, you've made your point. I'm sure there are others here who would like to add something.'

It's really important when emotions start to run high that the teacher take a democratic but firm lead.

So the role of the teacher is to lead, guide and provoke discussion. *What, when, how* and *who* questions are generally more helpful than closed questions. Sometimes the questions can be planned ahead, depending on the topic or issue.

If the group is obviously flagging or getting unwieldy, despite firm control, don't hesitate to call the meeting to an early close. Students are often not used to group discussion and it may take a few meetings to get them used to the experience of cooperation, sharing, taking turns, expressing ideas etc. Our persistence and modelling is often the best means to such an end. Keep the meeting moving by asking, directing, restating, inviting, challenging, at times provoking the members to participate. Use divergent questioning as much as possible.

Where classroom meetings (even short ones) are a regular feature of classroom life, teachers can use an agenda board where students can list agenda items for the next meeting.

A class meeting addressing put-downs

The teacher has a prepared poster of the typical put-downs she has been hearing in class (mostly whispered). She has previously reminded the class about this issue and pointed out that the class meeting will be addressing it.

She begins the meeting with a *brief* explanation of why the topic needs addressing and says, 'We are here to examine this issue and look for solutions together. These are some of the things I've been hearing in the classroom these last few weeks ...'

She invites student response and encourages them to share how they feel about this and *why*. She asks 'Why do people put others down? How do people feel when they are put down? How does this affect our basic treatment right?'

She has a student summarise the key responses on the board, leaving her free to keep the discussion flowing. Recording their responses gives genuine credence to their point of view. She knows that it is important not to criticise student responses at this point, but to clarify: 'Are you saying ...?' 'Have I got it right?' 'Let's write that up then ...'

The teacher *briefly* shares her point of view—not a lecture (they would turn off), but a brief reminder of why put-downs affect basic rights. She then invites the class to brainwave (brain*storm* sounds a little too violent!) suggestions for changing the language students use. For example, instead of saying 'That's a dumb idea' when a student disagrees with another student's idea, he can just say, 'I don't agree because ...' The ideas and suggestions are recorded without evaluation at this stage. Some students give unusual, even silly suggestions; by writing them up the teacher displays the silliness.

The teacher then invites the group to decide which ideas and approaches to put-downs and teasing we ought to use—and why. The test for using any suggestion is: is it reasonable? does it relate to the issue at stake? does it keep the respect intact? Suggestions range from positive-language posters, rule reminders (students themselves often resort to simple descriptors such as, 'That's a put-down'), ways of making a point without hurting others, and even fair consequences such as, 'Those who put others down in class will have to meet with the person they have hurt to work through an appropriate apology.'

The teacher will probably set up a review meeting to discuss how the suggested outcomes are working. Review meetings are helpful if the outcome of the first meeting doesn't fully meet its objectives.

Regular meetings are now being conducted in our classes at every year level (even with five- and six-year-olds). What fantastic experiences I've had, not only with the initial process of introducing the idea of meetings (always fun because the children are so enthusiastic), but also with teacher and children's responses (being listened to and being given the chance to work through issues).

Some teachers are nervous about classroom meetings and not always sure of their educational value. I always find the children just run with it so easily, and the teachers are usually surprised at the ease of it. While running a class meeting involves some trial and error, I've found that there are a number of things I can do to make it work well:

■ I try to schedule meetings for the half-hour leading up to a break.
■ I ensure that meetings are on days when I have no playground duty. Some children will want, or need, some one-to-one discussion or even, on occasion, some counselling. This gives me the freedom to do this.
■ I display a class poster (along with procedural outline) entitled 'Helpful ways to talk about problems without accusing people'.
■ When I hear a child begin (to address another student, or teacher) in an accusing manner, I signal (see p. 55), non-verbally, or if necessary verbally, to refer them briefly to the chart. I had one Year 7 girl who had real difficulty remembering and would often begin to share a remark in a put-down manner. I merely said, 'Careful', and pointed to the chart. She was never excluded from a meeting and was a very active participant.
■ I have some back-up for the 'no put-down' rule involving five minutes cool-off time (see p. 166). I find I can head off a potential put-down. In younger grades a put-down results in five minutes silence. In middle grades it is five minutes (cool-off time/thinking time) outside the room.
■ To help the chairperson in her role I laminate a copy of 'The role of the chairperson' and send it home (with the student) for a week leading up to the meeting. This gives the student an opportunity to discuss her role with her family. The children love it. We are also trialling a secretary role and an observer role. These are used only in upper grades, and the guidelines for the roles are also sent home. We have tried to simplify the secretary's role with a problem-solution sheet and an issue-idea sheet. The following are some examples of the role guidelines we have used:
Role of secretary: reads through agenda; reads previous problem and issue sheets; fills in problem and issue sheets; ensures problem and issue sheets are easy to read; records names of chairperson, secretary and observer for the next meeting.
Role of chairperson: opens meeting; doesn't take sides; remains calm and positive; ensures everyone has a chance to speak and be

heard; confines the speaker to the issue(s); limits individual's time for speaking; tries to involve and include as many people as possible and closes the meeting.

A warm-up activity

This is a useful way to 'unlock' the initial hesitation and unusualness of being in an 'unprotected' circle. The teacher starts with a brief turn-taking game. 'My name is Bill (or Mr Rogers). Two things I like to do are drinking tea and reading novels.' He then turns to Mark. Mark says, 'This is Mr Rogers, he likes tea, I mean, he likes *drinking* tea and eating (laugh), sorry, reading novels. My name is Mark. I like footy and skateboarding.' Mark turns to Courtney. To make the game a little easier, actions can be added. Courtney, a bit concerned, says, 'There's Mr Rogers (points), he likes ... this is Mark, he likes ... and I'm Courtney and I like ...' and so on. It can get confusing but it's a good warm-up. It opens the vocal cords and helps to free things up with a few laughs and with a bit of help from the chair.

Another useful activity is the quick unfinished sentence game. Begin with, 'Finish this sentence Andrea: "One thing that really makes me laugh is ..."' If Andrea can't come up with something, move on and come back to her. Then go round, in turn, with each member completing the sentence. Gene Stanford (1980) has a range of games for groups. See also Cranfield and Wells (1976), McGrath and Francey (1993) and Dempster and Raff (1992).

If you decide you want to run a class meeting, but feel apprehensive, try it out with a small group first, or invite a trusted colleague to assist you. We can best minimise uncertainty (we can never eliminate it completely), by thoughtful planning and colleague support.

I had a class meeting with a Year 3 group to discuss swearing in class. In a circle, we used De Bono's (1986) PMI approach (discussing and listing the plus points, minus points and interesting suggestions, neither good nor bad). 'All right, who wants to start? Kim, you've got your hand up.'

'She should get a battery and some wires (ha! ha! ha!) and tie it on her tongue (ha! ha!) and she will get a shock!'

'What do you think class?' Chorused reply—'Minus!' (Don't waste time on class wags. Briefly acknowledge and move on.)

'Paula, you've had your hand up.'

'Make her run around the playground till she is sorry!'

'Paula, how does that help her swearing? Michelle?'

'Get her mum down, she will smack her.'

'But who was swearing? Was her mum?' After several more illogical (minus) suggestions, Veronica said, 'Couldn't you say, like something—something will happen to her?'

'What will happen, Veronica?'

'I don't know, but something will happen.'

'Are you saying that we should warn the person who swears?' (and we modelled it) 'Yes, that's it!'

'What sort of warning?' Someone else suggested that we should tell the swearer, 'It's not nice to swear.'

Finally, we all agreed that a fair, clear reminder of our class rule on hurtful language would be the warning (a form of rule restatement). If the swearing was hurtful, the student would have to stay back, apologise and explain her behaviour. We would contact the parent only if the student continually refused to use the class rule about positive communication. We would (and did) help the student to use better words when she was frustrated, and positively reinforce her when she did.

What we think

Plus	Minus	Interesting	We decide
talk to her	battery	send a note home	1 Reminder of the rule.
say sorry	smack		2 Stay back and explain.
			3 Use better words instead of swear words.

Classroom meetings summary

■ Decide what the topic for discussion is *or* decide whether you want to use the group for a role-playing exercise, a self-esteem activity, a discussion on behaviour concerns within the class, or whether you want to use sub-groups (small groups of four or five who all discuss the same theme with the teacher moving around to assist, then back to a large discussion format).

▌ Decide on the time for the meeting. A vote can sometimes be used as a way of getting an agreed time.

▌ Decide beforehand how you get the chairs and desks moved into a circle. Let the children know beforehand that we'll be forming a discussion group at such and such a time. Often it's easier to get the children to organise the furniture.

▌ Establish the rules quickly and enforce them.

▌ Define the topic clearly. Perhaps begin with a warm-up activity, then get into it with as much divergent questioning as possible.

▌ Keep the group meeting on-task. Draw the threads towards a decision. Encourage a positive decision that reflects the fair rights, rules and responsibility focus. The essence of a classroom meeting is to open up and guide discussion towards responsible choices within the fair rules. A group secretary or recorder can be used to minute the proceedings and outcomes.

Similar approaches are found in Gordon (1974) and De Bono (1986). Gordon's steps are oriented to problem-solving by exploring several stages. Each stage is given a fair go before moving on to the next. See also Dempster and Raff (1992) for guidelines on conducting classroom meetings.

CHAPTER 6

Building a positive classroom climate

A good self-image is the most valuable psychological possession of a human being.

John Powell, 1976

Classroom climate

Classroom climate is the tone the class experiences in its normal daily life. Because a class is, fundamentally, a group of people, the relational dynamic is central to how positive the class is, how positive each of its members feels about belonging to *this* group. Because the class is a group engaged in learning, growing up in social direction, building a sense of identity and purpose, it is important that the teacher seek out ways in which the class can enjoy a more positive learning and social environment.

Factors which influence class tone

Obviously there are many factors which influence class tone, from the kind of lesson the teacher prepares right through to how she feels on a particular morning when she has a ghastly headache. Several factors, however, clearly stand out. We teachers create the environment as much as anyone, especially through our verbal and non-verbal behaviour. A number of questions need to be asked.

■ Do we have clear rules and procedures that are known and reinforced?

■ Do we speak hastily? calmly? clearly? Do we nag? How would our children describe us most of the time? Do we consider our use of language when correcting students?

■ Are we aware of what our children are doing? Do we encourage them, listen to them and notice their positive, cooperative behaviours as well as their off-task disruptive behaviours?

■ Do we cater for mixed abilities with a bit of variety in our approach?

■ Do we ever use small groups to encourage cooperative learning?

■ Do we show evidence of some humour from time to time?

■ How positive is our discipline style? Do we plan ahead for possible or likely disruptions?

■ Do we respect students even when we dislike them? How consistent are we in the way we discipline?

■ Do we follow up disruptive students?

Children are very forgiving when we fail, when we have a bad day, providing there's a basic consistency to our teaching. Establishing positive discipline and building positive class tone is one way of achieving that consistency.

Stages of a class

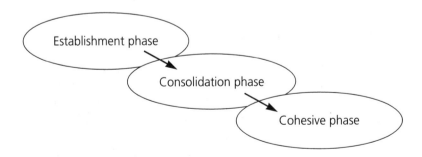

Basic stages of a class as a group

The establishment phase

During the establishment phase the focus is preventative—seeking to minimise unnecessary disruptions by having a thoughtful balance of rights, responsibilities, rules and routines. At this stage students are psychologically and developmentally 'ready' for teachers to clarify how *this* class will work (or at least ought to work, bad day notwithstanding.

The consolidation phase

Students naturally, and normally, test boundaries, routines, rules. It is important to teach, encourage and maintain what we establish, to affirm the gains of positive establishment. We don't just establish on day one and expect all to be fine because there is a set of published rules, a student diary and a school policy. We have to encourage, correct and build up our classes. We have to cater for mixed abilities and follow up and follow through with individuals who have problems with learning and behaviour.

The cohesive phase

The cohesive phase is marked by strong relational ties with the class and a positive working knowledge of the class and its individual dynamics. Management has moved into its relational phase. The psychological bond has been established. Through the establishment and consolidation phases we enable students to control many aspects of their own management and learning. During this phase cooperative learning, classroom meetings, peer-mentoring are the norm.

Establishing a new class

The establishment phase is a crucial time in the life cycle of a class and the teacher. The students expect their teacher, in that first meeting, to explain and discuss how things will be in *this* class, in *this* room, in *this* subject, *this* year. There is a psychological readiness, a developmental readiness, among the students on day one, week one that will never be quite as focused again. Teachers need to seize the teachable moment, as it were, and clarify those rights, rules, routines and responsibilities that will (in time) enable the reasonably smooth running of teaching and learning and social interaction in that strangely small arena called a classroom.

Even if students have gone over all this in other years, other classes, they need to establish a working understanding of each teacher's expectations. The more there is common agreement by staff in this area the more effective such rules and routines will be. It is always worth discussing with colleagues such issues as entry and exit from the classroom; initiation and establishment of *group* attention, dealing with initial disruptions (lateness, calling out, talking while teacher is talking, students without equipment ...); transitions from instructional to on-task time; 'working noise'; how to get teacher assistance and attention appropriately; lesson closure. While many of these issues may sound like they require basic preventative planning, I've worked with many teachers (not just beginning teachers) who have ad hoc responses to such crucial management concerns. Students very quickly sense whether teachers are in control of the establishment process.

By 'control' I mean a conscious directing of events so that students will feel secure in their knowledge of the reasonable parameters of classroom life, and confident that the teacher knows what he is doing. The teacher style needs to be positive, authoritative, and confident about expected and required behaviour (Doyle, 1986; Rogers, 1995).

A workable entry and exit procedure

Some teachers (especially at primary level) have the students line up. Even at some secondary schools (Years 7–10) teachers have the students in some basic ordered ensemble near the entry door. It is important not to keep them there too long waiting for two impossibly perfect rows! A positive greeting (especially in the morning, and with each class at secondary level) is important—basic as that may sound. Call the stragglers into line; briefly encourage those making an effort to consider others (this at primary level) and usher them in to take their seats or take their position on the mat (lower-middle primary level).

Before students actually go into the classroom it can help to remind the students of *expected* behaviours during the first few days or so. After greeting the students the teacher can give behavioural reminders or questions: '*When* you go into the classroom, remember to sit on the carpet area facing the board. Thanks', '*When* you go in remember to go straight to your seats (or work area, or …) and quietly get out your material so we're ready to start …', *'Before* you go in remember coats, hats, bags, lunchboxes …', or 'What do we need to *remember* before we go in?'

It is worth checking on how other colleagues actually 'do' this. The fine-tuning of a routine can make all the difference. For example, just sweeping (gently) your arm in a full-metre arc—with lower primary-level children—to show them where you want them sitting on the mat can help them to visualise it. A woodwork teacher can signal with his hands how he wants his students positioned around the workbench or lathe.

It can also be helpful to take primary-age children back out into the corridor if you think they haven't 'got it' for a second practice, with encouragement. Comments such as 'That's better, you remembered to sit in a half-circle' and 'It's helpful when the taller students sit at the back, ta' concentrate on their *efforts* at giving this routine a fair go.

Seating plans

Some teachers prefer to let students sit anywhere in the classroom, in friendship groupings for example. Other teachers allocate a formal (or semi-formal) seating plan from day one: alphabetical groupings, or names out of a hat, or boy–girl, etc. When drawing up seating plans we need to consider space, movement and likely noise level during group work. If it is known that the group is particularly chatty, or even noisy, it may be preferable to have paired seating, with students facing the front, and only move into groups at set times to minimise establishment of overly chatty work noise (see also p. 206).

Seating plans will need to vary with subject area, lesson needs and, to some extent, age levels. Several long rows of tables and chairs, for example, make it difficult to move around the room to give assistance during on-task time. I've worked in classes where teachers have allowed several challenging students to sit at the back. They then position themselves as a major attention-seeking bloc.

It is more difficult to change the seating plan and student groupings in weeks four to six *after* they have backfired. One solution I've used with upper primary and secondary students is to regroup the student seating by involving their reflective support. Each student receives a sheet on which is written:

> As your teacher I'm concerned with the level of noise and distraction during seatwork and I will be changing the seating plan. I want your assistance. Write down the names of two students whom you *know* you can work with and who won't hassle you (or vice versa) *or* make it difficult for you to get your class work done. I'll use your suggestions in the new seat plan. I can't guarantee you'll get every preference but I'll do my best. Thanks in advance, Mr R.

The teacher then works through their suggestions, sorts out the peer dynamics and makes up a new seat plan. I've seen many classes improve significantly with this kind of regrouping. The key is to emphasise why we need it, and to involve them in the process. If the class is seriously off-track it may be necessary to go through a re-establishment phase using a special classroom meeting approach (see pp. 244f). At this stage a colleague can provide useful moral support in running a problem-solving meeting with the class to explore what's going wrong (and why) and to work out how to work together to change things for the better.

Learning and using students' first names

Learn and use students' names as quickly as possible. Using a student's first name is very important at every level (even when we engage in corrective discipline).

There are a number of ways to learn names (depending on age). At primary level we can use name tags when marking the class roster and on their work tables or desks; and play name games. Using their names when answering a question (or receiving an answer) and acknowledging them in the corridor and playground will reinforce them.

At secondary level it can help to have a seating plan (drawn up quietly by a 'reliable' student) with tables or desks and first names. I do this with each of my classes, each lesson period, for the first three or four lessons. I explain that this is to help me to learn their names. It also helps with spelling of unfamiliar first names. I can then add phonetic versions of the names to my plan (I'm a visual learner) to make sure I've got the pronunciation correct. Students don't expect us to learn their names in one session so the name tags or seating plans can be used for the next few sessions. It is annoying to students when teachers don't make an effort to learn their names or speak in 'neutral tones' about them or their behaviour: *'That* girl in the last seat on the left ...', *'You,* don't call out!', *'You two boys* there, stop talking and face the front!' (I'd rather ask them their names, then direct them to face the front.)

Early disruptions

During the establishment of the lesson there may be a number of disruptions such as restlessness, rolling on the mat, 'testosteronic bonding', fiddling, lateness, talking out of turn, or talking while the teacher is talking. It is important to deal decisively with these disruptions as least intrusively as possible. ('Decisive' and 'least intrusive' are not incompatible.)

For example, if students are talking while the teacher is talking it may be enough to *tactically* pause (see also p. 57). If, however, two or three students continue to talk, a simple direction, or a rule reminder can often serve to refocus the situation. 'Michael and Damien, facing this way thanks (...) and listening.' Even a brief few seconds, pause after 'thanks' (...) can help convey the message. By resuming the flow of the lesson *after* the direction the teacher can convey that she expects their cooperation. If several students around the room are talking while the teacher is talking (or calling out, or talking out of turn) a general direction or reminder will be necessary. The teacher motions with the hand to 'block', as it were, their calling out, then gives a brief positive reminder. 'Remember our class rule for ...', or 'If you want to ask a question it's one at a time with hands up', or 'Hands up so I can see your voices.' With younger children a non-verbal signal can be quite effective (see p. 55) indicating 'Hands up', or 'Face this way', or 'Mouths quiet for now.'

When dealing with disruptions in class it can be helpful to:

∎ plan some key corrective phrases so we don't have to use reactive dialogue (see pp. 29f)

■ keep the corrective management positive where possible (use the *do* rather than the *don't*
■ balance correction with encouragement.

Establishing basic rules and routines

At primary level many teachers collaborate with their students in drawing up rules. It is best if there is a school-wide focus on key behaviours such as safety, fair treatment and learning. Discussion of a number of aspects around these themes increases group awareness and potential ownership of such issues as manners, respect, personal space, sharing resources, caring for property, teacher assistance, noise levels, cooperation etc.

It is helpful at both primary and secondary levels to have a common framework for rights and responsibilities across the school. Many schools publish such a document (in user-friendly language) in each classroom. At secondary level the home-room teacher, or the tutor will take the class through this document on day one. Students have a copy in their diaries and a large laminated or framed copy is on the wall in every classroom. School-wide rules can focus on these fundamental non-negotiable rights and responsibilities (see p. 122).

In the establishment phase of the year—in those first few lessons—we are, in effect, training our classes in our management and discipline style; getting them used to how we expect things to be and why. Our goal of course is to enable the students to be self-monitoring and considerate of others' rights but that worthy goal won't *just happen*, it takes time.

'I haven't got a pen'

I've been caught too many times with this one, especially at secondary level. In the first four sessions I take in my 'yellow box', a tough cardboard box (about 30 cm × 15 cm) with yellow electrical tape covering it, giving it a coloured 'body'. Each pen, ruler and pencil has a tip of yellow electrical tape (for visual learners) to track it back to the yellow box. I also include name tags, chalk-duster, chalk, whiteboard pens, etc. It is simply a preventative measure to minimise hassle (see p. 27).

If a student continues not to bring the necessary equipment over two or three subsequent sessions then the teacher will need to do some follow-through, perhaps looking at helping the student with a simple 'Remember your materials' plan, a small card listing the three or four items necessary to bring to class. It may help to have a small reminder picture against each of these items.

Working noise

It is natural that the noise level of the group will rise between up-front teaching time and on-task activities. Students will move from the mat to their tables, they will need to get necessary materials, or in a secondary English class they will shuffle around remembering they haven't got a pen or textbook or …

Before the teacher even directs the students to the on-task phase it is important to discuss:

■ the routine/expectations for 'working noise', 'table noise', 'part-ner communication' (or 'partner voices' as one of my colleagues neatly terms it)—some teachers even use visual *aide-mémoires* to teach non-verbally and encourage workable noise levels (see below).
■ how to distribute and retrieve materials
■ where to hand in completed work (a box, or tray)
■ how to get teacher assistance during the on-task phase of the lesson.

It is important to recognise that workable noise levels in class-rooms rarely just happen. They need to be planned, *taught* and encouraged until they become the norm.

Infant and middle primary

It can help, at this age, to use 'visual entry-points' to support students' learning and socialisation with respect to noise levels. Rather than having a stated rule alone, or saying 'Shh' each time it gets noisy, the teacher can make up a chart signalling different noise levels appropriate to the stage of the lesson or activity. Some teachers use a traffic-light poster which signals white for hands up, green for partner-talking at tables, red for stop. Children respond well to the positive use of visual and non-verbal cues.

Using a noise meter

I've been using noise meters at primary level now for well over a decade (Rogers, 1994). A noise meter is both a teaching and a monitoring device for encouraging workable communication levels. It is most useful in the establishment phase of the year. When it is used in a fun way children quickly see its relevance in the classroom. The meter itself is a 30-cm circle of card divided into different-coloured quadrants—white, green, yellow/amber and red. An arrow on a split-pin rotates from the centre. A large laminated drawing (35 cm × 45 cm) augments each quadrant (see drawing in Appendix XI). The first picture (corresponding to white on the noise meter) shows several students with their hands raised. The colour *and* picture symbolise the up-front or instructional phase of the lesson. At lower-primary levels students are depicted sitting on the mat. At upper primary the students are pictured sitting at tables.

The second picture (corresponding to the green quadrant, top right) portrays a couple of students on-task and quietly chatting at their desks (no doubt they're chatting about the work!). This picture symbolises 'working noise' or 'partner communication'. The third picture (corresponding to the yellow quadrant, bottom right) portrays two students talking quite loudly and has other students' irritated faces in the background. This is the reminder/warning cue. When the teacher signals the arrow to this quadrant and picture she is reminding, or warning, the class that the students are getting too loud. The fourth picture (red quadrant, bottom left) shows students clearly talking far too loudly. A 'ghost buster' red circle and line indicate that this is not on!

The teacher has blu-tacked the meter up on the wall (or chalkboard) in a fixed location which is clearly visible to all students. On day one as the students come in they are intrigued by the colours and pictures. They ask questions about it. The teacher says, 'Have a think about it, and I'll explain later, organise your lunch bag in the basket and remember your coat.' Later that morning the teacher will go over the normative rules and routines of *our classroom* using visual and written cues where appropriate.

The students are sitting on the mat, cued in by bell, or verbal reminder or a counting cue, or even a song. 'By the time I've counted backwards from 20, I want to see everyone sitting on the carpet ready for ... Off we go, 19, 18 ...' As each group sits, the teacher pauses to say, 'That's it Melissa', 'You're ready Jack', 'Relaxed and ready Ella.' She gives the good morning to all and points to the noise meter. 'Now, I wonder if anyone can explain what this picture means here.' Tactically ignoring the half-dozen who call out (with or without their hands up) she targets those students doing what is in the first (top left) picture. 'Yes, Bilal, you've got your hand up...' She then discusses the difference between hands up *and* calling out, and hands up *and* waiting (without clicking fingers or shouting out). She asks why it is important to take turns and have a 'signal' like a hand up. The arrow is on the white quadrant and she adds, as she points, 'When the arrow is on this white quadrant it means ...' Again she reinforces what is in the picture and what is happening as hands go up and students wait in turn. 'So, white zone means: hands up, wait your turn without calling out and one at a time.'

'Let's look at the green zone now. What do you think the green colour and the picture mean?' (She leaves the arrow on white to remind them that it is still hands-up time.) Here she discusses 'partner communication' and calls up two pairs of students to role-play different levels of working-time noise. Each pair of partners is asked to role-play different levels of noise. The teacher then asks the group which is helpful noise, which is too loud, which is okay and *why*.

(I recently used the noise meter in a composite class of eight- and nine-year-olds. I role-modelled 'partner voice' and discussed what made it 'partner voice'. The students used descriptions such as 'positive' and 'loud enough for students working close together'. I then used a 'playground voice' and we discussed the difference between the settings and the *effect* different voices had in those different settings. The students could clearly see the reasons for partner voices.)

Pointing to the green quadrant the teacher continues, 'Green is like a traffic-light colour; green for "go" but when we're talking at our tables we need to remember the other students nearby. What can we do to make sure they are able to get on with their work?' The picture is the visual reminder. The teacher points out that she ought to be able to say a student's name during work time (if she has to call across the room) without raising her voice. 'Let's practise, all of us. Have a little chat quietly here while I walk to the back of the room. I'll say three students' names in my *normal* voice. Those students put their hands up if they can hear me from the back of the room.'

Having practised green zone she indicates with her hand to the yellow/amber quadrant. She discusses with them the importance of the students controlling their own noise level ('consider others') at their work places. 'This colour (yellow/amber) is a reminder; when I put the arrow here it's your job to bring the noise level down. So you'll need to look up from time to time. To help you, I'll ask one person at each table to be a noise *monitor*. If I call their name during work time they can check the meter. If it's on yellow they need to quietly (and helpfully) remind their group to bring their noise level down to green zone; partner communication, partner voices.'

During the lesson the teacher hears increasing chatter at Krista's table. Turning the arrow to yellow she calls over to Krista, 'Krista— yellow'. The word 'yellow' is enough of a reminder. She continues moving around the room leaving Krista to do her job. Krista bends her head to eyeball her four fellow students. 'She did put it on the remember colour. We have to be more quiet.' As they bring their noise level down the teacher casually (ten seconds or so later) walks over to the noise meter and puts it back on green. She quietly calls Krista's name. Krista looks up and the teacher gives the okay sign with her finger and thumb and smiles. Krista returns the smile. Learning and socialisation are taking place. Most of all the students are beginning to take ownership of their individual and group behaviour.

I have also used the noise meter a number of times at lower secondary with some success. One particularly noisy class (all boys, Year 8) responded very well. I had used a little behaviour reinforcement by allocating a 'point' here or there when they remembered to approximate their behaviour to the white and green zones. They could also pick up (avoid the word 'earn') points if, when I put the arrow on yellow, they brought their noise level back *down*, by themselves, without me needing to remind them verbally (red zone). I wanted the colours, pictures and reminders (arrow to the colour) to be as non-verbal as possible to maximise on-task learning and teaching. I even gave points in white zone for hands up without calling out. If they got to 20 points they could stop five minutes earlier than the lesson ending and have free chat time or read comics (or even start homework!). If we didn't get to 20 points that lesson, the points could transfer to the next English lesson. They responded really well. Whenever I put the arrow on yellow you could hear the 'Pssts' and 'Oi look!' and 'Shhh'.

On the fourth session I decided to stop using the noise meter. One of the first questions of the day was 'Hey, Mr Rogers how come you didn't bring the pictures and the noise thing?'

'Well, Tom, I don't really think we need it now. The class is working really well. You're keeping the working noise comfortable during the lesson so I thought we'd go on without it.'

'Gees', he smiled, 'I really liked it when we had that thing!' (I think he actually liked the structure it gave as well as the points!)

I only ever use the points allocation for the more difficult, noisy classes as a behaviour-enhancement outcome (a more elegant term than reward). Again, like the noise meter itself, it is an establishment-phase prop. Its aim is to teach and encourage positive habits in the students; it is not an end in itself.

Variations on a theme

I like to use visual learning wherever I can, even for secondary students. A simple graph with a vertical and horizontal axis can be used to give the students visual feedback on their own working noise. The vertical axis is marked 0–10, where silence is 0, whisper zone is 2, the upper reasonable limit of partner communication is 5 and migraine level is 10!

The horizontal axis is marked off in five-minute slots. During the on-task phase of the lesson I go up to the board every five minutes and quietly mark a vertical bar (coloured chalk) indicating how loud they are in terms of their partner voices, or work talk. This gives visual feedback (non-verbally) to the class. With particularly noisy groups I use the points allocation system described earlier with a five-minute free time 'reward' for keeping below 5 on the scale. In a survey on rewards and punishments in British secondary schools students rated five minutes free time as a worthwhile 'reward'! Who would think five minutes would be so significant?

Cues for getting teacher attention

The need to *teach* cues for getting teacher attention will vary with age and situation but a simple rule reminder will always help, even at secondary level. 'If you want to ask a question during instruction time I'd appreciate your hands up (without calling out thanks).' If they forget, the teacher can use a brief rule reminder ('Remember our rule for ...') or use a non-verbal signal. Teachers will also need to teach appropriate cues for getting teacher attention during the on-task phase of the lesson.

When I was teaching a Year 7 class recently, several students called out for my assistance (even though the rule-poster was on the board with a simple cartoon headed by 'Hands up, fair go'). I looked at each, briefly, and raised my own right hand (touching my mouth with the back of my hand). I kept it low-key as I swiftly concentrated on the ones with hands up, numbering them off: 'Michelle 1, Adam 2, Halid 3. Be with you soon.' I had explained earlier in the lesson that they could go on with other work, or read the class novel, until I was able to give one-to-one assistance.

When the teacher gets to know the class well, the hand-up routine can be dropped. Its use, initially, is to *establish* fair communication patterns.

During the on-task phase teachers need to receive a simple cue for allocating their attention. Here are some possibilities:

■ Institute a 'Check with three before you check with me' rule.
■ Institute a hands-up-and-wait rule.
■ Have a class mentor system; students who have intellectual nous, social skills and peer goodwill can be called on to conference with a student if necessary to supplement teacher support.
■ Use a numbered ticket system: a student takes a numbered ticket (1, 2, 3 ...) and when the teacher displays the numbered card on

the board, the student with the corresponding ticket comes down for assistance. ('Come on down number 7'—you know, like in the supermarket!)

∎ Use a teacher help board. My colleagues and I have used this little prop with middle-school students. There are two large charts displayed at the front of the room. One chart is headed 'Remember'; it is a reminder that before students write their names on the second chart (the teacher help board) they need to remember:

1 'Check the work requirement yourself.'

2 'Check with a partner (remember to use your partner voice).'

3 'Check with a class mentor' (if there is a class mentor system).

4 'Write your name on the teacher help board and I'll come round (in turn) to help.' On average there are only three or four names at any one time, crossed off in turn as assistance is given.

5 'While you wait (your name is there, I won't forget) there are three user-friendly worksheets you can choose from until we can get a moment together.' (Or the students can reread the class novel, go on with a spelling activity ...)

All of this is discussed beforehand with the class. Have a felt-tip pen on a string up the front on the chart. Some teachers use whiteboard covering on the chart so the names can be erased in turn. The teacher help board lends itself particularly to a setting where the teacher is regularly on the move and cannot be always on the look out for hands up (for example, home economics, graphic design, textiles etc.).

Initiating and sustaining group attention

I was asked to take a home group, Year 9, one morning. My colleague had described them as 'seriously ratty' (plus a few other choice epithets). As I walked in, a girl pushed past me, 'I ain't going in, she's a bitch, I hate her!'—this to a girl just in front of her. A friendship fracas, I surmised. The student sulked, leaning against the wall outside the classroom. 'You look seriously uptight' I said.

'Maybe you need some cool-off time when you're ready come in and join us.' I walked in to see fifteen or so students talking loudly, some with their feet up, some wandering around. Some had even made a 'visual barrier' of chairs on top of tables and were gassing away behind the 'Berlin wall'.

I didn't want to shout, or stand and wait, or try the threat 'You waste my time and ...!' I didn't want to be psychologically 'done in' in that up-front vulnerability sense. I left the front of the room and wandered around the classroom. I introduced myself and asked politely, non-threateningly, for names. (One boy said he'd forgotten. I quietly said, with a smile, 'When you remember let me know. Mine's Bill Rogers.') I asked what sort of things they did in home group, etc. I quietly asked the group at the back if they'd help me put the chairs down and organise the back row. After six to eight minutes I went to the front and formally started. Armed now with at least half a dozen (remembered) names and having done some *mini-establishment* I had a much better time in the 'formal' attention-getting phase with this very challenging class.

It's tempting to settle group noise with a loud 'Right! Settle down! You're too noisy ...' This approach, coupled with some pacing at the front of the room may shut the class up—but at what cost? What will the teacher have to do in subsequent sessions? I've seen teachers shout and pace, and point out the noisy ones. 'Hey you, yes you! Didn't you hear what I said, eh?' I've even heard 'Shut *up*!' from some colleagues teaching next door to me. A teacher might get away with it once or twice but it establishes that loudness is the *norm* here. And that's the trouble. It 'anchors in' *our* loudness in competition with theirs.

Anchoring

Anchoring refers to the association of place, activity and expectation in the minds of the students. If we walk around at the front of the room, saying loudly, 'Don't talk, you are supposed to be listening!', we anchor into their experience a verbally agitated response. When we're standing at the front of the classroom, it will help to stand relaxed, feet a little apart (not the full stride, with hands on hips), with 'open' body language; not with arms tightly folded or hands behind our backs, sighing, with heads low, looking as if we believe, already, we're going to have trouble.

It is also important not to lounge at the front of the room or lean back against the wall. At secondary level it is normally not helpful (in the establishment phase) to sit at the desk trying to engage in productive instructional time *while* leaning back in the chair.

Anchoring calmness and expectation to our students is not easy. It is something we need to consciously do as we scan the room. It may be helpful to walk to the board (as the students file in), write up some key points, or put up a relevant poster, then walk to the front centre and wait. Some teachers use a signal such as a bell or a tap on a glass with a spoon (I've used that with many secondary classes).

As the residual group noise drops (in response—we hope—to our tactical wait time or signal) we can lift our voice just above theirs (*when* the residual noise drops) with the first direction. 'Settling down'—here a pleasant, firm voice. After a brief *tactical* pause (…) add the secondary directions. 'Looking this way thanks (…) and listening.' Of course tone of voice and manner are crucial. It can help to reflect on the sort of things one might say to signal, to initiate, *group* attention. 'Okay, everyone (…) eyes and ears this way (…) Ta' (as they respond). Voice tone is important; a clear and confident tone and a positive expectant manner will indicate much more than the words. 'Stop what you are doing (…) look this way (…) and listening (…) thanks.' A colleague of mine actually draws a face, adding eyes and ears bit by bit to indicate (1) eyes this way, now (2) ears listening then (3) a smile! With lower and middle primary-age classes a noise meter can be helpful (see p. 207).

Rather than target individual noisy students, briefly acknowledge appreciation to on-task students: a smile, or nod, or 'Thanks, Dean', 'Sean', 'Yes, Melissa, I see your hand up'. Gratuitous language ('Oh look how well Sophie is sitting. Well done! Oh, isn't that terrific!') is not necessary.

Get the students used to the fact that when we stand in *that* place, front centre, we want, and need, their attention. Explain what 'having their attention' means and why we need to have quiet at the beginning and end of the lesson. If we need to regain their attention we can go back to that positional place and use a familiar signal or cue: tapping a glass, raising a hand, clapping, saying a cue word ('class'), even singing a song! It is important to establish that we will not address the whole class until all students are attending. If we are giving a *group* reminder to pack up, or move on to another activity it is more effective to go back to the familiar, upfront, positional place and use the familiar cue. If the cue is a bell we begin with the bell *and* the verbal cue. A few sessions later we can use the bell alone (not loud, keep it gentle). In time we might be able to just stand and wait, signalling that when we are standing *there*, group attention is expected.

A positive greeting, settling time and positive ending to the lesson are all important to class tone. Like many aspects of classroom management these things sound like 'small beer' but, amazingly, some teachers forget or underestimate their importance. Even a little personal greeting as the students file in can enhance the beginning of a lesson—not conversations though. I've seen some secondary teachers waste several minutes talking to an individual student about an essay (or whatever) while the other students get quite restless. At the primary level we are often in the classroom quite early so we can have the opportunity for the little extended dialogue with a student prior to 'the bell'.

Plan for readiness time

Some students (especially at secondary level) take a few minutes to get ready for the lesson. If that were to happen each class period, that's over half an hour a day lost just settling or getting ready. It can help, at the end of the first lesson, to discuss with the class 'readiness time' and to plan for the next lesson. Discuss why we need to be ready on time (within a few minutes or so), what we need to be ready (materials, gear from the locker, etc.) and then set a target (Pearce, 1995). Ask the students how long they think they ought reasonably to take to have the appropriate materials and be in their seats, relaxed and ready to go on with the instructional part of the lesson. Students will respond with suggested times (five minutes down to 60 seconds!) from which a target can be set for the next session together. A student can be appointed as timekeeper to see if, for the next lesson, the class can be in their seats with relevant materials in, say, 120 seconds. As with all routines, the purpose needs to be explained and once the routine becomes the norm the 'props' supporting the routine can be dropped. A routine is never an end in itself.

Lesson closure, summary, exit from class

It is important to end the lesson positively, with a summary where appropriate and 'goodbye for now'. It is especially important at primary level to end the day with a class discussion of the day's events, notices and future events, and thankyous for their efforts in remembering 'the special things we do in our class to make it a happy and positive place to teach and learn in'. An exit procedure is also important. In some classes students just race off, even barge past each other, to the door.

I find it helpful in the establishment phase of the year to have a card on the wall indicating the three things students need to remember before they leave the classroom (see Appendix X):

1 Place the chairs under the table (on the table at the end of the day).
2 Pick up litter from the floor (do the next class/cleaner a favour).
3 Leave the room, after the bell, in a way that considers others. (The concept of 'considering others' is discussed on day one.)

I also have a little picture symbolising each positive reminder.

If they forget (some have been trained in the past to just race off), I call them back. 'Stop (…) Back inside and sit down thanks.'

'But it's recess, gees!'

'Back inside, take a seat, I won't keep you long.' They scowl and sigh. They sit down. A couple sullenly kick their chairs as they take their semi-recumbent positions.

If one of the students does a 'corridor runner' I let him go. 'I'll follow up Craig later, take your seats.' (See p. 96.)

Rather than pace the front scowling, 'Right! You wasted my time, so I'll waste your time!', I prefer to stand up-front and signal some calmness, some self-control (I can't actually *control* them), some waiting time. Their residual noise drops. 'Okay, this is *not* a group detention.' I scan their faces. 'This is a group *reminder*. When the bell goes it is a reminder to me, as well as to you, that the lesson has finished and it's my job to dismiss the class. Let's try it again. Remember the chairs.' Walking to the door to give an individual goodbye, I ask Jo to pick up a large, screwed-up piece of paper. 'S'not mine.'

'Maybe it's not, Jo; but it's under your table. Do the next class a favour, thanks.'

'All right (he responds to my grin), I'll put it in the bin if it makes you happy.' (He mumbles this as he walks off to the bin).

If I just let several students race off without some correction (supportive correction) in effect I say that what the students are doing is all right. When students exit from the classroom, whether they leave table by table, or stand behind chairs, or just 'leave quietly thanks', a *routine* can help. Even at senior levels, Years 10, 11 and 12, a reminder about considering others won't go amiss. If a student ignores the routine and races off, it is worth some individual follow-up (see p. 96).

At primary level I've used reminder cards on each table. The cards symbolise the essential things necessary 'for leaving your work area tidy and looked after'. A few little drawings can help to make the reminder card user-friendly. If the pack-up routines have been discussed on day one and then summarised on the reminder cards the teacher doesn't need to go over the minutiae each time; all she needs to do is refer to the reminder card.

Mrs D has a quiet reading area. Some cushions, a chess table, a sign saying 'Our quiet reading corner' with a picture of a child reading. Her room is not messy or too busy, but attractive. Some desks are against the wall, some in a rectangle arrangement. She's tried to arrange the children's seating relative to size. Books are neatly stowed (she does not allow sloppiness). She is firm on this. Books are special. The rules are called 'Our class rules' and are pinned up around the room. (This can be done up to Year 8; see Chapter 4.) Early finishers have a range of things they can do, from chess to reading, to special projects to worksheets.

Mrs D's students know how to come in and out of the room. Respect means that rights are respected. We don't all charge in and out to prove Darwin's theory! There is a movement rule.

There are set routines for lunch money and a master list of the canteen offerings to stop the 'What's it cost for a pie, Miss?' This also encourages independence.

We all work better when the environment is conducive to learning—not harsh, restrictive, cluttered, dirty, demeaning and embarrassing. Do you remember some of the places you've worked? Apart from the money, what made them *worth* working in? It's good for us too—not just the students. The benefits are an increase in positive, effective socialising and, therefore, a more positive learning environment.

Self-esteem in the classroom

If a child could tell us:

When you make me feel smaller than I am, I get angry, especially when you do it in front of other people. I often try to get back at you, by being a 'pest'.

When you correct me or put me down in front of others it doesn't work. Inside, I'm angry at you and I say all kinds of things that will show in my behaviour. I'll take much more notice if you talk quietly with me away from others.

When you try to get me to apologise, or ask me 'Why?' when I'm in conflict with others (or you) you'll see I'm not very cooperative; it will look like I'm not listening. I don't mind you taking action but can you find a way to 'turn the heat down' and provide a face-saving way out of it? After all, your social skills are better than mine. You're more effective, you know, when you stay calm.

When you apologise, you show me that you, too, are human, that it's not beneath your dignity to say 'I'm sorry'. Your honesty helps me feel warm towards you; it also reminds me that to be human is to be fallible. I can live up to that.

When you preach to me (or, more often, *at* me) you forget that I already know what's right and wrong. If you nag at me I might appear deaf (this is a way of protecting myself). If we have clear rules, expectations and consequences of behaviour, preaching won't change me.

When you go on about my mistakes, especially in front of others, I feel rotten, like I'm really no good. Sometimes I would like to learn to make mistakes without feeling I am no good. It's hard to build on failure.

When you're firm with me, I don't really mind. At least I know where I stand. All I ask is that you do it without making me feel stupid, hopeless and worthless. When you're inconsistent I just get confused. I even try to get away with anything I can. When your expectations are clear and your treatment fair and calm, I know where I stand.

When you're inconsistent I just get confused. I even try to get away with anything I can

When you demand reasons—you know, full explanations for my behaviour—I often don't really know *why* I did it. If you ask *what* I did and suggest alternatives, even ask me to suggest alternatives, that might be different.

When I don't get a chance to tell my side of the story, when you try to force or frighten me into telling the truth, I often tell lies, or like you, 'bend' the truth.

When you do things for me that I can do for myself, I feel like a baby—like I can't do it. If you keep doing that I might end up always relying on you and putting you in my service. You may end up labelling me as a 'learning failure', or a 'hopeless case'. When you go on at me about playing and not concentrating, remember I sometimes learn by experimenting.

When you remember the most important thing I'm most happy. You know—I can't really thrive without understanding and encouragement.

You are able to help me feel and believe I'm okay, I have worth, I can 'make it'—but I don't really need to tell you that ... do I?

The basis of a positive classroom climate: self-esteem and self-concept

Self-esteem is the *value* or esteem we put on what we perceive about our abilities, our body, our feelings, our social interaction. The trouble is that many children (and adults) process critical comments

The relationship between self-concept, self-esteem and behaviour

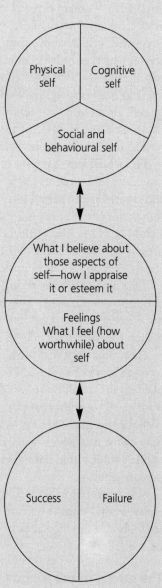

SELF-CONCEPT
The picture I build about myself—
what I conceive myself to be.

SELF-ESTEEM
How I esteem (or value) that
picture of self. I feel, then appraise
or believe, certain things about my
'self'. I do this largely from
messages I receive from others.
As I get older I'll be giving myself
messages of value ... or ...

MY BEHAVIOUR
How I perform in the cognitive,
social, emotional dynamics of
home, school setting. How I see,
and others see, my behaviour.

Figure 6.2   Adapted from Bernard and Joyce, 1984.

about *self* in critical ways. Unfortunately these external messages may become internalised as 'I *am* a failure' (rather than, 'I sometimes fail'); 'I *cannot* succeed at this' (low tolerance to frustration); I'll *never* manage, I *always* fail'; '*Nobody* cares'.

As children develop, they begin to build a cognitive picture or concept of themselves; an emerging 'I-am-ness', a perception and conception of themselves as *selves*. This picture or concept of self, as a self, is built largely by others and taken in by self, even confirmed by self. As a child interacts with parents, teachers, other significant adults and peers, she forms a concept of self in the intellectual, physical, socio-emotional and spiritual realms.

The who-I-am and who-am-I process arises from the way a child processes information from 'outside'. The way a child is spoken to and treated is processed through his feelings. Children don't reason things out like adults (and many adults don't reason things out!). If a child hears regular critical comments about his abilities or disabilities he will *feel* unsuccessful and may come to rate himself as unsuccessful (stupid, fat, ugly, useless, a failure).

Take a child who is trying to cut out a picture of a dog during a cut-and-paste activity. She obviously has poor fine-motor ability, low concentration and low tolerance to frustration, all of which makes the dog look like a map of Brazil. In seeking to help, a teacher might say, 'Look Shari, you should be able to cut that shape by now. Haven't I told you before how to use those scissors? All you need to do is follow the lines. Come on, I'll show you. You don't want to be a messy worker do you?' Shari may end up feeling, 'What's the use?' or 'I'm hopeless', or in some cases, 'I can't do this—why not agree with that adult judgement?' Children, like many adults, often rate themselves globally on a small aspect of performance.

Self-appraisal is powerfully related to how we feel. A child (and many adults) finds it hard to build on failure. If a child feels failure strongly (via the messages from others) he may well begin to believe he is a failure.

The power of the tongue

'Can't you understand that by now?' 'You *always* ...' 'No, that's not right!' 'Can't you get it by now!' 'What's wrong with you?' 'How many times do I have to tell you!' 'You *never* ...' 'I'm sick of reminding you' 'You'll send me to an early grave!' 'Others can do it properly, why can't you?' 'You stupid boy, you ...' Characteristic 'global' terms like these (sometimes just a slip of the tongue) are often interpreted by children as ratings of them *as persons*. Having worked with many children with very low self-esteem, it seems to me that the common thread is the message received from teachers or peers such as 'that's not right, you dummy!' Teachers who poke at a child's work, screw it up ('What rotten messy work!') and throw it in the bin, or demean it in front of others, demonstrate more than rotten manners.

The teacher who yells at the Year 1 student about the scissors, 'Hey, are you stupid or something? Didn't I just tell you to put those scissors away?' may get the scissors back in the scissors tray but he has said something to *all* the students. The 'ripple effect' of a teacher's verbal discipline affects more than the target audience (Kounin, 1977). The adult tongue is a powerful weapon. Some teachers use it intentionally to exercise dominance and help them to cope with internal frustration or anger about intransigent and disruptive behaviour. Others use it unintentionally because frustration takes over.

Our voices are our dominant working tool. Words strung out in sentences employ tone, strength, pitch and emotion. Words are things. They *do* something—they are instrumental. As far as possible, we should seek to develop an interactive style that is more reflective, more conscious of the effect of our verbal presence in the room—especially when we're frustrated or angry (see pp. 279f).

Developing a more positive verbal style is something to be worked at. It is a skill. It rarely comes naturally.

The way a child is spoken to and treated is processed by the child largely through her feelings. The message, 'Look, what's wrong with you, I've told you a hundred times how to do that!' is not processed as 'You have made a mistake', but 'Gees, you're hopeless, you always muck up!' often leading to 'I'm no good at this.' If children hear regular put-downs, global messages of 'You never ...', 'You always leave a mess', 'You always do untidy work', 'You're always late', 'I'm always telling you', how do we imagine they process them? As helpful reminders? How do we feel with similar teacher–learner messages?

Erik Erikson (1960, 1968) relates self-esteem to the long-term appraisal we pick up from significant others (parents, siblings, teachers). Healthy self-esteem is related to how we internalise those external appraisals. As teachers, we may not be able to influence the home messages; we can do a lot about the messages *we* give and how we give them.

Many teenagers negotiate their way in the world with poor pictures of themselves, especially their physical selves. Through the way they're spoken to, the images they see in the media and watching their peers, they rate their bodies: too fat, too ugly, nose too big, ugly freckles, funny-shaped legs, slobby-looking, etc. Human nature has a propensity for neat, global labelling. It's convenient, easy, simplistic, and even satisfies our desire to hurt, 'get back at', or 'teach so-and-so'. Such labels are the soil in which poor self-esteem is nourished, as encouragement, appropriate praise, trust and respect are the soil for healthier self-esteem building.

Children are more likely to build a stronger, healthier self-concept and value themselves more positively when:

1 They are achieving in some way, when they feel that they are able to accomplish *something*. Encouragement for specific improvement enables children to feel good about their progress. One of the harder tasks of teaching is enabling a sense of accomplishment by the way we organise curriculum for mixed abilities, learning outcomes geared to even small successes, and group activities that can give 'social strength' to the less successful classroom members.

2 They feel cared for and respected *as people*. One of the more profound statements I have heard many students say of their teacher is 'He (or she) treats me as a human being!' Here are some of the many typical responses I hear from students when we discuss teachers' good treatment: 'Friendly, they talk to you like a human being', 'They trust you', 'They make mistakes of course, but they fix it up with you', 'There's a climate of give and take', 'They give you a chance to talk' (this often refers to the students perceiving that they have an appropriate right of reply), 'They give you a fair chance before you get any punishment', 'They give interest-

ing work', 'They're not chauvinistic, they're not unfair about who is mucking around', 'They don't ridicule you or make you have unsafe feelings', 'They don't have temper tantrums.'

Emotional baggage

Simone struggles, deciding whether or not to get out of her warm bed. The first voice she hears says, 'Get up, come on, I said it's time to get up, I'll be late! Look, if you don't, I'll come in and get you out myself! Damn it, Simone, get up!'

Simone starts to put on her cold clothes. Dressed, she moves off to negotiate another lousy breakfast. She'll probably have to make it herself and her hastily organised lunch won't be much better. 'Look, what are you wearing that T-shirt for Simone? It's filthy. What's wrong with you? If you'd put it in the wash like I told you ...' Simone is awake enough to argue back now. 'Don't argue with me! Gee you really know how to upset me, don't you! All you think of is yourself.'

Simone finally makes a rough sandwich for lunch and walks to school. It's not always as stressful as this. It's been worse since dad left two weeks ago.

Simone is in Year 3. Each day she carries a weight of emotional baggage into the classroom. She has little to be hopeful or happy about—yet. School could help, for a short while, to change that. What she doesn't need is a teacher who replicates mum (at least mum on these days).

All students bring their emotional baggage into the classroom. So, too, does the teacher. The on-task and relational dynamics, therefore, need to consider that reality. This does not mean we can over-compensate for a child's difficult home life; it does mean that we treat our students with respect within a discipline framework that includes self-esteem as one of its goals.

Children learn best when:

- they feel confident and secure (they may even feel happy from time to time!)
- they are affirmed and encouraged
- the focus of learning is made clear
- learning tasks and experiences give opportunity for some success (It is pointless having the one algebra lesson in Year 7 for all students when it is manifestly clear that only half a dozen can cope with it.)
- the learning program caters for mixed abilities
- our dialogue with students is positive, and careful to concentrate on their *present* ability and present behaviour and future possibilities
- learning includes group tasks as well as individual learning tasks.

In short, children learn more effectively when they feel better about being in *this* group and coping with *this* work, when fundamental needs are being met. Students' preferences for subjects are often linked to their liking of a particular teacher. If we carp at Jono about what he can't do in maths, refer constantly to his wrong answers ('What sort of work do you call this?'), tear out a page (in front of the class) from his maths book because he was drawing in the margin and then proceed to humiliate him in front of the class, his effective learning is linked to how he feels about those messages. When we enhance self-esteem, we enhance the capacity for learning, and for growth.

Unseen baggage

Respect: at the heart of self-esteem

Peter is sitting outside the principal's office, waiting. Peter is a child who has been labelled socio-emotionally disturbed (SED). He presents as a scruffy, jaded-looking chap. His jeans are filthy, his sneakers ragged, his black dracula windcheater seems somehow appropriate. At seven years of age he's experienced much emotional and physical 'bruising' from home. He swears easily and loudly when frustrated. He finds it difficult to sit still on his chair in Miss S's class. He has been described as a 'pain', an 'A-grade attention-seeker', a 'shifty-eyed little bugger', a 'failure', a 'dummy'.

Today, he's been exited from Room 10 because he threw his books on the floor in a fit of low frustration-tolerance. Built-up emotion from home? Who knows? His teacher is not a psycho-therapist. He finds himself waiting for Mr D to return to his office and deal with him.

Mr D is a tough principal. He certainly does not like children like Peter. Eyeing him sitting there, morose and sullen, his voice is sharp, loud, frustrated. 'You, you again! It's always you. What are you here for today? No, don't tell me, it's probably another lie. I'm sick and tired of seeing you at my office! You're nothing but a nuisance, a damned nuisance!'

Perhaps Mr D is having a bad day. Perhaps he doesn't like this child. Perhaps he even hates him. Of course, Peter's behaviour is a 'pain'. This child has taken several years to learn a range of attention-seeking behaviours. They've got him where he is now. He's getting significant attention, from a male, right at this moment. Let's hope this is bad-day syndrome and not characteristic behaviour.

Can one respect a child like Peter? One of the confounding problems when dealing with such children is our spontaneous like or dislike of them. The trouble with this is that we may often be relying on our feelings to dictate our actions.

We often feel we should react angrily when we're angry—that's certainly what our feelings are telling us, so why shouldn't we? But, of course, our feelings are not proof of anything. It's like instinct. Many teachers and principals believe that their instinct for discipline is right. The trouble with relying on impulse, instinct and feelings is that they are devoid of guidance. As C. S. Lewis observed, 'Each instinct, if you listen to it, will claim to be gratified at the expense of all the rest.'

Because discipline is more than mere punishment or control, it is helpful to superintend our so-called 'natural' reactions (being natural does not make them automatically right). We best superintend our discipline by bringing some consistency to the treatment variable. In this way we are still able to be decisive and firm without simply reacting. I believe this is called respect.

Children like Peter are not easy to deal with. They've clocked up several years habituation. Teachers who are in any way effective with such children do not give up or accept excuses, don't resort to simple labels (he's a 'pain') and take a concentrated team approach (see pp. 299f).

Liking or respecting: the professional difference

As C. S. Lewis observed, respect is not a matter of forcing ourselves to like X, this disruptive person. ('Damn those stupid earrings, that ridiculous haircut, that whining nasal voice.') To psych ourselves into such a feeling is unhelpful to say the least. Showing respect for a child even when her behaviour is rude, arrogant and rule-breaking is a different matter. Respect is about speaking to and with her, acting towards her in such a way as to acknowledge that it is her *actions* that are wrong. Condemnatory, rude, sarcastic, caustic language is, therefore, unnecessary.

Respect is not a matter of pretending we like X either, it is commitment to an action, a treatment variable. We cannot say truthfully, 'I like Maria', because we know we don't—especially when she swears at us and wears us down with her attention-seeking behaviour. So, what do we do? Well, we certainly don't waste time bothering about trying to like her; we're on a safer course when we try to treat her with fundamental respect.

Respect is to do with *how* we treat X, and we can do something about that. Feelings will come and go. They are dependent, too often, on mood, digestion, amount of sleep, vagaries of time and circumstance. It is helpful, when our feelings trigger potential hate, rejection, frustration, animosity, to remember the treatment variable—respect; even in extreme crisis-discipline settings. If we just give in to our feelings, we will lose out on long-term discipline aims and perpetuate unhelpful, even stressful, teacher behaviour. Even our anger can be communicated respectfully (see p. 284).

Labelling and the expectancy effect

Labels are great for jars, not so helpful for people. It's easy to resort to labelling of others; a kind of shorthand description of another's social or intellectual traits. 'He's slow', 'She's always messy', 'She's a real idiot', and, a commonly heard one in staff rooms, 'He's a real sh——.'

The big problem with labels is that they're so often attached to definite beliefs. The user is reluctant to alter judgements, so that when George is on-task or behaves in a socially acceptable way, it's an exception. Once we perceive a student's behaviour via a label,

Labelling is suitable for jam jars, less suitable for people

actions by that student can be open to a range of interpretations. The more firmly we believe George is a pain, the easier it is to feel and act as if he will be what we think he is. Perception powerfully affects our behaviour.

Rating others through our perception and self-talk affects the dynamic of discipline and teaching. While not unsympathetic to how some students normally engender feelings of frustration or hostility, I believe it's a most disturbing step to then use such feelings as proof positive that one must label X in a derogatory way. It's far healthier to label the actions of X rather than X herself; children know the difference. We communicate our beliefs more powerfully than we realise. 'But I'd never call him a sh———!' That's not the real problem, as Robert Rosenthal observed.

In 1963 Rosenthal and his colleagues developed experiments to test 'self-fulfilling prophecy' or the 'expectancy effect'. Randomly assigned rats were divided into two groups and labelled 'maze-bright' and 'maze-dull'. College undergraduates who tested the rats only knew their rat sample as 'bright' or 'dull'. Ten trials later, the results showed the 'bright' rats nearly doubled the 'dull' rats in maze performance tests. Rosenthal concluded that rather than any real 'intelligence' differences raising the score of the 'bright' rats, it was the expectations of those working with them communicated through tactile and kinetic cues that had an effect on the rat performance.

This 'effect' has been widely studied with child–teacher relationships in classroom settings. 'You've got those terrors in Year 10! They'll drive you round the bend!' may well affect how a teacher operates with the group. When we label a child, hopeless, useless, an idiot, or dumb, we may find their relational behaviour (and ours) affected by that expectation and fulfilling the prophecy.

In building a positive climate, much will depend on what a teacher expects; not in a demanding way, 'I expect thus and so!', but in the normal treatment we apply. There *is* a difference between a teacher who expects children can and will do well, can achieve, can cooperate, will respond to the rule environment, and a teacher who communicates the expectation of (and may say it) 'I *knew* you'd blow it!', 'You *always* …', 'Can't you *ever* … ?', 'Oh! When will you … ?'. Again this is communicated through the teacher's verbal and non-verbal interactions.

We can communicate frustration, hopelessness, failure, by the perception–action process. It begins by rating and labelling (that is, believing) that X is a … The next step, of acting (or reacting) to X as if she is a … is often unconscious. To change the cycle means a change of thinking: 'I don't like what X does' is different from 'She is a real little so and so'.

All the discipline approaches discussed in this book are based on respectful language. They also treat children as if they are able to make better choices and are able to work cooperatively. Even if they don't, we will still treat them, not as if they are little animals, but with dignity. Even if we have to be decisive, we can still do so with dignified treatment (Chapters 2 and 3).

Praise or encouragement?

One way that teachers (and parents) seek to strengthen self-esteem is through the use of encouragement. Encouragement can be distinguished from unhelpful praise to the extent that encouragement concentrates on, describes and gives feedback on students' efforts or actions rather than their person. Rather than say to a Year 3 child,

'You're a good boy for working quietly', we simply acknowledge it, 'You're working quietly today', smile and move off to work with someone else. When a student gives a helpful, correct or thoughtful answer to a teacher's question, rather than reply with 'Good girl' or even 'What a good answer', we simply acknowledge it, 'Yes Cassie, that's right', 'That's one way of looking at it', 'Correct', 'Sure'. Giving an incorrect answer or not knowing, doesn't *make* a student stupid or bad. It simply means he, as yet, doesn't know, or may not understand or even be shy.

Global terms (good/bad) or praise evaluate a student's *person* whereas encouragement gives the focus of attention to *effort*. Praise is seen by some students as manipulative or even insincere, rather than supportive of the student trying to have a go. Some students don't believe a global rating of their work or behaviour ('Fantastic!', 'Brilliant!'). Some can't cope with that. It's not that teachers don't mean well, or are not sincere when they say 'great' or 'terrific'. *Descriptive feedback* (sincere) is enough. 'That's a tidy work area, you put the lids on the felt-tip pens, and made sure all the litter was off the floor.' 'You took time and care to tidy the library corner. That's what I call being thoughtful.' This acknowledges *what* is thoughtful.

Rather than call a picture or story 'nice' or 'lovely', comment on or describe *features* of the story that show thought, care, creativity. Some children, if told their story is 'good' or 'nice', will deny it. ('No it's not—it's a stupid story.') This may be part attention-seeking and part personal belief. The student can hardly argue with descriptive feedback such as, 'The way you described the rain falling on the boy's face matching his tears really got across to me the feeling of loneliness. It was very moving', or 'It's a pleasure to have a class like this because ...' (the teacher ticks off three or four points that give pleasure), or 'You went out of your way to help Dimitri with his maths this morning.' Encouragement is a comment on *how* the student's behaviour was thoughtful, considerate, careful. Often the description is enough for the child to get the point. 'I noticed you had the tap half-on so it wouldn't splash everywhere', or to the group (primary), 'I appreciated the way you came in quietly, went straight to your seats and got out your class novels.' I'll admit I've seen Year 7s and 8s appreciate that feedback. Every encouragement needs to be 'fair dinkum' in tone, not long-winded or sycophantic. Students will easily see through that!

A Year 6 class and a teacher knocks on the door for a brief chat. The class teacher stands at the door for five minutes. Most, if not all, students still carry on with their work, stay in their seats, use their partner voices. The Year 4 teacher makes a point of saying at the close of the lesson, 'I appreciated the way you all carried on working remembering to use your partner voices while I had a chat with Mr Davies. Thank you.'

Use descriptive feedback that encourages effort but still directs students to necessary improvement. This can be through written feedback or questions. 'The passage about rain and the feeling of loneliness really gets across what the main character was feeling at the time. (This shows appreciation.) Check the topic to see how loneliness affects the relationship with his dad—develop that idea too. Remember to check for editing. Hang in there, Mr Smith.' This is more encouraging than a final mark 6/10, or 'You *forgot* to …', or 'You've missed half the topic and not checked for spelling, etc.'

Some teachers give little encouragement because they believe that good work or behaviour is what is expected anyway. Yet even as adults we appreciate recognition of our effort and contribution. This is why students appreciate (at primary level) us showing their work to other teachers, or the principal. I've seen students at secondary level beam when their work is being shared and another teacher is giving positive feedback. 'That's a lively sentence using that word, Lisa.' 'I can see you're enjoying that Paul.' 'It seems like there is a different person sitting in this seat, Deanna (teacher has a frown) from the same looking person yesterday (wink).' 'You're using that Stanley knife carefully Craig.' 'Michaela, it might be easier if you hold the ruler with your thumb as well (…) Do you mind if I show you?' (rather than 'Don't hold it like that! No wonder it's messy'). 'That's an interesting thought!' 'I have faith in you because…'

Even if students do not always respond to our encouragement straight away we encourage because it is good teaching practice, not because it's a manipulative tool or because it 'works'. Some teachers find it helpful to keep a notebook to record observations of behaviour that can be utilised for encouraging feedback at a later date—it's easy to forget.

Where a student's work is incorrect or messy, it is better to note what he has done correctly and concentrate on the effort made, then ask if he understands the topic at hand, or suggest he has another go at spelling 'because', or say 'Let's try that again' or 'Show me, have you got that answer?' This approach can help to energise and motivate.

> During silent reading with Year 3, one of my students, who had severe learning difficulties, chose an encyclopaedia to read. Rather than say, 'No James, that's too hard. Let me get you another book', I encouraged him to tell me why he chose it. 'See these pictures, Mr Rogers, they're about road-digging machines.' We had a discussion about machines and used the experience during process writing.

Encouragement builds upon a student's strengths and assets. This is as true of academic on-task activity as of social cooperative activity. It works at crediting effort rather than merely praising the end result. This communicates to students that you believe in them and have confidence in their ability, stickability, judgement ... Students learn that they can 'do it' and helping others in the class reinforces that. (Group activity is especially useful to that end.)

Remember that failure is not the issue. Encourage the trying, the effort. Verbalise the encouragement. 'Come on Dave, keep trying. I see you're thinking hard, that's it. You've finished that part, that was the tricky bit, now let's work on the next bit.'

We should not over-pity them when they fail. 'Perhaps you're feeling it's tough, but I'm sure that you can do this. We (not just I) can help.' Look for effort, improvement, evidence of trying. Seek, as in all social behaviour-management, to assist them to take responsibility for their own feelings, emotions and behaviour.

Encouragement comes not just from the words, but also from tone of voice; body language; basics such as recognition of a student's presence, especially outside the classroom; the little special chat from time to time; the positive beginning and ending to the lesson, especially if we've had a bad day. A feeling of ineptness can be communicated to a student whether our actual words are encouraging or not. This is especially true if the *belief* behind our verbal direction does not separate deed from doer. To communicate, 'I like you, but I dislike what you did' (actions that hurt others and infringe their rights) is not easy. The balance between either overprotecting a student in her social and emotional development or punishing her with discouraging comment is the tension of creative teaching. What we are learning to ask ourselves as we manage children in groups, or as individuals in groups, is 'How does what I'm doing and saying affect a student's self-concept and encourage self-esteem?'

Acknowledging even the smallest effort, accomplishment or contribution often requires us to re-orient our view of our students, how we reinforce (positively and negatively) their attention-seeking or power provocation or inadequate behaviours. The way we *use* questioning is also significant. Do we restrict the student by closed questioning? We may simply set them up for failure. Open, exploring, discursive questioning ought to be practised alongside the closed approach. If a student is set up with a closed question (only one right answer is possible), we may set them up for a chain of small, unnecessary failures. Open questioning at least gives a student a chance to contribute to the answer.

Older students are often 'embarrassed' by public praise. A private word of encouragement will be more effective with upper primary and adolescent students.

Students also appreciate written encouragement to their parents. In a survey on attitudes of British secondary school teachers and pupils to rewards and punishment (Caffyn, 1989), over 80 per cent of students said a 'letter home about good behaviour would be rewarding' (for work effort or good behaviour); for example, 'Mrs Smith, Damien got six out of his spelling words correct and they were not easy ones.'

Avoid disclaiming or devaluing the encouragement. A normally talkative Year 3 student who often calls out puts her hand up without calling out. The teacher acknowledges this, 'You've got your hand up, thank you Rachel', but undercuts the encouragement by adding '... and if you had your hand up all the time it would be better for everyone wouldn't it?' Tim hands in his project with much neater writing. 'That's a neat and thoughtful presentation

Tim. You've spent a lot of time on the final result' but adds, 'and why can't you write just like that all the time instead of your regular writing—which can be rather messy, can't it Tim?'

Two kinds of teachers

When I first learned to sail, my daughter (then aged 10) and I arrived, nervously, at a narrow jetty at a lake to be met by a tough-looking female yachting instructor. With a bare hint of a smile she gave us her name and asked us to get into the sailing dinghy. 'Don't!' she said as I reached for a halyard to step into the boat. 'Don't you know how to get into a boat?' (She gave an overdone sigh.) 'Goodness, you step into it like this.' She showed me as she brushed past. I raised my eyes to the sky as I looked at my daughter. I was hoping it would get better—it didn't.

In the next hour, she whinged, criticised, grabbed at ropes, was sarcastic, 'humphed' and 'ummed' her way through a semblance of being a sailing instructor. Early in the 'lesson' she asked me to hold the mainsheet. I looked up at the sail (a sail is a sheet, isn't it?). Seeing my 'stupidity' she remarked, 'You were supposed to read the homework notes, weren't you? A mainsheet is the main *rope* for guiding the sail', and gave me one of those 'don't say I have to put up with another dope' looks.

At one point, when I was trying to steer the dinghy towards a fixed 'something' on the horizon, she said, 'Now keep it straight with the tiller!' I saw the bank loom close and I registered my concern. 'Don't you worry about that!' she snapped, 'I'm in control.' Bravely I replied, 'Actually I thought I was steering, that's why I was worried.'

'Look, do you think I'd allow that? Concentrate!' she said as I turned my eyes away from looking ahead and turned to face her. 'Watch where you're going—goodness!'

As we steered away from the bank under her control (my daughter sitting, worried, opposite me) Ms Napoleon asked, 'How old are you?'

'Thirty-eight' I replied. (What's she on about?)

'Can you drive a car?'

'Yes, of course.'

'And you can't understand the simple connection of rudder, steerage way and wind direction.' She droned on with incipient sarcasm. As we moved off on port tack she added a 'Concentrate!' and 'Watch the sail, watch the sail! Don't waggle the tiller!'

'Look,' I said (I was getting quite annoyed). 'This is my first time in a sailing boat of any kind. Now, as a teacher, I've found that the beginning of *any* new activity is helped by a bit of encouragement and understanding, however old one is.' I gave her 'Credo One' of my philosophy on learning and teaching methods. Water off a duck's back. 'I don't muck around' she said. 'You're in a boat, no time to muck around.'

For the rest of the hour she regaled us with seemingly a hundred and one bits of information, generally treated me as a child, huffed and haa-ed and, as we stepped ashore, said, 'Now make sure you do some reading by next week.' As my daughter and I walked to the car I felt like giving up. My self-esteem (our self-esteem) had been battered. But we laughed it off and I said, 'Will we try her once more?' (we'd booked and paid for two lessons). 'Yeah, but isn't she a pain dad!' I could only agree but said, 'We'd better get our money's worth.'

Next week was worse. We almost felt like we'd never learn to sail. Ms Napoleon projected failure and even stupidity on to us. (Maybe she didn't mean to, but her whole tone in the boat was, 'You should know. Why can't you understand? What's wrong with you?')

Well our self-esteem was stronger than her lousy teaching. We decided to try another teacher and signed up for a course with

The sailing lesson

another group. We arrived, on a bleak, windy, showery day at a small bay near Geelong in Victoria. There were six boats on a trailer. Sixteen people (including myself) unloaded the boats and placed them near the water. We stood shivering, facing the weather-beaten instructor and the vile, choppy sea behind him.

He smiled at us and called us over to a boat. He introduced himself and assured us all that we'd have a great day's sailing. Then he calmly and carefully explained each part of the boat we'd need to know about and how we'd need to mast it, put in the rudder, set up the sails, etc. Then we set it up on the beach, each crew with its own boat. He then showed us how to sit in the boat, how to tack, how to pull in the mainsheet and so on. All on dry land. We practised.

We *felt* reasonably confident (so far) under his clear and quietly confident instructions. 'The next step', he said, 'is the most important. What will probably happen is that the boat will tip over—no worries. All beginners experience it, we even practise it. I'll explain and show you how to get your boat back up should it tip you in the drink.' He calmly explained what to do, showed us how to right the boat and reminded us he'd be out there to help in his little motorised rubber duck (dinghy). 'Okay, off you go! Have a great time.'

With two others I managed to get our boat out from the shore. We steered it into the wind and were staggered at its power. In a few minutes we were soaked by the water sluicing up from the sides of the boat. Green as we all were, we tried valiantly to keep the boat on a reasonably even keel. Our 'green-ness' was obvious though. I couldn't seem to stop the boat keeling over, the wind seemed to push us further and further towards the drink! Surely we're not going to tip it! Liz yelled, 'I can't hold the rudder!' My fears were realised as we three sank beneath the waves with the sail flat on the water. The boat then turned right over as we coughed and spluttered our way to the surface. We remembered our drill. I made my way to the front to pull the bow into the wind and Liz reached up over the upturned hull to pull down on the centre-board.

The instructor saw us and putt-putted over in his motorised dinghy. As we three, shivering and clinging to the now-lifeless vessel, tried to recall his drill, he very calmly said, 'Well done Bill, and you too Liz, that's it, pull the centre-board down. I knew you'd remember the drill—good on you.' He trusted us to complete the procedure and as we righted the boat and climbed in he said, 'What will you do next?'

'Bring her round and set the sails?'

'Well done! Off you go!'

Wet as we were, we *felt*, not that we had made some great mistake but that we had passed a test. We were learning under the security of unbattered self-esteem.

Ten minutes later I put the boat in the drink again, as did the other member of our trio. Each time the instructor came over and smiled, calmly encouraged us, gave us confidence to keep on. He never took the initiative from us. .Even in stressful, cold and somewhat uncertain circumstances, he gave us only as much information as we needed—trusting us to know and do what he believed we could do. His calmness and clarity of instruction were most reassuring. He'd say things like, 'I knew you'd remember', or 'What will you do next?', or 'Which direction should you head?', or 'You tacked really smoothly that time. You're getting it Bill. Well done!', or 'Don't worry, you'll get it next time—it's not easy keeping the boat steady in a wind like this.'

By the end of our session with him, our confidence, self-esteem *and* skill had all increased. Even our failures were utilised. He also taught me a great deal about how to teach or, more correctly, how to *be* a teacher. He modelled:

- clarity in setting tasks and skills, and enthusiasm for the subject
- care for the individual
- consistency (in his encouragement and teaching style)
- encouragement to work cooperatively as well as learn individual skills
- the expectation that we would succeed. We did. Of course there were some students who were better at sailing that day, but we all experienced success. In this way our estimation of ourselves was positive, helpful, realistic, strengthening our belief that we could cope even in difficult situations.

The hard-to-manage class

The trouble with human nature is that it's in the hands of so many people.

Roy Clarke

Most teachers have experienced a harder-than-average class at some stage; maybe a class with a reputation. I know that as a younger teacher I was 'handed the reins' of a few choice classes from colleagues with a look of relief (mixed with glee?).

What makes a class hard, or exceptionally challenging, is not just one or two learning or behaviour difficulties, or the one or two attention-seeking boys—they would be 'manageable' if 90 per cent of the class were cooperative. A hard class is a class in which up to a third (even half) of the students are seemingly hell-bent on making teaching and learning functionally impossible. As one teacher said:

> It's like one thing after another; one 'brushfire' starts here another over there! Three boys loudly talking off-task, a couple of girls into long-term time-wasting; a few others wandering around ... and during the instructional phase it seems like ages before I can get them settled. Even then students will talk to each other while I'm talking.

I've worked with scores of teachers who describe their hard classes this way (and worse!). What happens is that the frequency and intensity of disruptive and off-task behaviour is not limited to one or two students. It is general and seems to occur every lesson/ every day. In the worst-case scenarios, classes will appear even to sabotage a teacher's efforts to engage them (Rogers, 1997).

Contributing factors

What makes a hard class?

■ The grouping together of students who are known to create behaviour problems. One of the most tempting, but least effective management strategies, is to put all the difficult students (at secondary level) into one class grouping. The question is: who is going to teach such a class?

■ Timetabling (at secondary level this can have a significant effect).

■ 'Streaming' or selective grouping of classes by ability (the 'vegie class'). This is more common at secondary level. These classes are sometimes given to beginning teachers or teachers known to have management problems. So much for teacher welfare! A skewed distribution of students (in terms of behaviour and learning) is bound to create management problems let alone limit the modelling of pro-social behaviour from student to student.

■ Who the class is given to, in terms of matching teacher to student grouping.

■ Subject area. Where students do not see (or cannot see) the value in a particular subject area (at secondary level) they will sometimes reflect that in their behaviour. Of course it depends very much on how teachers can work with natural disaffection for a particular subject area. Colleague support is crucial, especially at the preventative level, in getting the class off on the 'best foot' as it were.

■ Teacher attitude, beliefs and treatment of the class. If a teacher has a negative attitude at the outset, expressed in blame, frequent nagging and criticism, students will often team up to psychologically 'pay the teacher back'. I've seen many classes become 'hard' because of the way they are treated by some teachers; I've seen some students psychologically bully their teachers. While there can never be acceptance of such behaviour, one can understand how, sometimes, the spiral of antagonism and defeat occurs, where teacher and student become enemies and an us–them mentality ensues. Labelling the class ('those animals', 'those pack of ...', 'that classroom from Hades!') may block out the 50–70 per cent of class members willing to work with the teacher, plus others who can be refocused with some effort.

Early intervention is crucial. Dialogue with the class, the class (subject) teacher and a respected facilitator are required in order to defuse the tension.

Blaming the teacher or supporting a colleague?

Blaming the teacher is the easy solution (likewise blaming the class)—it's not that simple though. It can be dispiriting to turn up to a hard class every day (or several times a week) at secondary level. To add blame to a teacher's emotional load will only compound the problem.

There is no single, simple remedy for addressing the 'hard class' issue (Rogers, 1997). What is needed is a commitment to a supportive solution at the earliest stage. I've seen too many teachers break down in term two, three even four, when the issue should have been addressed in week two or three. Most teachers can recognise the difference between a bad day (when you had to move to the portable classroom because of a timetable change, and it was raining, and the key was misplaced ...) and a class, as a whole, that is hard to manage.

The teacher or team leader will need to initiate a meeting of all teachers who service the class. Some teachers may be reluctant to admit there is 'a problem with 8D' (for fear they will be seen as weak or ineffective). In this case the year level coordinator, head of department or team leader will need to set up an opportunity to discuss the issue supportively.

Initially this will involve a team meeting at which staff can discuss the common issues of concern (noise level, off-task behaviour, 'ringleaders' and 'followers', strategies already tried, successes and failures). The degree to which such a meeting is successful will depend on how supportive the school (or faculty) is when it comes to problem identification, analysis and action. It rarely helps when a colleague says, 'Oh, 8D—I never have any problems with them.'

Giving immediate support when a class is disruptive

It can be disconcerting to walk past a class that seems out of control; where a quick eye-sweep picks up several pockets of disruption and noise and borderline chaos. In such a situation it doesn't help to just walk quickly on, thankful that it's not your problem. Nor does it help to say silently, 'Well it serves him right …' My colleagues and I use what we call a 'safety valve option', an option left to the professional discretion of the colleague walking past:

▌ Knock on the door of 8D and ask if you can 'borrow a few students' (I've never been knocked back!) and direct them along the corridor for a chat about their behaviour in the class and what they need to agree on before they go back. I've had many such chats with overly 'testosteronic' lads. Direct them back in with the reminder to knock, and take their seats quietly.

or

▌ Knock on the door and inform the colleague, 'There's a message for you at the office.' This is code for, 'I'll take the class till the bell goes.' The message (when the colleague arrives) is, 'Have a cuppa—we'll have a chat about 8D later to see what we can work on.'

This assumes that such an option has colleague support (as an *option*). It is never an end in itself but needs to be backed up by thoughtful and careful analysis of whether the problems with the class are due to 'bad day syndrome' or ongoing.

The purpose of the meeting is to break the 'hard class' reputation and possible habituation of poor behaviour as early as possible, so it will be important to go beyond the natural complaining and expressions of frustration.

It may be that the class really is problematic only for a particular teacher. This may be due to the subject taught (that is, the attitude of students to *that* particular subject), or the style of management and curriculum delivery. In this case there may need to be one-to-one mentoring with that teacher and the class.

It can help if teachers visit their class in other settings and observe how different teachers manage the students they are struggling with. It can also help to build up a relationship outside our own subject area to see students learning and engaging in more positive behaviour. I have used this approach countless times with reasonable success—providing the teacher is willing to work on strategies to reassess and reorient the class as a group.

The establishment of the class is a crucial phase in group expectation about learning and behaviour. If, from day one, the teacher has been unclear and indecisive about basic rights, responsibilities and rules it will have an effect on classroom dynamics from that day. The crucial effect of the establishment phase cannot be underestimated. If a class has lost its way, though, in the first few weeks or so it will be important to *re*-establish the class; to go over the rules that may have been missed; to address seating plans (see p. 202); to refocus the working-noise levels (see pp. 206f); to go through even basic routines such as entering the classroom and settling at the work area; to revise communication protocols during instructional and on-task times for getting teacher attention (fairly and appropriately), leaving work areas tidy and exiting from the room.

It can help with upper-primary and secondary students to re-establish the class through a classroom meeting. This gives the class a chance to put their side of the story. The 'openness' of the meeting will depend to a large extent on the dynamics of the class.

'Closed' meetings

A senior teacher (well known to the class and held in some respect) outlines to the class specific concerns about their learning and behaviour. She does this in conjunction with the regular teacher. The emphasis is on describing behaviours of concern; not in a lecture format (bawling a class out or giving a lecture has limited effectiveness—tempting as it is!). It can help to have the behaviours and concerns written out in a large list (blu-tacked to the board) to give visual focus. The message of the closed meeting is:

- ▌ X behaviours are not 'funny', 'cool' or 'a game'. Students who choose to behave in these ways affect everyone's rights.
- ▌ Everyone in this class has rights and responsibilities.
- ▌ 'I'm sharing these concerns with your teacher and you all so you

know how we feel (and why). We haven't notified your parents (yet). We believe we can work it out with you. That's why we are having this meeting. Later in this session I want to discuss how our rights and responsibilities can work together, but I need to point out that we cannot and will not allow these kinds of behaviours (here be specific) in any of our classes.'

The tone of this meeting is serious yet it is not a lecture or a haranguing session. It is essential to focus only on actual behaviours (without labelling). Point out, too, that not every single student may have behaved (frequently) in these ways (those noted on the list) but that 'everyone here' is affected. 'That's why we need to discuss it with *all* of you.' Point out that some students in this class will be spoken to privately about their behaviour. The students are then invited to make a response to the noted behaviours (with firm reminders of the protocols for class discussion). Suggestions and responses are noted (on the board).

The senior staff member then hands out a revised class document outlining:

▌ the classroom rules
▌ the basic responsibilities of students (and teacher)
▌ the consequences for choosing to negatively affect learning and teaching, treatment of others, safety in the classroom.
▌ the positive aspects of working within these fair guidelines.

It often helps to reorganise the seating plan to refocus power-brokers and it is important that during this 'closed' meeting the class teacher takes some role so that it doesn't appear as if the senior teacher is running the meeting. All the way through the meeting the emphasis will be on 'we ...' (as both teachers are standing at the front addressing the class).

Invite the students to respond to the document. Any discussion will need to keep its focus on the non-negotiable issues:

▌ within the curriculum
▌ in terms of essential rights: to be *treated with respect* and fundamental dignity (put-downs, slanging-off, harassment will not be tolerated), to *learn* (without interference), to *feel safe* and act safely.

Point out there will be a review meeting with the class in two weeks time to see how things are going.

It can help too, to telegraph the probability that individuals who choose not to work within the classroom plan may have to face relocation to another class group. This should be said in a matter-of-fact way and not as a threat.

Open classroom meetings

Classroom meetings are addressed in Chapter 5. Suffice it to say here that the class, as a group, are encouraged to work with their teacher to address honestly issues of *common* concern, to give voice to the disaffected (especially the teacher!). But students, too, need a chance to share their perspective, providing they do so with courtesy and focus on the issues of concern without attacking teachers or other students. The key questions are:

1 *What* do you believe is working well in this class and why? (Start with the positive option.)
2 What do you believe is not working well (here in our class) and why? (The *why* is always revealing.)
3 What can *we* do (as a class, as a group), to make this class a more enjoyable place to be: a place where we can learn without interference but with support; where our noise level is reasonable, where we're looking out for (and after) one another not just ourselves? A tall order? No, it is a possibility. Assure the students that you value their contribution and that all contributions will be taken seriously. These questions can be developed through an open-forum meeting, in small groups (reporting back) or even in a written exercise through a questionnaire.

The three questions above are the first stage of action planning. The class action plan will be a published expression of class agreements about behaviour and learning, and consequences for disruptive behaviour.

It may help to have a colleague sitting in on such a meeting to give moral and teaching support. Certainly such a meeting should be planned with a colleague who has some experience and skill in the area of running classroom meetings.

Mini-meetings

Sometimes a support colleague can take the whole class for a full class period while the regular teacher withdraws three students at a time to another area where she can sit and have a mini-meeting using the questions noted earlier as a guide.

Meetings with individual students on individual behaviour plans

Senior staff can work with powerbrokers and significant attention-seekers (see pp. 170f) on contractual arrangements and behaviour plans that are focused on the individual student. These behaviour plans *highlight* personal accountability and responsibility, and spell out in a specific way (behaviourally) what those responsibilities are (see Appendix III). It is essential that the grade or subject teacher sits in on this one-to-one conferencing and planning process.

Accountability conferencing

If a student is psychologically harassing a teacher then early intervention by class teacher and senior teacher is essential. Some students will exercise their social power in abusive ways, ways that can garner support from their peers (in intimidatory non-verbal gesturing)—the chorus of noises, or cheers, the bouncing back and forth of comment or gesture so the teacher is uncertain as to where the noises or comments are coming from. When a teacher seeks to confront this in class she may be met with 'Who me? What did I do?' (especially if the bullying is non-verbal or of an ambiguous nature).

In such cases the teacher concerned needs to meet with each perpetrator *separately*, with a senior teacher facilitating (not as a group—with a group of 'bullies' there is diminished responsibility and minimisation—'We weren't the only ones!'). The teacher can then face each student (with the senior peer present) in an accountability conference (Rogers, 1997) based on the following:

■ Describe, *specifically*, what the student has been doing/saying in class in terms of behaviour. Mirroring may even be relevant if the teacher is comfortable with such an approach. This is particularly effective when addressing harassing gestures or tones of voice. It will help to have the student's behaviour written down and refer to this during the accountability conference.

▌ Describe how such behaviour affects our feelings as a person and, more importantly, our job as a teacher and others' learning.

▌ Point out that this behaviour (refer briefly to list) has to stop and why. Here the facilitator can refer to the school's code of rights and responsibilities.

▌ Invite the student to respond and clarify what he will do to change 'how things are in 8D' and how he needs to change his behaviour that contributes to 'how things are in 8D'. It can be helpful to write this down. It adds to the serious tone of the accountability conference.

▌ The senior teacher invites the student to meet again with the grade or subject teacher and the senior teacher in a week's time to review how things are going with him and 8D.

In larger schools it may be possible, if the behaviour problems of individual students are very disturbing, to separate them and place them in other classes. It can be helpful to give those individuals a 'choice' first:

▌ to work within an agreed personal behaviour plan (consistent with the class rules and responsibilities); or

▌ to be de-enrolled from the class (where they are presently persistently disruptive) and enrolled in another class.

Group reinforcement for behaviour modification

Early in my role as a consultant in discipline and student welfare, I was asked to work with a class of Year 8 boys at a local secondary school. I didn't know what I'd let myself in for. 'Can you do something with them? They're a bit testy!' said the principal. From the raised eyebrows and 'hangdog' look, I had the impression that he held out little hope of success.

I'd been reading up on group reinforcement (for behaviour modification) and had tried it out on a few classes at other schools. With that experience in reserve, I walked down the passage towards one of the rowdiest post-primary classes I'd ever faced. You could hear their yelling from twenty metres away. Four-letter words were being hurled around along with screwed-up paper balls and half-eaten apples, and there was the 'playful punching' that seems to be a ritual with boys.

My host teacher, after being rudely addressed with nicknames, let me in the classroom. B block in the science wing was filthy. Throwing their bags across the floor and talking at a noise level akin to that in baboon cage number 4 at the primate compound, they began sitting down, in a fashion. The talking didn't stop. Fortunately, I'd made an attempt at a plan. Mr S lamely introduced me to 8D. The noise level didn't drop. They were completely unabashed about ignoring anybody up-front. I wrote my name on the board, and across the centre wrote: CLASS EXPERIMENT. 'Good morning. My name is Mr Rogers.'

Getting the group's attention

Facing the tumult, I casually drew from my bag a big pack of potato chips and a big pack of mini-chocolate bars. Don't shout bribery yet! I'll explain.

I'd read up on using edible reinforcers in groups on a points-for-reinforcement basis. The program relies on the power of peer reinforcement within teams where points are granted to the team and 'rewards' are a key outcome (along with increased teacher sanity, a 'calmer' class, and a demonstrable change in on-task learning). The *coup de grace* is a small bag of chips for each member of the team once they have a certain number of points. Other 'rewards' can be utilised in following sessions. I was now going to try to explain something of this to 8D. Novelty, I hoped, would act as a kind of circuit-breaker on their ritualistic hooning. Not for this group a discussion of rights, rules and responsibilities; just knowing manipulation.

As I drew the potato chips from my bag, the chaotic noise level dropped enough for me to speak and be heard! I waited until the class were looking, listening and almost quiet. Speaking in a firm voice and ignoring the odd clownish comment and seat-leaving, I said, 'We're going to run an experiment this week. I'm going to split you all into four teams, and I'll need four team leaders. Each team has a chance to win a prize. These goodies here.' I beckoned to the edibles.

Choosing team leaders

Well, the calling out started. 'I'll be a captain!' 'No me!' 'I wanna be one.' 'Over here, Sir!' Not looking at any of the students I added, 'When you're settled I'll explain.' I waited for quiet and steamed on. 'Okay, the way I'll choose the leaders is by giving you all a small piece of paper. Write on the paper two names of people in this room who you would like to be a leader—a leader of a team you'd like to be in. Any questions?' To help them I had listed the qualities of a group leader on a poster (someone you respect who can assist the group in working by the fair rules, who will keep the group focused on the learning task and enable cooperation within the group) and blu-tacked it to the chalkboard.

Immediately, calling out started again. 'How many names?' 'Can I put my own name down?' Tactically ignoring the calling-out behaviour, I was expecting someone, anyone, to actually put up a hand. Someone did eventually put up a hand without calling out. 'Yes? Thanks for putting your hand up by the way (firm eye contact). What's your name and what's your question?'

'Can we put our own names down?' As I answered, I let them know points would be granted for behaviour that is fair, that keeps the fair rules. (I'd work out the *actual* rules with them later.)

The reinforcement began to work. I only noticed, attended and answered the on-task students with their hands up. I took a risk by not reinforcing calling-out behaviour. It worked. They smelt the game plan and saw the edibles on the desk. We steamed ahead. 'Okay Tom, pass out the bits of paper, please.' He swaggered off but passed them around. Amazing. There was still plenty of noisy chatter but it had dropped six decibels (or so it seemed to my ears) and they were actually writing.

Choosing teams

'Okay, collect leadership selection slips please Tom. Thanks. Now I've got a list up here of all your names. What I'm going to do is sort through these names and see who have been chosen as leaders. Then we'll give each leader a chance to choose from the list of class members. First we'll find out who the leaders are. I'll need a couple of helpers.' (I ignored students who called out at this point.)

The two helpers sorted out the most recurring names into a final four. While they did this with their regular teacher, I had a discussion with the class about basic rights and rules.

Rules

'We'll need a few basic rules for our class over the next few weeks while we have these teams. What sort of rules?' We had a brain-storming session where I only attended to those with hands up. 'Thanks Huan for putting up your hand, it makes life so much easier.' 'I appreciate you waiting with your hand up.' 'Nick, what's your question?' 'Yes, down the back with your hand up. What's your name and what's your question?' In the first week of this experiment, the social reinforcement was given for each occurrence of on-task behaviour. Later the reinforcement was discriminate and focused on specific, rule-keeping behaviour.

We ended up, as we always do in these situations, with a commu-nication rule, a movement rule, a learning rule and a safety rule. We later added a rule (or due process) for settling disputes or prob-lems between students. The focus for each rule was a key word: *communication, learning,* etc. To save time it can help to have several, brief rules already written up and simply stick them to the board and use them as a basis for discussion (see also Chapter 4).

By this time we had the four names for the leaders. I read them out as I wrote them up on the board, in chart form.

NICK	HUAN	FRANK	CON

'Would the four leaders please come up to the front desk, thanks.' (The noise level, due to the novelty of the experiment, had dropped significantly. I was speaking at a reasonable level now.) Frank and Con swaggered up. 'On you Frank' called out a wag from the back of the class. Huan and Nick looked bemused. Children choose leaders by two broad criteria; power-brokerage and a form of 'moral' leadership. Clearly Nick and Huan were initially surprised at their peers' approval of them as leaders. I asked the leaders to select students for their teams from the class name list (one at a time to get equal distribution). No problems here. I stressed they had to do this until each name had been chosen. I kept them moving quickly until all names were crossed off. Collecting the four lists of team members, I asked the leaders to go back to their seats. I then addressed the whole class.

'All right, we've got the teams.' I read the names as I wrote them up on the board, reading the last name first in an attempt to give a minuscule measure of self-esteem to the person chosen last in each team.

Reinforcement and the points

'Now—the really important part.' Rustling the bags of goodies I said, 'Each team can receive points for keeping our fair class rules, getting on with our work, packing up, and entering and leaving the room in a fair way. I'll put the points on the board under your team leader's name. My job is to be the umpire. My decision is final. If anybody makes objections about the points or makes things tough for the group, they'll miss out on a point. The umpire's decision, like in footy, is final. Okay? But I know you'll all play fair (wink). Any questions?' Again, only on-task questions were accepted. There were only a few calling out now. The reinforcement was working.

'In a moment, I want each leader to move with his team to the part of the room indicated on the board here. (I'd allocated four areas for the team leaders to move to with their teams.) Move the chairs or desks any way you want, as long as you do it quietly. I'll be giving points for fair rule-keeping. Off you go.' Well, I expected some noise, but in a few minutes they had grouped themselves together without kicking any chairs around (as had happened in the first hair-raising five minutes). I reinforced many behaviours in that short time. 'Frank! (he turned with a worried look as he passed kids moving in the opposite direction), thanks for moving quietly with your group; especially the way you got your team organised with the chairs. Well done! Point for your team.' A smile of relief appeared on Frank's face.

Giving the groups a task

There were now four teams quietly facing the class teacher and myself. Each team had 'earned' a few points or more even at this early stage. 'Thanks for settling down so quickly. The first job for each team—by the way Con, your team has four points already; well done—is to choose a name for your team. No footy names thanks. You've got two minutes. Off you go.' There was positive working noise and we ended up with:

SPEEDOS	KNOBS	RAMBOS	ACES 5	
NICK	HUAN	FRANK	CON	
				POINTS TALLY

We made up a chart with the permanent team names, captains and points—we used this chart over the next four weeks.

I called Con aside, quietly, from his group. 'Con, I noticed you spoke quietly to your team members as you moved the table—a point for your team.' His team members smiled, the other teams heard, most were spurred on. The tone of the room was much more positive. My job now was to pick up quickly on-task, rule-keeping behaviours, sometimes giving a point, sometimes not. The basic principle is that in reinforcing one team member, and giving a point (or verbal reinforcer), this acts as an advertisement for the other teams to observe and, hopefully, imitate.

Our second task was to give each group the job of writing one class rule. We'd already discussed the class rules and had a rough draft up on the board with the key headings. The task was:

1 Write a rough draft developed through group discussion (for example, a communication rule).

2 Confirm the rule with the class teacher (who may do some fine-tuning).

3 Write a brief description of the rule under a bold heading such as 'communication', or 'movement', or 'learning', or 'safety' on a large piece of coloured card. (Later, we displayed these around the class at each science session with 8D.)

Each team wrote up its rule. At the end of the class session, the teams were 'rewarded' with some edible reinforcement depending on the points granted: one, two, or three packets of chips to be shared around by the group leader. The team with the most points got to choose between the 'rewards'. The class was reminded that next week they could 'earn' points by the way they entered and left the room and that points would accumulate each week. Next session, I added, there would be a wider range of BEOs (behaviour enhancement outcomes)—canteen vouchers, pencils, free-activity time, depending on points accumulation. 'Okay, pack-up time. Desks back, chairs up, we'll see you next science session.'

As they all left, the noise level went up, and several students forgot to push in their chairs. Quickly I said, 'Huan, I noticed three of your team put the chairs away without being asked. Two points already for next week.' Almost immediately several others put their chairs away. All they got was a smile and a brief, 'Thanks, see you next week.'

In the following four sessions we had our ups and downs, but the students were really beginning to settle down well and were actually working on the set science curriculum. Normal, but improved, science lessons were planned with groups in mind and as much 'hands on' activity as possible.

All discipline problems were settled with a focus on the rules They were *our* rules. We only had a few major disruptions (a chair kicked, the old 'f—— unfair!', a bit of attention-seeking) but these were handled within our clear discipline plan. The tone was positive.

In week five we had a class meeting to assess where we'd been and what we'd achieved. Seated in a circle, we began our discussion (see

Chapter 5). Essentially, the students agreed that the class was much better, that they were *working* and that it really didn't matter whether they had the treats. We celebrated with a barbecue that week.

Remember, this degree of behaviour modification works best with classes who have a nasty reputation. The only times I have used group reinforcement with edible reinforcers has been with groups such as 8D. Generally speaking, the novelty of such an approach wears off after Year 8. It has been used with extremely difficult groups of students aged four upwards.

The fundamental aims of the behaviour modification experiment were as follows:

1 To change the power-brokerage in the class membership through leadership selection.

2 To change the dynamics in the room through organising mixed-ability groups. The points process is a novelty to enhance the clear, fair rules and positive behaviour. The points and behaviour-enhancement outcomes are a way of reinforcing the positive behaviours.

3 To enable the class teacher to see the students in a new light, especially as the teacher needs to focus on more positive social reinforcers and build a more positive discipline plan to make the process work.

4 To allow the students to see a change in 'climate'. They, like their teacher, experience a taste of normality through engineered reinforcers, but more importantly through social reinforcers. Both experience those small successes that make teaching a bearable, even enjoyable activity.

The use of students themselves to maintain social order, rights-enhancing behaviour and to motivate one another is well established in the literature. Studies show that task performance among 'delinquent adolescents' (by the way, I'm not saying 8D was delinquent!) was at its highest when they were reinforced for their work by their peers, rather than by an adult (Brown, Reschly and Sabers, 1974).

Variations on a theme

1 Each group accumulates points, session by session, and the teacher has a raffle at the end of the 'experiment'. A group reinforcement phase would normally run for four to five weeks.

2 Each group contributes to class rewards by having set work goals. The teacher contracts various tasks at various levels. Clear examples of required work are provided. Students move from task to task.

   Points are earned for on-task and rule-keeping behaviour. All points go on a class chart that has a goal of 1000 points. When the whole class, through individual and cooperative behaviour, reaches 200, potato chips all round; 500, a coffee break; 750, a 'free' activity; 1000, a barbecue or special trip. Points are allocated for on-task behaviour using a timer set at random intervals. When the timer goes off, on-task students or groups are allocated 10 points.

The question of manipulation

Is group reinforcement manipulative? No—the students are well aware of what's happening, it's all up-front—they know the game well! I've had children say, 'You're bribing us!'

'Yes, any other questions? No? Good, let's get on with it.'

There is no question that group reinforcement can be a marvellous group circuit-breaker, especially where long-term habituation has resulted in a class with a 'reputation'.

If a student says, 'This sucks, I don't want to be in it', don't get drawn in. You're the referee. 'Okay, you can sit over here Michelle, and work away from the group.' Invite her in again next week. But don't force, or coerce those *very* few who sulk, refuse, or play power-broking games.

With less difficult classes, the same process can be used *without* any formal reinforcers (points and edibles). Simply operating the class through a group process with chosen leadership often changes the climate of power-brokerage in the room. I have done this successfully with Year 9 and 10 classes.

Like most techniques, we get better at it with practice. One colleague, in her first session, pulled out the chips, turned her back on the class to write on the board, and a furtive Year 7 boy raced to the front, grabbed the chips, gave a victory salute and bolted down the corridor! In the second week the program was more successful as she was better prepared with colleague support (and a private chat with the chips-stealer). *Be prepared.*

If you feel you would like to develop group reinforcement with 8D or their equal, but don't think you could make it work, then team up with a colleague and plan it together.

Using group reinforcement in the classroom

1 Clarify why you want to use group reinforcement. Be clear in your own mind that this is a short-term program—*it is never an end itself.*

2 Be prepared. Plan the steps well beforehand. Have the charts, paper, pencils, name list and edibles ready. Know what your opening lines will be.

3 Explain the process to the class. Explain that this is a short-term activity (and you may want to explain that it will be fun). Explain the rules. It can be helpful to have the rules written up, in point form, on cards with bold, clear headings (see Chapter 4). Express the rules positively, or, as in the example noted earlier, employ a rule-making phase. Then explain how points will be granted to each team.

4 Organise leaders. Distribute small pieces of paper for students to write two names on. When collected, identify the most recurring names. These will be the leaders. Have work to do for students while you sort out the names (or have a colleague in the class to assist the process.)

5 Form teams. Call the leaders to the front. Ask the leaders to choose from a class list, *one at a time*, to form their teams. Have a sheet of paper for each team leader. The choosing is done up the front of the class (away from public gaze) with the teacher and four or five leaders.

6 Form the groups. Explain that the teams are to group themselves quietly in the room. Ask the teams to choose a team name (no footy names or silly names).

7 In the first couple of sessions, give points regularly. Make it clear that you are the referee; no debates will be entered into. Write up points as soon as you give them. Be ready to give points especially to previously disruptive students.

8 Have a clear discipline plan. Expect cooperation and compliance. Reinforce specific behaviours that are cooperative and on-task. When using corrective discipline, be brief, clear and rule-focused. Remember to be positive.

9 Have the prizes ready. Give out the edibles to the winning group near the close of the session. In the last week, you may want to give a small prize to each class member as well as group prizes, or even have a barbecue or hot chocolate session to celebrate.

It can be helpful to complete the experiment by holding a class meeting to see where you will go from here (see Chapter 5). By this time, the group will be amenable to a healthy discussion.

Group reinforcement with younger students (Kinder to Year 2)

With younger students, the same principles can apply. As Brown, Reschly and Sabers (1974) have observed, such a process can significantly modify even the behaviour of aggressive pre-schoolers who display kicking, fighting, biting and other anti-social behaviour:

1 Explain to the children that they are going to do something 'special' starting today (and for the next few weeks). 'We are going to work in groups. I have chosen the groups. I'll tell you what group you are in in a moment, and each group has their own colour.' Blu-tack four or five (depending on the total number of students) large, coloured discs on the board. Later, attach the names of group members to those discs. Some teachers form the groups using 'rows' of students, especially if they want to modify (in effect help the *children* to modify) working noise and increase positive on-task behaviour. Many of my primary-school colleagues have used the noise meter (see p. 207) as part of a reinforcement activity.

2 Explain the process. 'Now, you can win special rewards for your team by working well together in our groups—by helping, sharing, working quietly, putting up your hand, sitting quietly on the mat, putting the scissors and clag away.' (It can help to have key behaviours published on cards.)

3 Explain expected behaviours, positively, through the classroom rules. Have a large card for each rule with two or three pictures on it depicting expected behaviours (see Chapter 4). For example:
   I Our Talking Rule (hand up, not calling out, listening to others).
   I Our Movement Rule (lining up quietly, on-the-mat behaviour, moving-out-of-seat behaviour during the on-task phase of the lesson).
   I Our Working Rule (helping one another, borrowing by asking, cooperation and respect). (See examples in Appendix X.)
You can model this behaviour by a demonstration of manners, asking politely, using partner voices, walking quietly, etc. and by little role-plays with the students. This phase of the process

involves reinforcing expected behaviour in a positive way. During the reinforcement phase, look for specific behaviours, within these rules, either to comment on or to reinforce tangibly.

4 Organise the groups by equal distribution, or in middle–upper primary by the name-choosing method noted earlier (each child writes the name of her preferred leader and returns it to the teacher). Each team member has a small coloured badge and a designated table. Team leaders can be chosen as focal points for identifying the team.

5 Explain the points and the goal. The children can earn points for their helpful, cooperative behaviour. Each point earned by the team goes on a chart. The chart is a metre-long poster with divisions to note in the team points. The goal is to get their big coloured disc (their team) to the end of the road (the chart). Points are coloured in by a member of the team as allocated and in the team colour.

Reinforce *specifically*. 'Chris, I noticed you had your hand up and you waited. Point for your team.' 'Esta, you sat down quickly and quietly. Point for your team.' Edible reinforcers (energy-enhancers such as jelly beans) can be given each 15 to 20 minutes for all teams that have at least a few points. Towards the close of the day, as points accumulate, begin to give a running commentary. The team that reaches the goal first can choose the special prizes (a special pencil for each team member, a free activity, stickers). All teams will eventually reach their goal. Some teachers divide the goal into sub-goals.

6 Use supportive discipline. By concentrating on positive behaviours, team members start to reinforce one another (peer support). Refer to the rules where there is disruption, or simply and firmly direct the student back on-task. Where a child is significantly disrupting, direct the child to the time-out area for two to five minutes (see p. 166), set a timer and expect the student to settle and return to the group. Rather than take off earned points, just don't give out any points to a group that has a member in time-out in any one class period.

7 Assess the outcome and plan for maintenance of the improved behaviour. The aim of this exercise is to use novelty and group reinforcement of clearly expected and defined behaviours to *break the circuit of overly disruptive group behaviour*. Normally a process such as this would run for only three or four weeks; then you would see if the desired behaviours had generalised. Of course, the process of cooperative group behaviour can continue without the organised reinforcement. An excellent book on cooperative learning is Joan Dalton's *Adventures in Thinking*. See also McGrath and Francey (1993) and Hill and Hill (1990).

Variations on this approach are limited only by a teacher's ingenuity, but the fundamentals are:

∎ clear rules
∎ positive expectations
∎ specific encouragement and reinforcement
∎ building of self-reinforcement through peer reinforcement and support.

Group reinforcement is a short-term, circuit-breaking activity that can and does bring success back into group life for students and teacher alike, forming a basis for future growth as a classroom group.

This approach should not be dismissed lightly by ideologues who are not in the front-line with an unruly bunch of four- and five-year-olds with little or no social skills. It is a vehicle for social reinforcement to train and guide behaviour towards that self-control which is the aim of all responsible discipline.

The basic principles of behaviour modification

Behaviour is shaped by the reinforcement it receives. The kind of consequences occurring after an 'act' help to determine the way in which behaviour continues.

On-task behaviour

On-task behaviour can be strengthened by reinforcement:

∎ Where reinforcement is systematic, it can aid the direction and maintenance of behaviour.

■ Reinforcement (negative or positive) is to be distinguished from mere punishment.

■ Where on-task behaviour is reinforced by teacher 'reward', the on-task behaviour is likely to be repeated.

■ Where it is possible to tactically ignore observed off-task behaviour and reinforce the student when on-task, the 'ignoring' will often aid in minimising off-task behaviour (see p. 59).

■ Where behavioural consequences are applied instead of mere punishment and combined with regular, positive reinforcement, the on-task behaviour is likely to increase (see also pp. 232f).

Reinforcement and discipline

When using reinforcement for behaviour modification key features of discipline are presumed.

■ There are clear rules and an understanding of consequences. The rules are discussed with the class and are recorded on cards placed around the room. Rules are few in number and positively expressed.

■ There is a plan by the teacher to use a 'steps' approach in handling classroom disruptions. Know what to do first, second and third when a student is disruptive. This should be supported by clear, in-class time-out and exit procedures if necessary.

■ There is colleague support. Teachers can be significantly assisted by having a trusted colleague observe their practice and assist in planning the reinforcement process. Support staff (psychologists and specialist teachers and consultants) can also be supportive when working with very challenging classes.

The principles of reinforcement are useful for all general classroom practice. They are tied in with respectful treatment and encouragement. Always be on the look out for behaviour to reinforce, even just by a nod or a wink. It beats nagging, slinging off and repetitious verbals like, 'I'm not going to say it again.'

Where normal rights-rules-responsibility discipline is not working, behaviour modification can be a positive and productive means to enable students to move towards on-task goals. I've used group reinforcement with many wild, chair-throwing classes to bring the class back to some reasonable sanity and success from which we can move on to less external means of classroom management.

The process works best when the reinforcement is partial—the student does not know when the reinforcement will come. The goals, of course, are self-reinforcement, the enjoyment of naturally occurring approval, and attention from the teacher and peers.

Ideally, any systematic reinforcement program should be short term as a step to the laudable goal of self-reinforcement; no one wants to keep a student on a 'token economy'.

Behaviour modification should be used with dignity. It should be explained to the student what we are doing and what we expect, what the reinforcement is and why the student is receiving it. 'Behaviour therapy does things *for* people, not *to* people' (my itals) (Ross in Poteet 1973, p. 84).

The hard-to-manage class and first-year teachers

First-year teachers have enough problems without being 'thrown in at the deep end' as so many are. There is that twin culture to break into: the culture of the school itself (each school has its own idiosyncratic culture of timetables, lines of communication, policies, routines/procedures, etc.) and the culture of teaching, with its special language, bureaucracy, hierarchies and literature.

So many first-year teachers are given a brief pep-talk and then left to negotiate these cultures with little or no structural or professional support. That common practice of timetabling the toughest or most unpleasant classes (8D for a double maths period on Friday afternoon!) indicates a singular lack of concern for first-year teachers. This is the beginning of their career! This practice is often cynically passed off with the comment, 'Well, we had to wear it, we had our turn, why can't they?' This attitude ignores completely the practical welfare issue. Surely the 'harder' or 'tougher' classes should be taken by the more experienced teachers, or at the very least a system of team-teaching should be set up so that the establishment of the 'harder' classes will be psychologically and professionally less stressful. It might even be valuable, for professional development, to invite beginning teachers into 'harder' classes to see how experienced teachers manage (Rogers, 1997).

I have found it very beneficial to establish peer (colleague) support groups. First-year teachers are invited into a regular group meeting at set times (generally weekly for the first few sessions, then fortnightly). A senior staff member (or two if the first-year intake is large) could facilitate the meetings, which would have these general aims:

■ To make the beginnings of a teacher's professional life as smooth as possible (instead of the basic handshake and 'Here's the toilet, there's the timetable, you've got 10E for double maths and there's a staff meeting every Monday').

■ To assist in ironing out and giving support with routines, procedures, policy matters, etc. Even a decent map would help, and a teaching buddy (a more experienced teacher who knows the school) to answer questions in the first few weeks.

■ To guide the group through some of the pitfalls that can occur in the first year, especially in the area of classroom management.

■ To provide a regular focus for sharing of common needs, problems, concerns, ideas, etc.

■ To provide a climate of moral support and the opportunity to offer 'structural' support if needed, especially for the time-out and exiting of difficult students, behaviour contracting with students, and parent conferences.

Many groups of first-year teachers with whom I have worked evidence a genuine sense of being supported when a process like the one described above has been implemented. Comments like 'not being isolated', 'feeling that others care', 'we can laugh with each other', 'learning not to take things so seriously' are common.

Leadership

Group spirit, group dynamics and the climate necessary for sharing, growth and skill development arise when effective leaders build such groups; leaders who have demonstrated skill in relationship building, communication and effective modelling skills.

Group facilitators have to build a group spirit from disparate personalities, drawing out weaker members, encouraging and building up others, allowing non-judgemental comment on displayed attitudes and ideas inimical to positive teaching practice. Some teachers, for example, feel that it's all right to embarrass, humiliate, ridicule, put kids down, or scream. Group facilitators encourage discussion on ineffective management practice without putting down colleagues who may be managing students inappropriately.

Here are some areas that first-year teachers may wish to explore in peer-support groups:

1 How to make effective and positive rules with classes (Chapter 4).
2 How to make a discipline plan (building and rehearsing some basic management skills and techniques) (Chapter 3).
3 How to use and apply behavioural consequences with students (Chapter 5).
4 How to handle conflict without getting into no-win situations (Chapter 8).
5 How to follow up on major disruptions beyond the classroom (consequences, conferencing, contracting) (Chapter 5).
6 How to use group approaches (Chapters 5 and 7).
7 How to create a positive class climate (Chapter 6).
8 How to interface curriculum and discipline (Chapter 6).

These areas can be explored in workshops throughout the year which are interspersed with inservice programs for all staff. Speakers may be invited to work with the peer-support group as they workshop these areas.

Peer observation

As a feature of ongoing professional development, members of the first-year peer-support group can be encouraged to observe one another's classes. Through an agreed agenda and focus, they can give feedback on what they heard, what they saw, how they felt in their colleague's class. This feedback provides valuable data for generating change. Peer-group members may also elect to rehearse skills prior to classes and ask their 'peer observer' to give feedback. This observation phase forms an invaluable link between workshop discussion and modelling, and the application in class. Many members, after several peer-group meetings, feel comfortable enough to share their experiences (often with humour!) with the whole group.

Evaluation

At the close of the year the peer-support group should meet to evaluate its progress. Often this can be carried out through a half- or full-day 'retreat' from school where experiences and reminiscences are shared and evaluated. These can be written down and shared with the incoming teachers the following year.

The success of the colleague peer-support process relies on:

- effective and committed leadership (embracing enthusiasm and willingness to persist in the long haul)
- support and back-up from the administration
- clear objectives, timelines for meetings and a trusting and positive attitude engendered by the facilitators
- opportunities for practical, professional development through regular workshops
- opportunities to give assistance to members of the group by linking up colleagues to help one another, bringing in other support persons where required, and giving assurances to struggling members that the school can and will provide whatever assistance is available.

The first year of a teaching career can be somewhat bruising. First-year teachers especially shouldn't have to go it 'alone'; there is much that a school can do to provide practical support. Peer support is one way of doing just that; peers supporting peers.

Some responses from teachers involved in first-year peer-support groups

Peer support saved my sanity. It was through the program that a group of us were able to work on effective strategies to enable us to teach effectively, discipline fairly, and remain sane at the same time. There were three things that I found most useful as a result of our meetings. The first and probably the most crucial is for teachers to get together with their students as soon as possible to establish a set of fair rules around which the class will operate. These must range from behaviour to movement and to anything else and must be accomplished with clear consequences and be followed by the teacher as well as the students. The second most useful technique was so simple yet so brilliant. The two 'magic' questions: what are you doing and what should you be doing? In my experience this year they have not failed me. It does not matter how many times you say them or how repetitive it sometimes feels—it works! Peer observation was another crucial element of my success and I believe should be examined in college before we are sent into the 'jungle'. The procedure is simple. Take a trusted peer or two and go into each other's 'nightmares' (I mean classrooms). You simply observe then discuss. Not only does it reaffirm your beliefs but you can be *constructively* criticised without awkward, embarrassing feelings that often go hand in hand with being told 'you did it wrong!'

Possibly the most significant thing that I have learned during these meetings is to analyse students less and analyse myself more. I have found that once I began to honestly criticise and accept my shortcomings as a teacher, then work determinedly to eradicate those shortcomings, my stress level, anxiety, anger and frustration slowly receded.

As one aspect of my teaching improved I realised that I could spend more time and conscious thought upon improving other aspects of teaching, but it was the recognition of the need for me to change that helped me.

Through my observation of my colleagues' classes, I was clearly able to see a great many aspects of teaching (not child-minding as I was tending to do) that I had not really seen, felt or practised since my teaching rounds (which I had enjoyed).

Because of this program I feel I have changed from a child-minding, assignment-feeding, aimless machine, to someone who tries and at times succeeds in actually providing the means by which students can learn and/or experience something new, different or worthwhile.

Peer-group support—although initially yet another onslaught to the battered ego—has proved very useful.

I found it demystified the 'successful' teacher, offering objective advice, techniques and skills.

I can remember the first day, weeks, of my teaching career: the unfamiliar surroundings; feeling new, green, and knowing that others too may perceive you that way; the room, the equipment (or

May the force be with you

lack of it!), not knowing how to ask for all the bits and pieces of equipment and materials; dealing with grumpy colleagues (especially when they are your seniors); not really knowing the real culture of the school (not just the paper-culture dropped on you in the pile of policies and papers and student profiles). Then there are the students. They can see you're new and if you're *young* and new (especially at high school), it's not easy. The normal culture shock though, can be eased if you are given support from day one.

It was the little things. I was welcomed by the head of department (maths). She took me around to all my peers and introduced me to my teaching 'buddy' for the next four weeks. She even wrote down key people I'd need to know on a piece of paper (you know how easy it is to forget when you're swamped with info as a new arrival!) to help me remember. I was shown the photocopier (and given a number) and the staff room. I had a tour. Each face I passed I was introduced to. Most of all I wasn't talked down to.

The first day we had a meeting (there were two other first-year teachers and some teachers new to the school). We discussed how we could:

- establish our classes (see Chapter 6)
- deal with basics such as marking the class roll with a 'waiting audience', dealing with latecomers, settling a class, dealing with the 'no pen, no materials' student
- develop a basic discipline plan, including some key language examples (see Chapter 3)
- draw up a time-out policy, especially using the buddy system (see p. 168)
- follow up and follow through with students and seek colleague (especially senior) support (see Chapter 5).

Later meetings went over how we had fared, our experiences, troubles, little triumphs and joys, even our crises.

One classic was a student who had set fire to his pants in science when being stupid with a bunsen burner! Thankfully, because of colleague support, the crisis was able to be managed. Another first-year teacher showed how she was able to deal with a student who had vomited all over his work (and others) and how she managed to stay calm, dealing with the mess and the class and the student. We all discussed what lessons we could draw from this, as well as having an appropriate laugh. The freedom to laugh at ourselves and the situation has always proved therapeutic. The point was we all shared concerns, anxieties, and even asked dumb questions. Most of all I felt I belonged.

The above was only one of the many such comments heard from a first-year peer-support group we ran with teachers in 'difficult' schools in the northern suburbs of Melbourne. We ran meetings over term one and two (weekly, then every three weeks). Many schools now run specific colleague-support groups for beginning teachers and even for teachers new to the school.

Summary

When addressing the hard-class issue it is important to recognise the pivotal nature of colleague support. When we are feeling defeated in the first few weeks of the year by a group of recalcitrant Year 1s or Year 8s, the least helpful thing to do is to try to go it alone in the mistaken belief that others will think of us as failures or as weak. Early intervention is the key to 'cracking' the hard class and any intervention will benefit from a team approach in which there is:

- an honest sharing of common concerns (it's rarely a hard-to-manage class for only one teacher!)
- problem analysis beyond normal frustrations and whingeing (after all, we've all got to teach them)—see if there are any *contributing factors* that affect the manageability of the class
- a search for a solution that will help the whole class to refocus on the common rights, responsibilities and rules (class meetings may be a useful approach)
- a search for ways to work one-to-one with key powerbrokers
- support for the class teacher.

Questions to consider

Colleague support

- How important is *colleague* support to you—as an individual teacher?
- How would you assess the general climate of colleague support in your school?

■ What *kind* of support do you want from:
  - colleagues?
  - team-leader or coordinator?
  - head of department?
  - principal?
■ How often, and in what ways, are your contributions (and even worth!) acknowledged and recognised (even in small ways)?
■ What problem-solving support is offered/available (for example when behaviour problems with an individual or class arise)?
■ What structural support is offered (for example time-out provisions, monitoring a difficult student, teaming together to run classroom meetings)?
■ What suggestions do you have for improving colleague support in your school?

Developing a whole-school approach to behaviour management

■ Do you have a whole-school commitment to common/preferred practices when it comes to behaviour management? To what extent? In which areas? What are they? Are they published (for example a common time-out plan and due process)?
■ Is there a common framework for behaviour-management plans:
  - at the classroom level (common classroom rights and responsibilities, common consequences for serious behaviour issues, common routines for establishment)?
  - at the playground level (and other duty-of-care areas), such as wet-day timetabling, corridor supervision, bus duty?
  - for working with behaviourally disordered children?
  - for the 'hard class' syndrome?
■ Are there any areas in which you need to fine-tune, modify, adapt, or change your current whole-school approach? If so what are those areas? What are your suggestions for change, and how might you go about such change?

Conflict resolution and managing anger

It is natural that the parties involved in a conflict should settle their conflict. It is their business. Their interests are at stake. They started it anyway.

E. De Bono, 1986

If we say that conflict is inevitable, we are not being defeatist or unnecessarily negative. We are merely making a statement of basic reality. Whether the conflict arises out of predisposing factors (problems at home, place in the family, general immaturity) or classroom conditions themselves, the issues are as follows:

■ How do we as classroom leaders minimise the likelihood of potential conflict?
■ How do we manage conflict *at the point* where emotional heat is exchanged? (especially our own anger)
■ How do we work for long-term resolution and positive working relationships?

Keeping students in a small room for 50-minute periods with a curriculum that doesn't cater for mixed abilities or take into account some of the backgrounds of our students, or the nature of social change itself, and expecting them to sit and be quiet and submissive,

Stages in conflict

Pre-conflict phase
1 Antecedent conditions
   - effect of child on 'environment'
   - effect of 'environment' on child
2 Conflict
   - as it is perceived by the parties (cognitive)
   - as it is felt by the parties (affective)

Conflict phase
3 Conflict behaviour
   - by one or both parties (argue, yell, scream, abuse, hit, fight, tantrum, swear, annoy)

Post-conflict phase
4 Resolution characteristics
   - communication
   - mediation
   - withdrawal
   - intervention
5 Aftermath
   - genuine resolution where needs are discussed, negotiated and resolved—if not, hostility or revenge

Figure 8.1

is a recipe for conflict and teacher stress. Conflict is, in a sense, a natural by-product of the group life of classrooms. Some students will actually seek it as a form of social identity (Dreikurs, Grunwald and Pepper, 1982).

Teachers define conflict in various ways. For some it may be a child who merely answers back, for others it may be those frustrating and petty annoyances: 'No pen, Miss!', 'What do we have to do again?', late students, students with sulky voices and annoying body language, or the 'dropped' swear word. In this chapter, the conflicts being addressed are those more serious issues that are likely to cause significant frustration, anxiety and anger in teachers: swearing, overt defiance, aggressive behaviours (kicking, hitting, shoving, pulling), verbal aggression directed at others (including the teacher).

The most common form of classroom conflict which occurs is where the nature of the transaction easily becomes a win or lose situation for both sides. There is no question that children, adolescents, the students we teach, can at times cause us great frustration and anger. As one of my colleagues said of a female student who frequently spoke in a tone of voice that had 'contestable' and 'I don't care' all over it, 'I tell you, that Lisa, she's got a slappable face!' I understood.

Conflict is basically the presence of two (or more) competing needs or demands at the same time. Mick is frustrated and gives quick vent to his emotion. 'F—— this work!' (Need met, frustration partially ameliorated.) Teacher gets angry. He needs to 'control' the outbreak of swearing and manage his own frustration with this four-letter word provocateur. The climate now exists for conflict. How the conflict proceeds will depend largely on how each party defines the ongoing transaction. Weber (in Rex, 1981) describes conflict as a 'will to act' being resisted where the other party acts against the actor's needs—an incompatible difference of objective. For the teacher it is often expressed simply as the student–teacher situation over which control is difficult and stressful.

Wishing and hoping for the halcyon days of 'Yes Sir!', 'No Sir!', ordered rows and neat polite children is professionally and psychologically stupid. Conflict, at any level, will come. How we minimise it and creatively channel it will depend to a large extent on the kind of personal, organisational and managerial planning we employ to resolve it.

Frustration and conflict in children

A good deal of conflict with children arises out of frustration: internal frustration (induced by family or social climate or an inability to manage task demands) or external frustration induced when outside pressures create conditions under which reasonable coping seems difficult, even impossible.

Younger students and those less mature tend to react to failure maladaptively (Vernon, 1969). Less able to think out an appropriate course of action, they get frustrated and will not tolerate the presence of that frustration. Much of the swearing we now hear in (some) classrooms is engendered by simple frustration. As Milgram and Shotland (1973) noted in their research, the presence of frustration is an extremely powerful determinant of anti-social behaviour.

If Cara answers me back because she is frustrated, *what I do* will determine (as much as anything) how the conflict proceeds. I can increase or decrease the frustration by what I say and do. If I slam my hand on the desk (I must win, I'll show this little swine she can't answer me back. 'Listen you, who the hell do you think you are speaking to me like that?') and speak in a hostile fashion, it will have a different outcome than if I restate the rule, give a simple direction, defuse, or take the student aside (see Chapter 3). I may not be able to stop the child from *feeling* frustrated but I can do a great deal about how I respond to her acting-out behaviour in the immediate emotional moment and, later, when she and I have calmed down.

Students who react quickly

One of the problems in dealing with students who react quickly is their failure to interpret a social situation beyond the few cues of frustration ('I'm angry!'), there's a threat ('That bastard took my rubber!'), and the belief 'I must win'. Dodge (1981) describes such students (mostly boys) as 'low searching' in their perceptual cues. They 'globalise' a threat and do not take in all the available social or situational cues (high searching). 'He stole my rubber!' ('stole', not 'took without asking'). 'I'll belt the bastard! How dare he!'

Teaching in a graphics class, some years ago, I watched Michael (a tough, street-wise student) wrestle with a student who had 'borrowed' his rubber. It happened so quickly. Apparently Darren, a mate, had 'borrowed' his rubber from one desk away. After Michael retaliated with a grab and, 'Give it back you f—— poofter!', the two fell on the floor to wrestle and to grab the rubber which had now bounced under the table. I managed to direct both students aside from the group and ask what they thought they were doing. As with many such students I've worked with, they saw conflict in terms of a power struggle. Even when I pointed out that they were 'mates' the response was: 'So what!—he don't care if I hit him a bit—like it's just getting my rubber back and that.'

'Fellas (…) I care. In our class we sort out our hassles without fists and feet.' I directed them back to the graphics project and followed up with them after class (see p. 96).

Many of those 'quick responding' students see the transaction as *merely* one of win or lose. Enhancement of self at the expense of others is not simply a prepubescent or adolescent characteristic, of course. Many adults don't subjugate that win–lose predisposition (Bryant, 1977), what Bernard and Joyce (1984) call the 'uncontrolled behaviour syndrome'. In 1965 Fannin and Clinard noted that many working-class boys saw themselves as tough, powerful and aggressive, and felt that such traits were not only desirable but that social placement was correlated with these traits. In a research study I conducted (back in 1985) with over 500 pre-adolescent students, boys showed significantly more hostile and aggressive resolutions of conflict than girls.

Gender differences

Boys are predominantly more aggressive in resolving conflict than girls. This is seen in play behaviour, differences over property, opinion and friendship patterns. Girls tend to be much more verbally active in conflict resolution, or will call on an adult to mediate or arbitrate. Boys are more pragmatic, more utilitarian: a punch, snatch or strike is quick and easy! Even in play settings, boys are more active and aggressive than their female counterparts—a fact borne out by study after study (Williams, Bennet and Best, in Papalia and Wendkos Olds, 1982; Rogers, 1985). Little wonder that boys see 'power' basically as the ability to win over someone else—often by verbal or physical force. Talking takes time and effort.

The research data on male proclivity for aggression in conflict is a salutary reminder to male teachers especially about their *modelling* of conflict resolution in their classrooms. Where girls are aggressive, it is often expressed as verbal aggression; the mouth is used instead of the fist. However, I suspect this is changing. As a recent TV documentary indicated ('Four Corners', 28 April 1997), women and adolescent girls are becoming increasingly more aggressive in conflict situations.

Classroom conflicts

In classroom conflicts, boys exhibit more negative behaviours: negative attention-seeking (calling out and often being reinforced for it); antisocial aggression; physical aggression (pushing, pulling, grabbing). Even in their self-reporting, boys will describe males as more aggressive, more dominant, more hostile in conflict settings; as if such behaviour is the norm. Most of the complaints regarding confrontations in classrooms come from boys. As early as pre-school age, the sex difference in conflict is clearly observed: boys retaliate more, thus becoming involved in more hostile encounters; girls either submit or employ more 'devious' strategies to gain their objective. Of course, much of this pattern is to do with modelling, and social expectation through nurturing in the early years. School, especially the playground, still reinforces such patterns (Maccoby and Jacklin, 1974, 1980).

When it comes to the resolution of conflict, children (normally) can be expected to move through the following stages though, like some adults, they regress under stressful circumstances:

1 Physical aggression towards other children or adults (biting, hitting, kicking, pinching, punching) and towards inanimate objects (throwing, hitting something).

2 Undifferentiated aggression (tantrums, foot stamping, running crazily) and aggression towards self.
3 Verbal aggression towards others and towards things ('You b—', 'You f—— idiot', 'That bl—— book!', 'That sh——hammer!'); towards self, covertly or overtly ('I'm an idiot', 'I'm useless, no good!').
4 Socially acceptable means:
   ■ bargaining, discussing, expressing and explaining one's feelings
   ■ seeking alternative goals
   ■ seeking third-party mediation
   ■ cooperative resolutions.

Our goal as teachers, of course, is to enable children to work, play and socialise with others cooperatively. Developing the sustained ability for non-hostile resolution of conflict is a hard task for teachers and is related to how teachers develop self-esteem, a fair rights–rules–responsibilities dynamic and workable and positive communication channels for handling conflict at the point of crisis and in the long-term resolution.

Conflict resolution employed by children

Aggression: snatching, punching, pulling (hostile mode), verbal abuse
Adult intervention: 'Mum!' 'Dad!' 'Teacher!'
Threat: 'I'll dob if you don't!' 'I'll hit you if you don't give my rubber back.'
Diversion: trying something else to divert attention
Reasoning (basic): 'Give it back.' 'Don't do that, it's mine!' 'Why did you snatch my rubber?'
Reasoning (mature): talking through issues and problems to resolution.

Children display all the characteristics that adults display when facing what they perceive as 'conflict'. Girls, generally, are more likely to use an adult mediator and to use threats, or reasoning. Certainly they show more likelihood of mature reasoning in settling disputes than boys who lean heavily on aggressive modes of resolution.

Teacher frustration, anxiety and anger

Damien doesn't like school much. Already, in Year 6, he's scored an impressive record of unmanageable behaviours. He comes to school dirty, has holes in his jeans, is quick to swear and is often aggressive. Many teachers are thankful that he is not in their class.

He's already butted in several times during morning talk, to the teacher's annoyance. Now, as the on-task activity in maths begins (applied number), he starts one of his interminable conflict rounds. Of course he's got problems at home, of course he has learning difficulties and his social skills are not good. There are countless numbers of students like Damien in our schools. His teacher has been fair and reasonable in her discipline behaviour. Damien throws his books off his desk and says loudly, 'What do I have to do this sh—— work for?' He sits, arms folded, in 'dumb insolence mode'. It's a scene. Whatever the teacher does, there is a lot of interpersonal emotional heat being generated.

How does the teacher feel? She probably feels very frustrated. She may feel threatened (What will the other children think? What will the teacher in the next room think?). What makes her feel this way? Is it just Damien's four-letter defiance? Has he some special magic to make her very upset? I've worked with many teachers who have gone right off at swearing, as if the swearer had 'lit a fuse'. I've seen some teachers throw kids, in a fit of anger, across a room. 'He made me so angry!' How the conflict, and the student, are defined is very important.

While not unsympathetic to teachers' feelings, I think it is important to identify where intense feelings of anger or powerlessness come from when we are faced with provocative children. Our feelings do not just happen. When we get frustrated, even angry, several things are happening and happening quickly. We are perceiving a child's behaviour as highly threatening, we are believing that we must do something about it. We have attitudes that quickly rise to the surface. We experience, on the one hand, emotions of anger and, on the other, physiological arousal (tense or vigilant muscle reaction, increased heart rate, etc.). We also react or respond to the threat.

Anger is a very powerful emotion. It can, at times, overtake rational control. As Emily Dickinson aptly says, '... a plank in reason broke'. We *naturally*, and at times justifiably, get frustrated and angry at some student behaviours: persistent calling out, butting in, clowning and other expressions of attention-seeking, persistent laziness and task avoidance, lying, cheating, stealing, indifference and rudeness.

It is *natural* to get angry at injustice and persistent unfairness. Anger is an emotion linked to our very survival. It can enable us to respond, react or protect; when others are unfair, unjust or hurtful the arousal of emotion (that is anger) can enable our necessary response. However, it is not appropriate to handle all anger-arousing situations in the same way. Most anger situations, as Tavris (1982) points out, are 'social situations'. Sometimes we need to address conflict spontaneously, with assertive language (see pp. 77, 108). Sometimes we need to demonstrate our anger coldly and calmly after due (and thoughtful) consideration (Scott Peck, 1978, pp. 67f).

We can't stop *getting* angry, it's what we do *when* we're angry that counts in how effectively we manage the conflict cycle (see Figure 8.1).

Anger, obviously, cannot tell us what to do. That's why it is important to have a general approach to managing our frustration, our anger, and the typical conflicts that elicit these emotions. Any approach will need to include the sorts of skills that enable us to respond in the immediate emotional situation (this will largely address use of assertive language), the back-up supports when students go 'over the top' and will not settle (this includes structural support such as effective use of time-out), and how we follow up and follow through with the resolution of conflict beyond the immediate emotional moment.

When we get angry we tend to behave in one of three basic ways:

1 with reactive anger
2 with passive anger
3 by utilising anger.

Reactive anger

'No one is going to swear in my class!' 'I must not lose face!' 'I *must* win.' Belief, emotion, physiology and behaviour combine to produce shouting, yelling and rough treatment—counter power. The conflict *is defined* as a power struggle. The emotion of anger is seen as proof positive that 'I *must* act angrily', especially when dealing with stressful conflict. We feel we must do something, we are compelled. If our emotion is the primary motivator to action and the emotion is anger, we must act angrily. Of course *reactive anger* is often irrational, often over-rates the threat and is counter-productive in the long term. ('No little sh—— is going to swear in my class!') When teachers become reactively angry they tend to provoke, or feed, such behaviour by their counter power. They often don't care about their anger, or its effect on others.

Although emotions don't tell us *what* to do, they certainly describe (quite naturally) what we are experiencing; We can't choose our perceptions, but we can learn to manage our response to our perceptions.

Passive anger

When we react with passive anger we hold it in for fear of 'letting go' and acting irrationally. Non-assertive teachers often feel that anger is a bad thing, especially when they've seen some models of it in other teachers. The emotion of anger is one of the most powerful of human emotions. If we internalise our anger it will be to our cost, even if we hold it back for high motives. All that energy has to go *somewhere*, as teacher stress records show: days off, inability to face that class again, physical distress or sickness. If we restrain the emotion in the setting of the conflict itself, we may only release it later, at home, on some poor, unsuspecting loved one who has nothing to do with the original cause of the anger. If we do nothing about the anger or the conflict that precipitates the emotion, we rarely resolve it.

It is unhealthy to ignore our feelings or pretend that we are not *really* angry when our body is clearly saying 'I am twisted up, I am furious. My heart rate is up, my hands are sweating, my muscles are tense.' Behind such thinking is the irrational belief that a good teacher shouldn't get angry. We *need* to express our anger and find appropriate ways to make our needs and feelings, or others' needs and feelings clear. We need to focus on issues, or behaviour—

clearly forcibly—without ending up in an aggressive verbal slanging match with others (students or teachers!).

Utilising anger

There is nothing wrong with anger *per se*; the emotional energy is there for a reason. There is a demand on our coping ability. How do we rate it, perceive it and control it? We can't stop the ire rising when Sean says, 'P—— off!' to a reasonable request. If we plan ahead, we can do something about using the emotion assertively to express our feelings appropriately, and manage the due rights of all.

If we just react, or sulk, or withdraw, or curse back when we're angry we learn nothing about this useful emotion. We have a *right* to get angry on issues that count but because anger is such a stressful emotion it needs management. High emotion clouds our perception and our thinking processes and affects our actions. Planning ahead will enable us to manage emotions; not to eliminate them, but utilise them.

Perception and emotion

How we perceive the conflict will affect the degree of emotion we experience. We often forget the place of belief and perception in our behaviour. Many angry teachers I have spoken to will recount a list of conflicts which made them angry, and while they can't remember what they *said* when angry they can recall why the child shouldn't have sworn or answered back or defied them. In effect they are explaining the social reality by attributing their anger to causes outside of themselves. Behaviour doesn't just happen, it interfaces powerfully with both emotion and belief; we are not made angry just by events themselves; we contribute to the anger process too.

Take swearing as an example. Where swearing is another form of defiance (and not merely a slip of the tongue), we could ask ourselves where our feelings are coming from when we become angry about it. If we believe, and say to ourselves, 'Children must not swear! They should not use filthy language like that! They should respect me! Swearing is awful!', where does such demanding thinking get us?

Anger is, like all emotions, powerfully linked to our beliefs. One affects the other. The actual swearing does not *simply* cause the anger we feel. The cause of our feeling, and the intensity of it, comes from what we currently believe. While we may strongly dislike swearing per se, if we demand Frank shouldn't swear (when in fact he just has), that demand can significantly affect our emotional state and stifle productive handling of the conflict.

Of course it's preferable that students (and teachers) find appropriate avenues to handle their negative feelings, but to demand that they act as we say they *should* creates unnecessary stress especially when such demands are often refused. There is a preferable, realistic and much less stressful alternative: to say, 'Well, I dislike swearing, but it is a reality. Now, how can I better handle it in the short and long term?' It's unpleasant, frustrating and annoying, but it's not the end of the world. This is not excusing the swearing, it is simply distinguishing between a *demand* for desirable behaviour and a *preference* for desirable behaviour. All the demands in the world won't stop swearing, especially conversational swearing (see p. 291). They will make us more stressed about the swearing behaviour. No student who swears, challenges our authority, or defies us has the inherent magic to really upset us, unless we attribute to them that they do have the power. We can acknowledge our frustration but we do not have to slip into a win-or-lose mentality. There are other, productive ways to handle feelings of anger such as assertive statements, *tactically* avoiding the debates and arguments of power-provocative children (an ancient ploy), not over-attending, and giving clear assertive choices rather than threats and demands (see Chapters 2 and 3). In effect it means converting our old 'involuntary emotional habits back to their original state' (Bernard and Joyce, 1984, pp. 86–87).

The issue of anger management and conflict revolves around the twin issues of:

■ emotional coping: managing the intensity of frustration or anger at the time of the conflict.

■ *dealing* with conflict in a way that doesn't create too much stress and doesn't wreck the interpersonal dynamic in which frustration and anger are aroused. Poorly handled anger interferes with effective management goals. Teachers who just *react* angrily to interpersonal conflict often create longer term conflict by demanding, blaming and holding judgemental beliefs.

Physical reactions

Because the body reacts to emotions, it is important to be aware of what is happening to it. As we perceive a threat, we become emotionally involved and the emotions affect our bodily responses. The heart rate beats above the normal range, the neck muscles become tense, and the face becomes red as the heart pumps the blood to the excited areas. We may grit our teeth or clench our fists. The body is getting ready to do something. But what? We can't hit, strike or strangle that intransigent creature (unless it's self-defence)!

These bodily signals are important. This is the natural way our physiology prepares us for conflict, signals us to recognise and utilise our anger. When conflict arises:

- Consciously recognise what is happening.
- Clench the fists to concentrate quickly on the body's reaction, then unclench.
- Concentrate on breathing more slowly. By quickly doing this we acknowledge what is happening. The pattern of 'tense and release' emphasises and acknowledges the anger and gives us a brief breathing space; we do something about the emotional arousal. As we speak clearly and firmly we also *do* something about our frustration.
- Count to three, exhale and respond. Speak firmly and assertively to the student about our anger, the situation, the right being affected by their behaviour, the rule. Give a clear direction or choice and avoid prolonged argument. If the conflict is low-level, call the student aside to speak with him about his behaviour.

How we *define* the conflict at its earliest stage will normally determine how successful or unsuccessful are the resolution and aftermath. This is why we need to make a conflict 'plan'.

Basic protocols of anger management in conflict resolution
1 Get angry (and express anger) on issues that really count

Avoid getting angry over common misdemeanours such as not having pencils, sulkiness in student body language, 'conversational' swearing, homework not handed in, not having textbooks. Save expressions of anger for situations that carry some emotional, social and moral 'weight' such as racial or sexual harassment, put-downs, bullying, aggressive behaviour and behaviours that necessitate expressions of anger that demonstrate the link between our anger and the rights affected.

2 Know what makes us angry

Be aware of the factors and situations that lower our tolerance for potentially stressful situations and especially for people we know we can't interact with well. Be aware, too, of how we may be 'coming across' to others when we're frustrated and angry. It is worth reflecting on what we get characteristically angry about. Is there anything that can be done preventatively on *those* days, with those particular students, in that timetable slot (blast—not 8D again!)?

3 Address the situation

Attack the problem, not each other; it's easy when anger rises to start giving 'you' messages. 'Listen you! I said get it out of your mouth. I'm sick and tired of telling you about your damned chewing gum!' 'But other teachers let us!' ... and the argument starts.

Whatever the situation—chewing gum, noise, task-refusal—address *that*. Have some characteristic verbal repertoire in mind to say when precipitating ('anger producing') student behaviour arises. 'Holly, if you want to ask a question put your hand up' is much better (said assertively) than, 'You always yell at me, what's wrong with you? Can't you put your hand up or what?' Try to stay on the issue itself, as briefly as possible. Hyperbole such as 'I've told you a thousand times!' doesn't really help. It also doesn't help to get locked into a win–lose argument when students engage us in 'secondary behaviour' (see p. 29).

4 Avoid put-downs and criticism of the person

As an adjunct to anger, it is tempting to try to 'get back'. But remember, we may be in the wrong too. If we are, we ought to apologise. 'Sorry Maria, it was wrong of me to scream like that. I was uptight about what you said. I didn't mean ...' Avoid comments about students' home environment (over which they have little control) or words like 'idiot', 'stupid', or worse. Distinguish between the person (however unlikeable) and their actions and behaviour—*that's* what we're getting angry about. When there is a fine line between the two it is even more important to concentrate on the behaviour.

5 Acknowledge the emotional climate

Rather than just venting our feelings it is more appropriate to share our feelings briefly. 'I am angry about ...' is better than 'You swine!' 'I feel ...' is better than 'You drive me up the wall, you stupid twit you!' 'I feel angry about ...' concentrates on what we are feeling about the behaviour. There is no harm at all in telling a student we are angry and why. There may also be some occasions (for example when Damien calls Maria a slut) when *acted anger* is appropriate. 'Damien! I am appalled at what you've said! That language is *totally* unacceptable here.' (Drop the voice now, to a firm level.)

As Ginott (1972) points out, anger situations are high-attention situations. We should describe what we *see*, and act in a way that unambiguously conveys what we feel and why.

> The students have given the relief teacher a hard time. Mr R, the class teacher, faces his students, focused, but his face expressing the anger and hurt he feels about their behaviour. His face is set, he stands upright, he scans the class, his hand making the point (without pointing) as he gestures ... he stands still as he scans his class. 'I am really upset, in fact I'm appalled, at the behaviour of many of the students in this class ...' He *briefly* describes their behaviour. He lifts the voice, tactically pauses, scans, makes his point. He is assertive, not aggressive. He finishes by directing them to spend ten minutes writing down what happened, how they think the teacher must have felt and what they can do in terms of restitution (now) and what they will do whenever a relief teacher comes 'to our class' in the future. Anger, when it is assertive, can really make a *significant* point.

> A female colleague of mine was walking past a group of Year 11 boys in the playground. She heard a wolf-whistle (she tactically ignored that) but didn't ignore the 'whispered' sexist comment about her body and clothes. She walked back, faced each pair of eyes silently, then said, 'I heard it. I don't want you, ever, to refer to my body. At all! I don't like it.' She dropped her voice to a serious, unmistakably firm tone, 'I don't expect it. Do you understand?' She scanned their

eyes, some now averted. There were a few grunts and 'pawing at the ground' with feet. She walked away. There was that 'social silence' that says that what just happened was significant, pivotal.

She heard a student mutter loudly, 'Gees, only joking!' She turned back and said (again with that serious, quiet, assertive tone) 'I don't see it as a joke. I don't like it and I *don't* want to hear it again—do you understand?'

It didn't happen again. Nor did she bring it up in class—in fact she developed a positive working relationship with that group of Year 11 boys as the year progressed.

Gordon (1974) has noted that 'I' messages enable the teacher to take some responsibility for his own feelings of frustration or anger while at the same time communicating the teacher's need. It is a way of taking responsibility for our emotion and is often *read* less antagonistically by the student. 'When I find the books left out, Caroline, I have to waste a lot of time putting them all away' is enough for a clear 'I' message. It explains to the student what the situation is, and it implies a desired action. It can be followed, if necessary, by a simple direction. 'I get frustrated when everyone calls out at once. Remember our class agreement for ...' 'When ... then ... because ...' is another form of conveying need and rights. 'When you call out (or butt in), then I feel annoyed, because it's not giving others a fair go.' The key to using 'I' statements is the confident tone and manner of the speaker. If what we say sounds like we're pleading, with overdone frown and defeatist body language then it is the indecision that is heard not the assertion. 'I'm really angry about what you've said, I expect an apology' is better than standing and demanding one. We move off if an apology doesn't come. We've said we expect one. It looks like we have saved 'face' as far as is possible in a stressful setting. We've also explained why we're angry. Follow up later.

During the on-task phase of the lesson you can continue 'I' messages by directing a student aside. It is important to think about the sorts of 'I' messages that are appropriate when one is frustrated or angry. Respect is an attitude, expressed in our actions; feelings come and go.

6 Keep the heat down and avoid a power struggle

Conflict (sometimes high-level) is inevitable and even unavoidable at times. The potential struggle often created by conflict *is* avoidable. When we use the language and action of win or lose we only *define* the conflict in the most restrictive way. If there can only be one winner, we will tend to employ any behaviours (however damaging) to reach that goal. *Aim for resolution.* There are several stages in conflict (see Figure 8.1). What we do at the point of conflict determines how successfully we resolve it later.

In the heat of the moment it is important to calm ourselves before we attempt to calm the other person. This doesn't mean we are unemotional but we are controlling the expression of our anger. It is possible to communicate 'calmness' even when we're angry. If we try to use an angry tone of voice we'll only increase the emotional arousal. I've seen teachers respond to whining students in the playground: 'Miss, miss (as the Year 1 child pulls at the teacher's coat), Miss! No one will play with me ...' The teacher turns, glares, extends the pointing finger, 'Well, I wouldn't play with you either! You're a whiner you are! I'll tell you something for nothing—people don't like whiners! No wonder no one will play with you!'

Watch the volume. There's little point screaming and yelling (unless a real danger can only be attended to by a raised voice). Shouting; a constant, raised voice tone; an argumentative stance; and sharp, caustic, staccato language all convey that we can't communicate in a normal, firm voice. Sometimes it is appropriate to acknowledge the other party's anger. 'You sound very upset, annoyed, irritated, angry ...' Students have bad days; like us they get tired, cranky, have emotional baggage they bring to school (and our class). It can help to remind students that if they're angry with us—about something we've done or said, to tell us. To use words. It will often help to give them examples; this is normally best done one-to-one outside the classroom time.

If we're *too* angry to speak, we should explain that to the student and avoid the open-emotion slanging match. 'Look, Danni, I am too angry to discuss it with you now. I'll talk about it later.'

Provide a face-saving way out for both sides. A gracious route away from conflict can only occur if the teacher takes the initiative.

Avoid escalation of conflict—follow up at a calmer moment

It is unlikely the student will care enough to want to save face—especially if his agenda is power.

Keep the heat down by:

▮ directing the student aside away from his peers (if possible)
▮ making the rule clear (without nagging)
▮ making the 'choices' clear (clear choices within the rules rather than forcing or threatening)
▮ remaining 'calm'
▮ speaking assertively rather than aggressively (see Chapter 3) in the emotional moment
▮ following the issue through later *after cool-off time,* explaining how the conflict affects you or other students.

7 Call in a third party

If the conflict is getting unmanageable, call in a third party. Have a well-developed exit and time-out plan (see Chapter 5). Don't hesitate to have a student removed if the situation is *clearly* getting unmanageable and our fair steps have not achieved the desired control.

8 Follow up classroom conflict *(see p. 96)*.

Follow-up may also require a mediator (preferably a teacher effective in student–teacher negotiation). The object of follow-up is to work at a mutually acceptable solution. Use a problem-solving approach. 'Linda, we need to sit down and talk about what's happening in class.' Explain the facts as we see them. Explain how particular behaviour affects class rights (or rules for younger students). Include the student in this. Generate solutions: the possible and the achievable. Select appropriate solutions and necessary consequences. Use reflective listening: 'Are you saying …', 'As I hear it, you mean …', 'Let's go over that again', 'I can see you are angry Linda', 'How do you feel when …?', 'What will you do …?' The teacher, the student and the third party mediate and plan consequences and future behaviour.

Keep away from self-blame. We would not say to a student that she is bad for feeling angry or expressing her anger. We might disagree on the way she expressed her anger. Some teachers respond to anger-expression in themselves by blaming themselves. 'I shouldn't have got angry …' (We probably should have got angry.) 'I'm an idiot for …' Even if we expressed our anger unhelpfully—even stupidly—it doesn't mean we *are* a failure, or are intrinsically bad. It means we didn't express it thoughtfully. We can always apologise (where appropriate) or explain, and we can always learn to be more effective and responsible in expressions of anger next time.

Swearing and defiance

During a Year 7 textiles class Adam, minus a front tooth and sporting a tough jeans jacket replete with studs and swastika, was trying to stuff a piece of dowel up the back of his felt crocodile. The theme was soft-toy making. He was making a crocodile. 'F—— this dowel!'

he said, loudly enough for all to hear. What is the teacher to do? Before we get angry we need to consider how swearing occurs in a classroom setting.

A lack of social skills

When we get frustrated as adults we probably say, 'Oh bother, I've just snapped my pencil!', 'How annoying, I've dropped my hammer on my foot.' With our well-developed social skills, we work within the parameters of social convention, curb the 'sh——!' and drop it elsewhere. Not so Adam and many others. I've heard muttered 'sh——', 'buggers', 'bloody' and the f—— word in every type of school. Many of the students who drop the four-letter clangers do so out of social-skills deficit or sometimes to set their teacher up. I find it helpful to distinguish between the kinds of swearing that often occur in a school setting.

■ Conversational swearing. This is most common outside the classroom. Several lads are talking about the latest blockbuster (Mission f—— Impossible) 'Did you see that f—— explosion where the whole car f—— blew up?' In this sense the f—— as used in student conversation is part habituation, part social peer-pressure. Teachers can remind students of positive language without preaching or moralising.

■ Frustration-engendered swearing. Sean drops a catch in footy. Lisa gets a drop of acid on her paper in the science class. In these cases, 'sh——' is an understandable reaction. Swearing comes easily to some students. It may be appropriate to simply acknowledge the student's frustration and give a rule-reminder and, perhaps, follow up with a one-to-one chat later. Sometimes the swearing may be indirectly targeted to the teacher. The teacher has directed a sulky Year 8 boy to return to his seat. As he moves back to his work area he mutters a swear word under his breath. The teacher tactically ignores the sulky body language and briefly notes what the student has said. Walking across, he says, 'I heard that Peter. I'll chat with you later.'

'Don't care.'

'I do Peter.' The teacher moves off, giving take-up time.

▌ Swearing directly at students or teachers as abuse or defiance (see p. 295).

Teachers can, and do, use repartee to defuse some conflict situations, especially swearing.

The student says 'sh——' clearly enough to be heard. Poor lad has dropped his new silver pen which has now broken and the spring has popped out. The teacher walks past and says, 'Where?' the student looks up, 'What?' 'Where?' replies the teacher. The student gets the joke, giggles and the teacher quickly redirects. 'Okay, Sean, pick it up—the pen I mean.'

Rebecca turns to her friend, during an art class, and says (loudly enough for her immediate audience to hear), 'F—— this useless, blunt knife'. The teacher bowls in a smart one-liner. 'I didn't know you could do that with a Stanley knife.'

Other students may laugh, if they hear, and that's the point of the defusion. By using light humour, the teacher is, in effect, taking the 'heat' out of a potential conflict. She may follow up with the student later and have a chat about the four-letter word dropping.

Some teachers object to the use of humour when dealing with swearing, claiming that it excuses the behaviour. Not so. It is a way of defusing potential conflict *at the point* where emotions are running high.

Consider the teacher who starts a big debate about swearing.

'What did you say! You know swearing is not allowed in our room!'

'Gee, I didn't mean it', says Dean. Who knows whether he did or didn't? He folds his arms and sulks as if to say, 'Don't pick on me!'.

'And don't you sulk at me. You know the rules the same as anybody else. I don't care if you swear at home. You will not swear in my room. Do you understand?' (He obviously feels compelled to preach at Dean.)

'You always pick on me—fair dinkum!' 'I do not pick on you ...'—and so on.

The teacher has now got another conflict on his hands beyond the initial swearing. It was a bad move to refer to Dean's home background. One of the cardinal rules of conflict resolution is to maximise face-saving on both sides by eliminating unnecessary embarrassment and hostility.

Of course many teachers are reactive in their behaviour because they feel angry, but behind their anger is a firm reasoning process that embodies such self-talk as: 'I must win here', 'Children shouldn't swear!', 'I must prove who is boss', 'I'm the teacher', I can't lose face!' The teacher's belief quickly raises the feeling of anger because reality doesn't fit the belief; stress arises as much from firm, set beliefs as it does from the four-letter language of Dean or Rebecca.

Power struggles in conflict situations

Many teachers believe they must use counter power (more power, more force). 'It's the only message that so and so will understand!' They believe that they must compel the rude students of this world to submit to the rule, to their requests, demands or whatever. The trouble with pouring on more power, however, is that it never influences; it coerces or forces. Gordon (1974) has pointed out that merely falling back on power in no way educates or persuades a student. The student will either fight back (especially if she is after power), submit, or withdraw for a while until the pressure is off. Power *by itself* doesn't change the conflict; it is almost always counter-productive.

When we challenge students, in a heated voice, 'Who the hell do you think you are, you little ...? You'll apologise now!', students whose goal is a power exchange will often simply resort to counter power; the combatant mode of conflict resolution.

When we play the win-or-lose game we are committing ourselves to only one way out. And of course, the more credibility we give to the threat (of such power-provocative students) the more we unhelpfully empower the student. By giving a clear, firm 'choice' in a situation of defiance, we put the responsibility back where it belongs. But if we demand and threaten, and back the student into a corner in front of his peers, often there is a no-win situation established. This common conflict cycle leaves the teacher uptight emotionally, the child still hostile and an effective aftermath more difficult. As well, the teacher will not get sympathy or support from the rest of the class.

The win-or-lose approach will often escalate the conflict to unmanageable proportions simply because the teacher has then to behave as if he *must* win; hence power tactics come into play. In an emotionally charged dynamic like a classroom, it takes a significant change in thinking and belief as well as strength of will not to use coercive power. As the conflict begins to reach its peak, the issue of competing needs becomes obvious: the student's need for emotional outlet (frustration, anger, confusion) or for expression of power (defiance, humiliation of another, ridicule) and the teacher's need to be seen to be 'in charge' in some way, as well as to protect his rights to teach and other children's rights. If the conflict is significantly affecting fundamental rights the teacher will need to exercise the time-out option to enable formal cool-off time for all. Later it will be essential to work with the student on some resolution of the conflict beyond time-out itself. Once we define the student as the enemy, we may believe we have to play war and there is no room to manoeuvre.

If we want to manage better our anger, or frustration, or fear (of not being able to handle the conflict) then we will need to examine what we are thinking. Here is an example of a different perception.

▪ 'Now I know Jono's probably into power provocation. He's defiant, rebellious. If I pour heat on, he'll only further believe he gains his goal by provoking and challenging me.'
▪ 'I don't *need* to yell, scream, abuse, or threaten. I don't have to be *inevitably* upset. I don't have to have my personal peace destroyed.'
▪ 'Okay, I don't like this, but I can stand it. It isn't the end of the world. Let's try those steps I worked out before to handle conflict. My influence will be reduced if I simply try to compel or force.'

Dropping standards?

Many teachers will see this approach as a dropping of standards. Not so. We can, by our example and teaching style, often reduce swearing more effectively than by all the moral preaching under the sun. If we have made a clear rule about swearing, we will need to decide how best to enforce it. On some occasions we may defuse or quietly remind; on other occasions we may assert, forcefully, our displeasure. Denunciation won't stop a student swearing; neither will suspending every swearing student. As in all discipline trans-actions, we'll need to decide our approaches *in advance*. If we have already communicated our expectations, moralising (as distinct from a reminder or an assertion) won't help.

Swearing at teachers

Students swear at teachers for one of three reasons:

- As a form of testing out a power relationship.
- Because the teacher has been hostile in the first instance. ('Why are you late?' 'Where's your late notice?' 'Listen, I've told you before if you don't hand the work in you stay in after school!')
- Because they don't handle their own emotions. They say 'Get f——!' or 'P—— off' as a quick solution. It's not easy for an angry student to *say*, 'Excuse me, I'm quite angry about the way you just slammed your hand down on my desk and demanded I stop talking to my friend.'

If a student does swear *at* the teacher, or speak defiantly, the teacher should restate the rule, assertively express how he feels and (briefly) why that language is unacceptable. In some schools any form of abusive swearing means formal time-out; in others it means immediate suspension. Even if the school has an unambiguous policy about abusive swearing it is still important for the teacher and student to resolve (later, after cool-off time) the issues leading to that conflict. It will often help to have a senior colleague involved in the resolution process to support the teacher, but not to merely act on the teacher's behalf to 'fix' the student. Never ignore swearing as defiance. Take the student aside if, and when, appropriate and:

1 Restate the clear rule about swearing and assure the student that there will be follow-up. 'Ben, you know the rule for swearing, I expect an apology. I'll speak with you later.' Speak with a clear sense of controlled anger and use decisive body language. Avoid the dropped shoulders, pained expression and pleading tone that says, 'What have I done to you that you speak to me like that? It hurts, Ben, when you swear at me like that.'

2 Use an assertive message. 'Excuse me, I don't *ever* speak to you like that. I don't expect you to speak to me like that.' Use direct eye contact, but keep some distance away. Make the point clearly. It is not a fight, it is an assertion. It is important not to stand there in combative mode because it is not a fight until, or unless, we define it so. Move off, and expect an apology, later, when the student has cooled down. It is also important not to be devastated by the abuse. 'I don't have to be inevitably upset just because he swore at me. I can speak with assertive anger to make my point without letting it traumatise me.'

3 Direct the student aside, or away from the group, and briefly discuss the rights-infringing behaviour and how you feel about it.

4 It can be appropriate, if you are comfortable, to use repartee or humour to deal with those students who 'set you up'. It is one of the most powerful approaches for the so-called hard-case students who swear 'to the gallery', or lay the 'bait'. Repartee is very effective because it defuses the interpersonal heat. I have seen many teachers effectively minimise audience-seeking and power-seeking swearing. When using repartee it is important:

- not to be malicious or sarcastic
- to take the heat *out*, not increase it
- not to comment on the student but rather on the words used
- to be 'quick off the mark'.

When the other students laugh along, quickly divert their attention back to the task at hand.

'I hate you!' whines a Year 9 student.
'Thanks for the compliment! Now get back to work thanks.'

'Get stuffed!' (muttered loudly under his breath)
'If I could find a taxidermist willing to do the job—possibly.'
What's a taxidermist?'
'Someone who stuffs people.'

'Bullsh——!'
'Where? You have to watch that stuff. It smells and attracts flies.'

Student mutters, 'Holy sh——!'
The teacher adds, 'What denomination?'

Remember, you're trying to minimise the generation of heat (interpersonal aggression, anger, hostility), provide reasonable 'face saving' on both sides and protect the due rights of all class members.

The domino effect

Of course other students will laugh when teachers defuse potential conflicts and some teachers argue that this is a bad thing; that it teaches students that we excuse swearing, and only encourages it. Not so. There are few students brave, silly, arrogant or stupid enough to swear in the presence of their teacher. That is why defusion is effective. It communicates quickly that the teacher:

■ knows the game
■ will not put wind to the sails
■ is confident about what she is doing
■ has intentionally used repartee to defuse potential conflict.

The matter of the wrongness of swearing can be followed up later—when the audience isn't there. Don't worry, the tribal 'tom-toms' will soon pass it on that the swearer has had to face the consequence of his behaviour.

Simone has a permanent scowl on her face. When her teacher hands out some work, she says in a loud voice, 'This work sucks!' The teacher calmly walks over, picks it up and says, 'So it does!', with a lilt in his voice. The class laughs at the teacher's words and the teacher quickly gets the class back on-task. Later, when they are working, the teacher goes over and asks Simone how it is all going. Although he doesn't particularly like the scowler, he tries to speak civilly to her when she's on-task.

Miss J is writing algebraic formulae on the Year 9 chalkboard. She turns to face her class and one little wag calls out, 'Miss, someone just did *that* when you had your back to us!' and he demonstrates by sticking his two fingers up at her, grinning to draw group attention. Unfazed, and skilled in defusion and deflection, she recognises teacher-baiting and with all eyes on her says firmly, but without aggression, 'Well, I'm glad I didn't see it. Okay (directing group attention back to the task), we were discussing algebra.' She is brief, decisive, firm in body language; and not drawn by teacher-baiting.

Don't use defusion if you're tired, uptight, jaded, really frustrated or upset; use it on your good days.

If you don't like, or feel you can't use, defusion then employ the other approaches described. Defusion is a personality-based style of conflict resolution. It is most effective when the teacher has a positive working relationship established with the class.

Always follow up later with consequences. Ask for an apology, have a conference, make a behaviour plan. Use detention, during which the swearer writes out:

▋ what he did or said
▋ why he thinks he did it
▋ what he could have done instead (if he were uptight, angry, upset, etc.).

Contact senior staff and parents when frequent intentional and aggressive swearing is a regular pattern of behaviour in a student.

Working with behaviourally disordered children

Matthew was sitting in the time-out area yet again. His teacher had sent him there for verbal aggression in class and not doing his set work. Sitting at a desk, in the time-out area, he was reluctantly catching up. He showed me his book. The teacher had put a big red cross through the day's diary entry (Year 1). I asked him why he thought the teacher might have done that. 'Cos it's really messy!', he answered. I asked him what he was in the time-out area for. 'I sometimes fight with words.'

'Oh, yes.'

'You know what my problem is?'

'No', I replied.

'Well, like my head and mind get a sort of headache. It's ADD. I have to control ADD.' He seemed quite earnest about his 'problem'. 'What's ADD?' I asked. 'It's like from my head. And then it comes to my mouth and I fight.' I simulated a boxing position with my hands, 'You mean with your fists, Matthew.' He laughed, 'No, fighting from my mouth. But there's a solution.' I was surprised at his use of the word 'solution'. 'Oh, yes, what's that then?'

'I'm going to get a prescription.' He didn't know for what—probably Ritalin.

Attention Deficit Disorder (ADD)

Many of us have come across children diagnosed with ADD (ADHD where the hyperactivity factor is a dominant feature of a child's behaviour). Such students:

■ are restless
■ are easily distracted and inattentive
■ can be very impulsive (often not thinking about consequences of behaviour—sounds like half the boys in 8D!)
■ have significant problems with concentration
■ have poor social relationships (this often affects their self-esteem)

■ have obvious difficulty in waiting for their turn
■ are hyperactive
■ lose items (especially those for learning tasks).

This list of typical behaviours, though, could fit many boys (it's mainly boys). We have to be careful that we don't label all attention-seeking students who call out in class, shout out answers, roll on the mat, rock in their seats, wander in class or are restless as having ADD. ADD behaviour is *learned* as well as conditioned. And while there may be physiological factors that contribute to, and affect behaviour, we need to be careful not to make the child the 'victim' of his predisposing factors. ADD is the most widely used term applied to disruptive behaviour in schools these days. ('Half my class is ADD!')

Recent research suggests that ADD is a genuine behaviour disorder that can affect up to 10 per cent of all male children, that it is an inherited condition (from the male line) and that it has some physiological, as well as psychological, basis.

Because ADD-type behaviour overlaps with attention-seeking and general naughtiness as well as other behavioural problems it is important to have a thorough psychological analysis, or a paediatrician's assessment rather than rely on anecdotal evidence alone. This assessment will need to involve parent and teachers.

Many children diagnosed with ADD or ADHD are prescribed Ritalin or Dexamphetamine by paediatricians. The medication works by stimulating parts of the brain that enable focus and attention; conversely it cuts out social contextual 'interference' to further support the child's ability to 'tune in'. Medication is a common response to ADD by medically trained practitioners. Green and Chee (1996) point out that ADD affects the children's learning and behaviour and any medication programs should always be supported by behaviour management programs.

I have seen some (not all) students dramatically improve in their behaviour and on-task learning with medication, providing the teaching staff also have some behaviour therapy in place as well.

Teaching new behaviours

Matthew believed that 'the tablet' would fix him. I had to point out that the tablets might help him but *he* would have to *learn* how to control *his* behaviour. When working with any behaviourally disordered children the focus must be on the learning of new behaviours, to dehabituate the old patterns and rehabituate the new. Reliance on medication alone is not enough. As one ADHD child said to one of my colleagues—'I can't be good today, because I haven't had my good behaviour tablet!'

Behaviour profile

As with *any* behaviourally disordered children, what we need to assess is the frequency and intensity of the disruptive behaviours. There is a big difference between the occasional and the every day or every class exhibition of disruptive behaviour.

Behaviour also needs to be looked at in terms of context. Is his disruptive behaviour frequent or intense with specialist teachers or teachers other than the regular class teacher? At secondary level is his behaviour *generally* disruptive across all subject areas or selectively disruptive? Is the behaviour more than bad-day syndrome? (Students' behaviour is sometimes worse on Mondays or Fridays.)

A behavioural profile is a starting point for team-planning and dialogue with parents. When behaviour is frequent, intense and general in its disruptiveness it severely affects learning, social relationships at school and the tolerance level of teacher, other students and parents alike. Early intervention is important before the pattern of behaviour becomes routine for the child and the peers who have to work with him.

Support processes

Set up support processes for the teacher and aides who work with the behaviourally disordered child (Rogers, 1994), for example:

▌ Identify the problem, analyse it and monitor the behaviour.
▌ Draw up a well-conceived time-out plan. It is important the student associates that any potentially disruptive behaviour, or significant disruptive behaviour will *always* result in time-out of

some kind. If teachers treat disruptive children as if they can't really help their behaviour or learn new ways of behaving because they have a dysfunctional home life, or are socio-emotionally disturbed, or have a 'condition' like ADD they only reinforce the students' lack of behavioural choice.

I Organise classroom rotation. It can help to relocate the child in another class (at primary level) for at least one timetable period, once a week—just to give the class teacher a break (this is to be distinguished from time-out).

Individual behaviour plan

Develop an individual behaviour plan with the child to teach him the behaviours he needs to cope with both the academic and social demands of classroom and playground life. This is discussed in some detail in Chapter 5. (See also Rogers, 1994 and 1997.)

Monitor the plan

Monitor the plan daily with the child and give regular feedback (each class period) to the child, and regular feedback to the parents or caregivers. It can be helpful if regular, weekly feedback is monitored by the principal as well, to encourage the child within his plan.

As with any behaviour therapy it is essential to balance corrective approaches (short-term discipline, consequences and punishment) with supportive approaches (counselling and behaviour therapy).

Working with angry children

I Consider the difficulty even adults have in managing their frustration and anger. Try to appreciate the difficulties a child may have with self-control. (This doesn't mean we excuse the child's inappropriate expressions of anger.)

I Teach children the difference between anger as a feeling and what to do with anger; it's not bad to be angry, or to have angry feelings. We should make this clear to children; even as adults it is unhelpful to blame ourselves for *having* angry feelings—it is what we do with them that counts.

I Teach anger-management skills to children (see Rogers, 1994, Bernard and Joyce, 1984). The one-to-one teaching of strategies needs to occur in a non-pressured setting (away from the classroom) with an emphasis on support for behaviour change. While all children can benefit from social skills generally (see McGrath and Francey, 1993), children with low frustration tolerance and high impulsivity will need to learn to recognise where their frustrations come from and how to address their emotions in a practical way that doesn't hurt others. This may be as basic as counting backwards from 20, self-imposed time-out, or even handing a small card to the teacher that signals what he is feeling inside. ('I'm feeling very upset right now. I would like just five minutes cool-off time please.') A simple card like this can help young children in settings outside their own classroom.

Anger-management skills include muscle relaxation, reframing self-talk, writing down 'angry thoughts', switching academic tasks, communicating anger verbally. As with the learning of any skill the key aspects will include modelling and rehearsal and feedback (see p. 176).

▌ In the heat of the moment when a child is angry it is important that the teacher acknowledge the child's frustration or anger (as well as their own) and refocus the situation for the child to make the behavioural options clear. 'I can see you are upset (or annoyed, or angry) because … (focus on the behaviour you observe).' 'I feel annoyed (or very concerned, or angry) because you're trying to fix up your problem by arguing, and pushing and shoving. What's our rule for settling problems here?'

▌ With students who are in conflict with each other ('he stole my rubber', the two children who come in crying from lunch recess because they won't be friends any more) it may be important to direct them to separate and take some cool-off time for a while. It is also helpful to acknowledge their emotional state and assure them we can follow up later. Bring them together later and invite them to work within a mediation process (where both can 'win' and have their needs met) or have the teacher decide on a solution. Any process of mediation needs to be based on trust and in a climate where teachers have to generate a problem-solving ethos that puts appropriate responsibility back to children.

▌ Teachers can easily be put into the role of judge and jury by children, and while teachers will need to arbitrate in serious situations there are many conflicts between children that can be mediated by children with guidance and skills taught by the teacher. 'Do you want time now to sort this through or later at recess?' It may well be appropriate (at primary level) to give ten minutes during the school day where they can sit in the corridor to work through key questions. 'What happened?' 'How am I affected by this (be specific)?' 'What can I do/we do to fix this problem we have?' Younger children will need an adult or an older child (upper primary) to assist in the mediation. Mediation can also be undertaken by trained older children in the school, children who have undertaken skills training in conflict mediation and 'peace keeping'.

■ Structural approaches by the teacher can involve modifying the seating plan, the time allocation and the design of learning tasks. (ADD children, especially, find long periods of quiet and concentration very difficult.) It may help the behaviourally disordered child to work with a responsible peer who can act as academic and social mentor.

■ Above all, take time, and give time, for conflict resolution.

A long-term plan

If a student is repeatedly disruptive over several sessions, in several class settings, the teacher needs to consider the school's long-term plan for supporting teachers and giving assistance to the student. Such a plan should address the following questions:

■ How are students targeted for special assistance?
■ Do we develop individual behaviour plans for such students? How? Who is involved in the development of such plans?
■ What support is offered to the grade/subject teacher?
■ Is there a team-approach to working with such students? How does that team-approach operate to support the student and his teachers?

Encouraging long-term change

Long-term change takes time. It is unrealistic to expect success overnight, when behaviours have been built up and practised over years, often under inconsistent adult tutelage. Students *can*, and often do, get strong reinforcement from teachers and parents for negative behaviour. (Hostile attention, nagging or rough treatment by an adult is still a form of attention which some children actively seek.) It will take significant resolve, goodwill and support to make any impact with such students, and it is important that we:

I consistently show respect to the student through the steps we take to manage their behaviour and the plans we develop with them (see Chapter 5)

I encourage the student's approximations and efforts towards cooperative behaviour, and make such encouragement situation-specific

I don't excuse aberrant behaviour but apply consequences when the 'heat' dies down. I once watched a principal trying to get a student to wipe spit off a window. In full view of a third of the school, the almost apoplectic principal tried to drag the Year 6 student's hand to the spattered window. He couldn't make him, however hard he pulled. The student was dragged swearing, back to the principal's office. Who won?

We can't make the student do anything

What infuriates many teachers who have to deal with difficult students is the sense of powerlessness that such students can create by their resistant behaviour. In disciplining such students, in balancing corrective and supportive adult direction, we need to accept the fundamental premise first: we can't *make* a student do anything. We can direct, restate, ask, encourage, even command, but the more we use teacher force alone, the more we lose (face, control, temper).

Some of the 'hard' students have long-practised repertoires in baiting or setting up teachers. They get what they want—reaction, attention; in short, 'belonging'. If we are going to be effective, we will need to be aware of their deeper problems as well as the acting-out behaviour they present when an audience is available.

Wayne was persistently noisy at his desk. When asked to move, he replied, 'No!', or 'Why?', or 'Why are you always picking on me?' What could the teacher do? Drag him bodily, kicking and screaming, two metres to an isolation desk? He was aggressive and sullen by turns. He swore, argued and was persistently defiant.

This type of situation is best handled by a basic plan communicated to the student prior to class and *backed up by colleagues*. Such a plan was used in Wayne's case (Year 6).

The teacher had to resist his first impulse (thump him!). When students like Wayne seek to belong by aberrant power-seeking, it is totally ineffective to meet them with a win-or-lose strategy. The teacher was clear in his own mind that he would decide how he would behave in *response* to, rather than as a reaction to, Wayne.

The teacher was assured that if Wayne was overly disruptive, a colleague would support him with a time-out approach. He was encouraged to see that such a process in no way suggested failure on his part. (Male teachers are still expected to be able to effectively manage the Waynes of this world simply because they are *male*.)

The essence of the plan was to make a number of points clear to Wayne (at a non-threatening time and with the principal involved):

▌ He was more than welcome to be part of the school and enjoy classroom life and learning.

▌ The teacher could not and would not make him do the work. This took him by surprise because he was used to the task-refusing ploy to gain significant attention in class. The teacher would not, however, let him disrupt others' rights to learn or be safe.

▌ If he did his work the teacher would give him all the help he wanted and needed. The teacher wanted him to be part of his group.

The class rules were re-established and a written plan developed to enable Wayne to focus on and take some control over his behaviour. This plan was taken from class to class (see Appendix III). It was made clear to Wayne that if he continued to make it difficult for others to work, or to be safe, or made it difficult for the teacher to teach, then he would be given a clear direction, a clear reminder of the rule, or invited to explain his behaviour after class. If he refused to cooperate, he would be given a choice to stay and work by the fair rules or leave the classroom and face time-out.

Of course, for low-level disturbances, the teacher may well be able to tactically ignore. If the student shows any on-task behaviour, then the teacher will give due encouragement (not praise).

Employing conflict resolution steps will minimise hostility with students such as Wayne. Even confrontational students can be effectively dealt with when a teacher (or support teacher) remains calm. On some occasions such students have been re-enrolled in to another class. It is understandable that sometimes, even with the best will, a bond may not be possible between some teachers and a student like Wayne. There should be no professional shame attached to this. Colleague support is essential both within the school and from outside the school (consultants, psychologists, social workers).

It can take a long time to achieve any success with someone like Wayne. In the process, his rights must be fairly balanced with those of his peers. We cannot change Wayne's home environment but we can do a lot about how he is treated at school.

With extreme cases like Wayne we may never win. We may even have to resort to expulsion from the school (although the sad reality is there are few off-school options for behaviourally disordered students). This is the hard reality that can, at times, make teaching a frustrating profession. However, we can work together, develop a joint plan and minimise stress for teachers and the other students who have to live and work with behaviourally disordered students like Wayne.

Abby, a Year 3 student (and a ward of the state), displayed strong attention-seeking behaviours which included throwing off her shoes and socks (sometimes at the teacher); spitting and swearing; constant calling out, task refusal and avoidance. She came from a severely disturbed and broken home life and was in transit to an institution while awaiting foster parents.

The school decided on a joint teacher plan. With school-wide colleague support, a behaviour modification schedule was drawn up and Abby was given a book with weekly target behaviours. Those behaviours were rehearsed with two teachers and Abby (see Chapter 5). A discipline plan was worked out with a series of steps (see Chapter 3) so the teachers knew when and how to intervene. When teacher A's frustration reached a significant level, Abby was taken to teacher B's room (with her behaviour modification book). In this way the management of Abby was shared between two teachers. With consistent, firm, calm treatment she progressed remarkably well and in a few months had settled back into some sort of steady routine. Routine, consistency and firm, caring adults are crucial when dealing with deep-seated and ongoing disruptive behaviour.

Effective teachers working with such students are marked by:

- their willingness not to give up
- their basic calmness
- their willingness to respect the unlikeable
- their consistency of treatment within the group so that the disrupter is not seen to have markedly different treatment (getting away with it)
- their encouragement, regularly expressed, for the smallest effort (they expect positive change, but not overnight!)
- their provision of opportunities for success
- their willingness to enlist the help of others
- their judicious sense of humour and refusal to take all such acting-out behaviour as personal attacks on them.

Aggressive behaviour in the classroom

Teaching a Year 3 art class one afternoon, I had finished explaining the object of the lesson, and had asked some students to hand out materials, when suddenly, apparently out of the blue, Ric raced for the door. I grabbed him quickly as one student said, 'Watch it, he runs off sometimes!' As I held him by the arms, as firmly and calmly as I could, he struggled and grunted and kicked. I had no idea why he had exhibited this explosive anger—his class teacher had given me no prior warning. I had no idea how she might have handled his behaviour or whether this was characteristic of Ric.

He finally calmed down and I led him back to his chair and explained the task. He sat sulking, arms crossed, head down—dumb insolence. I already knew that pleading, arguing, fighting (power struggles) or plain aggression was ineffective so I left him in dumb-insolence mode and, as a safety measure, moved my chair near the door and taught from there. A few minutes later Ric jumped off his chair, ran for the door, head down like a bull, and charged into me to get to the door. I took hold of him and held him with my arm around his chest and arms as he kicked, screamed and struggled. I spoke calmly to him as he tried to escape. 'Don't worry, Ric, I'm holding you till you stop being angry.' As he relaxed, I relaxed the hold until he was quiet and I led him back to his seat. Six more times he made the bolt for the door.

I later found out about his extraordinarily twisted home environment (including bashings from dad) and the fact that I was the only male teacher he had had at that school. Had I known about Ric's background I could have sent for senior teacher support for time-out although we had no formal time-out policy at that stage (see Chapter 5). As it was, I was still able to teach; as calmly as one can holding a child while speaking to other students. 'Maree, that's developing well, can you hold it up so I can see.' 'Suki, could you hand out the charcoal at your table?' 'If you've finished Paul, you can clean up and read a book.' All this *while* holding Ric until he calmed down enough to be led back to his chair. Tiring.

Many children cannot say to us, 'I am angry about ...' 'I am angry because ...' They tell us they are angry by *acting* angrily. They rarely foresee the outcome or predict the consequences. In

dealing with anger that erupts into aggressive behaviour it is important to be well prepared, for example:

1 Find out about any predisposing factors. Where possible, get parent support. In Ric's case we felt that such 'support' should be minimal for the child's safety.

2 Develop a maintenance plan. Establish when and under what conditions the disruptions tend to occur—who with, what time of day, what is happening in the lesson. Accurate records assist in diagnosis, strategy development and evaluation.

3 Develop a plan with *all* the teachers who come into contact with the child. Consistency is especially important. If one teacher ignores, another screams and yet another tries to ameliorate, the child will either end up confused or play one teacher off against another. A team approach ensures consistency *and* stability. Where possible also enlist professional psychological assistance. The plan should include steps to deal with any conditions leading up to the conflict (seating, curriculum, directions); steps to deal with the actual disruptive behaviour itself; and a contingency plan if the child's behaviour is overly disruptive or distraught. It is crucial that, where aggressive behaviour (to self or others) is concerned, a teacher acts quickly:

- Speak calmly but firmly. With lower primary-age children it may be necessary to hold them to establish the importance of your leadership at that point. This is especially important if the child is hurting others (pencil-jabbing, persistent pinching, biting, hitting or hair-pulling).

- Give clear, brief directions and reminders about the rules.

- Apply consequences rather than punishments (we don't excuse their behaviour). There is a belief amongst some teachers that we should just 'be hard' with kids like Ric. 'It's the only language they understand!' That, in essence, is the trouble. We need to teach them another language.

- Use time-out *immediately* if necessary. Colleague back-up and assistance is essential with aggressive students of any age.

- Develop a plan with students to enable them to deal more successfully with the frustration that triggers such behaviours.

Such plans may include behavioural modification techniques (see Chapter 7) as a short-term mechanism to get success into the child's social and learning behaviour. An important part of any personal behaviour plan is the designing of 'escape hatch' mechanisms. 'Next time you feel angry I want you to tell yourself that it's okay to *be* angry then go and sit in the cool-off corner or come and tell me.'

Encourage all positive attempts at management of anger. Above all, find ways to show respect and care at times when the student reveals reasonable social behaviour. It is so easy to alienate such students. Barracking for them is hard work and requires plenty of colleague support. They have 'failed' miserably and their self-esteem is often low. While we should never ignore their anger and aggression, we should help them to redirect it (see p. 302).

Sexist remarks, innuendo or touching

Sexist remarks, innuendo and touching (including crowding, pinching, provocative gestures) are largely a problem for female teachers and can be quite debilitating to those unprepared for it. They can include everything from comments about boyfriends to remarks about parts of the body. No teacher should ignore this or excuse such talk. We have a right to personal dignity. Of course, like all conflict, the way it is managed will affect the nature and extent of the resolution.

Assertive messages

Be clear in your own mind about unacceptable behaviour. 'Gee you've got a great figure, Miss!' is different from specific remarks about body parts. If it is offensive, say so. 'I find that remark offensive.' Move away, or block with your hand those crowding behaviours students sometimes exhibit. Keep the response firm, brief, clear and intentional. Don't labour the point but make it unambiguous. With younger children who are touching or holding us out of natural affection, we will need to be much more diplomatic, distracting the child aside from his peers to explain our concerns.

Rules

Discuss appropriate treatment behaviours during the establishment phase of the year (this will include discussion on put-downs, hurtful language, harassment of *any* kind).

Choices

If a student continues with offensive behaviour, give a clear choice to work by the fair rules (the way we treat one another) or leave the classroom. Make the consequences clear. Be sure to have an exit plan as a contingency measure for such students (see Chapter 5).

Conferencing

Ms M had heard the words 'slut' and 'pro' dropped behind her back during the Year 9 history class. She knew which of the boys were 'setting her up'. She had tried confrontation, only to meet denials. 'We never said anything, Miss!' Upset, and naturally angry, she let it go for a couple of weeks only to break down, crying at a faculty meeting. Only then did the offer of support come. A meeting was convened with the three boys, a support colleague (male) and the teacher. (Unless the teacher is too upset she should participate.)

When using this approach, it is important that all parties affected know what is going on. Get the facts straight. Give due right of reply. Explain, again, the rights of the aggrieved party. Expect appropriate apology. Work at a mutually workable solution with consequences clearly outlined for future behaviour (see also pp. 105, 207f on accountability conferencing).

How we deal with sexism and harassment will depend on how provocative the student has been. If it is clearly light-hearted, a rule reminder, a brief defusion, or a quiet aside may be appropriate, but if it borders on the sexist put-down, deal decisively with it or get support. Most schools have a sexual harassment/discrimination policy.

Summary

Frustration and anger are dominant emotions (anxiety is prevalent too) among teachers. Anger is normal and can even be a healthy emotion. When situations are dangerous, hurtful, or severely affecting others' rights, we are bound to get frustrated, even angry, and are properly employed utilising that anger. We will handle it better when we understand it. What signals it? What do we characteristically think, say and do in anger-arousing situations? Can we do it better? Like any teacher behaviour it can only be more professional when, at the end of the day, we take some responsibility for the way in which we manage conflict. By discussing it with our peers and making better plans, conflict and the attendant emotions can be utilised towards resolution.

Questions to consider

- What are some of the classroom behaviours, circumstances or situations that make you angry? Can you pinpoint them? When do they occur? In what subject areas? With which students?
- Are you able to specifically recall what you *currently* do in managing high-level conflict (conflict that sees you highly frustrated or angry). What sort of things do you find yourself saying? Can you recall? What sort of things do you think (or say to yourself) when you are angry?
- If you have angry or aggressive students, how do you normally deal with them?
- What behaviours do you want to change in yourself or others? (In effect, we are the only ones we can directly change; we can change the way we address situations and relationships.)
- What specific alternatives can you propose to your current approach?
- List some practical alternatives to address *your* particular situation (a clear policy for conflict mediation and resolution with students; a clear policy on the use of time-out across the school; clarification of the support role of colleagues; especially senior staff).

Conclusion

NO ONE, no one who is a teacher that is, pretends that discipline and classroom management are easy tasks. Schools, more and more, are expected to have the widest of curricula from the 3Rs to bike education, social skills training, human relations education, computer and information technology, and environmental education. How often do we hear the cry in the media, 'Why don't schools teach them ...?'

We are required to cope with wide individual differences, cater for the emotional needs of our students and provide the best learning environment for all. Ministers of education frequently harp on about the 3Rs, and at other times stress the need for inclusive curriculum and more human relations education. Many teachers are reporting significant stress as more and more bureaucratic demands are made on their time, their goodwill and their energy. We are also expected to pick up the unfinished guidance and discipline tab that some parents leave behind. Most teachers do this with diligence, hard work and good humour.

In this demanding role of teaching there are some situations over which we have minimal control: the students' home background; the particular school we were sent to; the regular changes that proceed from the Department of Education; limits to funding; the portable classroom we got landed with; the timetable. There are, however, some areas of our practice that we can have significant and effective control over:

∎ the way we organise the curriculum and present it to our students
∎ how we organise our classroom space and aesthetics

▌ the kind of rules and routines we make with our students
▌ the way we cater for mixed abilities
▌ the way in which we can build up workable relationships with our students (we'll even enjoy most classes, and like most of our students!)
▌ the support network we can build with our peers
▌ the control we can exercise over our discipline and management style.

Most of all we can work with colleagues on the situations, circumstances and student behaviours that stress us. Colleague support will always make a difference to our coping ability and the quality of teaching.

A teacher once said to me, 'I understand all this discipline skill stuff but you know you can't teach an old dog new tricks.' But we're not dogs! We're people. We *can* change. Like most significant change it won't come about by accident, without some 'failure', or hard work, or support. Developing more effective and positive discipline practice will require the same reflection, effort and rigour that we apply to any area of the curriculum.

Today, personal dynamics in classrooms are subject to high emotion and fallibility but that only increases the need to plan for the sorts of things we ought to say and do when we discipline. It is possible to develop personal and school-wide discipline that is more decisive and less reactive without losing that fundamental humanity that not only makes teaching bearable but even enjoyable. If this book can stimulate that kind of reflective change, based on strong colleague support, it will have achieved its purpose.

Personal running records

Personal running records are important management tools:

1 They can assist in profiling the kind, number and content of disruptions. Teachers will sometimes say, 'He *always* calls out!' Now we know that's probably hyperbole, but it's helpful to know actually how many times and when. Such records are diagnostic data much as we would use running records for literacy and numeracy.

2 They are a useful record if support services are called in (another teacher, senior teacher, psychologist, special education teacher or consultant), and when conducting a parent conference.

3 They give a guide as to whether or not our intervention programs are effective. We can look back at particular occasions of disruption and see whether the behaviour management strategies or individual behaviour plans we are using are having any effect.

4 They assist teachers in reflecting on their practice: what they are actually doing, how often a given method or process is tried and whether there is a successful outcome. It is important that, as teachers, we become more reflective and appropriately evaluate our actual discipline and management.

5 They provide a focus for problem-solving discussion with our peers.

Disruptive behaviour analysis record

Incident (brief specific, description)	AM PM (or lesson time)	Gender	Task student is undertaking	Is behaviour directed at particular students? Who?	Teacher's action (be as specific as possible)

On the other side of this record the teacher can note severity and intrusiveness features of the students' behaviour (see also Rogers, 1994).

The 4W form

NAME _____ CLASS _____

What I did (against our class rules)

_____

_____

_____

What rule (or right) I broke or infringed

_____

_____

_____

Why I did it (my explanation)

_____

_____

_____

What I think I should do to fix it up

_____

_____

_____

Teacher/parent comments

_____

_____

_____

Signed _____

Date _____

Behaviour plans

1 Formal contract form

I have discussed my behaviour with the following persons

_____

_____

_____

and have agreed to work with them in changing my behaviour.

Behaviours I have agreed to work on

Be specific here. Focus on the class rights and rules.
It is better if the student uses his/her own language,
with teacher assistance. 'What do you want to try to do?'
'What do you need to work on?'

How will I do it?

Again be specific.

How my teacher/s will support me.

This aspect is often left out of a contract.
It is important to include it.

Comments on the student's progress.

Keep comments as positive as possible.

Signed _____ Student
Signed _____ Class teacher
Signed _____ Parent (if necessary)
Checked by_____

2 A self-monitoring behaviour agreement

This can be tied in with the 4W form.

Keeping tabs _____ *Jason* _____ Year ___ *7B* ___						
Week _____ Day _____ *Monday* _____						

How I behaved	Period 1	Period 2	Period 3	Period 4	Period 5	Period 6
1 *Hands up without calling out.*	***					
2 *Stick to my task, or the work set.*	**					
3 *Completed the task.*	**					

*** I'm happy with the way I went.
 ** Just okay.
  * Not okay. I'm not really happy with the way I went.

■ This behaviour agreement can be adapted for use with younger students (from Year 3 onwards). They should be encouraged to write any extra comments on the back of the card.

■ Use the phrase 'keeping tabs' to highlight behaviour ownership and self-monitoring.

■ The teacher, student and teacher-support (year coordinator, home-group teacher, school counsellor) will have discussed how the student can 'keep tabs' by working within fair rules; giving herself clear messages of encouragement; asking whether she has achieved the goals and whether her behaviour is helping her or not.

■ Each teacher who has this student needs to be aware that she is trying hard to manage her behaviour. They should be encouraged to support and maximise her efforts and assist in the program of behaviour ownership and change.

■ The agreement should be reviewed as often as the teacher or team feels necessary.

Behaviour goals

I can do it	MY BEHAVIOUR GOALS	Step by step
STOP DOING …		START DOING …

STOP DOING …
- _____
- _____
- _____
- _____
- _____
- _____

START DOING …
- _____
- _____
- _____
- _____
- _____
- _____

Is what I'm doing really helping me here at school? Is it really okay in terms of other people's rights?

GOALS These don't help:	GOALS These do:
- _____	- _____
- _____	- _____
- _____	- _____
What I need to stop doing:	What I need to start doing:
- _____	- _____
- _____	- _____
- _____	- _____

On the back of these behaviour agreements the teacher and student can note idiosyncratic reminders plus, of course, daily feedback acknowledgements.

Gentle, assertive role-plays (GARPs)

I have used GARPs as a teacher-training tool for students at university and at school workshops. Positive discipline skills are workshopped and the GARPs provide the testing ground for application. Teacher-training courses tend to treat discipline *practice* minimally. I believe it is possible to be far better prepared not only by knowing what we can do, but trying out how we might actually do it. We are more comfortable in discipline, and less stressed, when we have a discipline plan. A plan helps us to juggle the multi-task demands that teaching and discipline create in any one teaching session, on any one day. Combined with inservicing, teacher-support networks and the willingness to try a new approach, GARPs can be a highly useful vehicle for effective learning.

To improve their professional practice teachers need three things:

1 some realistic assessment of their current practice either by self-monitoring or by peer observation
2 a clear understanding of a possible, achievable new or improved repertoire
3 an opportunity to practise the new repertoire and get feedback.

Facilitators will ensure that no one is pushed into the unknown or put into an embarrassing situation. The role-plays are scripted so that those playing the disruptive students don't over-play the behaviour which is being managed by the teacher practising particular discipline strategies. When used in the context of trusted peer support, GARPs can provide a practical framework for getting a handle on a new repertoire in the safety and security of a role-play situation.

Action and feedback

Teachers know how important 'hands on' learning is; to be involved in *doing* the learned thing. Whenever we try to learn a new skill, or improve existing skills, we can turn to books, or current research, or attend an inservice or college course. Important as these learning experiences are, they cannot reproduce the emotional climate of a classroom setting. We can, of course, practise discipline skills in front of a mirror, or mentally rehearse an approach ('What will I say, how will I do it?'). These are valuable ways of internalising a new repertoire and giving confidence. What a GARP does is simply create enough of the classroom conditions to make the practice of a skill as realistic as simulation can allow. This is followed by immediate feedback. Teachers often miss out on *targeted* feedback, which is the link in the learning chain. It is fundamental to the impact of new learning on actual practice.

Feedback hits the spot when:

- it concentrates on specific behaviour
- it is non-judgemental
- it is as immediate as is possible (following the trial of the new skill)
- it encourages and builds on strengths
- it is used to fine-tune the skill again as soon as is practicable.

GARPs have been used at all levels of the teaching profession to enable such feedback. It goes without saying, of course, that GARPs are a voluntary teacher activity. They can be enormous fun (when facilitated with care) and can provide a simple opportunity to experiment with new discipline and classroom management skills.

Organising GARPs

GARPs can be used as part of an inservice, a training course at a tertiary institution, or a peer-support group within a school. They need willing volunteers, a facilitator, full knowledge of the process by the facilitator, and a willingness to accept a small element of risk. The facilitator should have a sense of humour and the ability to get on well with a disparate group of personalities, know how to give feedback and have the necessary classroom experience. The facilitator should also be thoroughly familiar with the skill repertoire being practised; its theoretical base as well as its methodology (see Chapters 2 and 3).

The sorts of disruptions teachers want to role-play in a GARP vary. These are the ones commonly used.

The up-front phase of a lesson

The following scenarios are examples of student management issues I have role-played.

Students who:

■ walk into class late
■ haven't got equipment or say 'What do we have to do again?'
■ call out across the classroom to get the teacher's attention while the teacher is working with other students
■ talk loudly and off-task
■ argue over property ('She's got my pen')
■ wander aimlessly about the classroom
■ demean the task ('This work sucks')
■ refuse to do the task
■ use low-level swearing to each other (or frustration-engendered swearing)
■ bait the teacher ('You can't make me do anything')
■ play-fight
■ require time-out situations.

In a GARP we are trying to simulate the level and extent of a typical disruption (even multiple disruptions) but with the teacher's cognisance. We are therefore looking for specific verbal and non-verbal teacher behaviour and management practice which can be exercised when managing that disruption.

'Scripted' disruptions

As suggested before, an open-ended role-play can be formidable. Give teachers the licence to role-play disruptive students and they will easily go 'over the top'. If a role-play is going to be a learning experience (in this case primarily for the person role-playing the teacher), then it will be important for that learning to have boundaries within which the learner can feel secure.

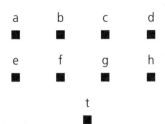

A group of 8   t = teacher
a–h = the class of students

During the GARP, one member of the group elects to play the teacher. The teacher-learner in the role-play is required to deal with disruptions occurring during the instructional phase of a lesson (15–20 minutes is plenty), then to move around the room dealing with on-task disruptions (another 15–20 minutes). The time may be extended to suit the needs of the group. The teacher will be aware of the kind of disruptions that will occur and will be ready to try out new language and non-verbal behaviour skills. She will have to decide what to do to manage the disruption, what language or intervention skills to use.

The 'students' are seated at desks in any way the group feels comfortable (see diagram above). Each has a card scripting a disruption:

> Call out twice to get the teacher's attention. If she ignores you, fold your arms and sulk. Throw in a snort as you go into sulk mode. That's all. Ten seconds later put up your hand and wait, without calling out.

> Call out with your hand out. 'Miss! Miss! I've got a question.' Do this for a count of five seconds. Stop. If the teacher doesn't respond, do it again thirty seconds later. And again one last time. If she still doesn't respond do it again. If she does—comply.

> Turn to your mate and whisper while the teacher is teaching. Do it until the teacher says something to you.

> Put up your hand and wait until the teacher notices you.

No student is to role-play beyond the clear script. Variations on up-front cards can be:

> Click your fingers with your hand up to get the teacher's attention. Do it for a count of eight to ten seconds.

Butt in and say, 'We did this stuff last year in Mr Davies' class!' Then look around to get peer approval, lean back slightly in your chair and wait.

The main thing is to script what you want in the way of disruption and then tailor it to the skill the learner-teacher is wanting to develop. The teacher knows that there will be, for example, calling out, tapping and whispering while she takes a mini-lesson up-front for three minutes. The teacher begins a mini-lesson on applied numbers, ready to handle three students calling out, two whisperers and a tapper. The limit of disruptions is decided by the learner-teacher and the group. The facilitator will often stop the GARP during the process and get feedback, asking the teacher, 'How did you feel when Michael was calling out and clicking his fingers?' The facilitator will also invite non-judgemental feedback from those role-playing the students, who now act as colleagues giving supportive, descriptive feedback.

General questions for feedback
'Were you conscious of what you were doing?'
'Were you clear, in your own mind, what you wanted to say?'
'Do you want to try it again?'
'How will you approach it this time?'
'What will you say?'
'Can I help?'
'Were you aware of the *actual* words you used to Michael and Deanne? What did you intend?'
'Try to recall them.'

Feedback questions for those playing the role of students
'Michael, did you feel Maria was assertive enough?'
'Was eye contact established?'
'How did she make her intentions clear?'
'What did you understand by her non-verbal actions?'
'Any other comments?'

Fine-tuning

The teacher should now utilise the feedback to try again (she may do this more than once). The facilitator may say, 'Maria, this time try tactical ignoring of Michael but use a clear direction to Deanne. What do you need to say? Okay, rehearse it. When you want to make a point, try extending the hand like this. Let's try it.'

The goal is to build up a repertoire that is modelled in the teacher's behaviour. This should include:

■ the expectation of compliance (direct eye contact, brevity of direction or instruction, tone of voice, and take-up time)
■ effective eye-scanning skills and tactical ignoring
■ a non-argumentative stance
■ general assertive (non-aggressive) body language
■ matching of teacher assertion to the level and extent of the disruption
■ rule-focusing and *conscious* verbal repertoire
■ re-establishment of working relationships as quickly as possible
■ minimal attention to off-task behaviour, conscious attention to on-task behaviour

It is better for the teacher to try again, on the spot, several times (if she feels comfortable) to get that tone of voice or gesture right. The facilitator will assist in this fine-tuning by modelling the desirable behaviour if necessary.

The on-task phase of a lesson

The same process is used when role-playing the on-task phase of a lesson. During the role-play, the teacher tries to decide what to deal with next—the student wandering out of his desk or the one calling out from three desks away? Prior to the GARP, members of the group will have discussed the sorts of skills they want to practise. Here are some examples of cards for use in role-play settings:

Go into task-refusal mode. Sit at your desk with your arms folded and do no work. Look around you. No noise.

Call across to the teacher every ten seconds or so. 'Miss, Miss, come over here!' If she says anything, keep quiet for a while and try again.

Stop after two or three times. If the teacher ignores you, finally put your hand up and wait.

Get out of your seat and wander over to a mate. Start a whispered discussion

What the teacher knows

In 'managing' the disruptions (via the role-play) the teacher knows what sort of disruptions will occur but not necessarily who has the cards. If the teacher wants to try out an approach more than once, the cards may be shuffled around to increase the sense of realism. At any point in the GARP, the facilitator or teacher can stop to reassess and get feedback and use this feedback to try again:

'This time, Maria (the teacher), see if you can *tactically* ignore Michael. Give him no direct eye contact and only go over when you are aware (using effective eye scanning) he is on-task. Otherwise, your directions were clear and decisive. You may need to lift up the eyes a bit and give a general eye-sweep of the class if you are at a student's desk for more than a minute. Want to try it again?'

It's then a good idea to swap roles. The time can be extended, of course, as people feel comfortable.

Included here are some examples of the sorts of scripts which can be used. These need to be varied to accommodate age and setting. For example, we can model a Year 1 child hiding under a table and refusing to come out as easily as a Year 8 procrastinating student— as long as the behaviour is scripted and agreed upon by group members. It is the facilitator's role to plan the GARP with the 'trainees', to facilitate immediate feedback during the role-play, and to debrief and guide discussion on what has been learned from it.

While the teacher is up-front, take a piece of paper and screw it up into a ball and toss it up and down in the air. Quietly giggle to your mate.

While the class is working, get out of your seat and start a conversation with a friend. The teacher will redirect you. Argue slightly, go back but sulk. After a while pick up your pen and start work.

You are a noisy pest. When the students have been asked to get back to work, turn around and start a discussion (with moderate volume)

with another student. The teacher will warn you. Settle down, but resume after twenty seconds. The teacher will restate the rule. Settle down but resume after twenty seconds. You'll be given a choice, but resume. You'll be asked to move. Initially procrastinate with 'Why should I?', then move off. After this, say nothing.

You are daydreaming, and have not started work. (It is 'work' time.) Start talking to your friend. If the teacher gives you a direction, stop talking. Resume a few minutes later. If she comes back, stop. Resume. She may ask you to move. If so, comply—sulkily.

Click your fingers and call out several times. Then go quiet. Try again by clicking your fingers and loudly calling out. Stop when the teacher disciplines you. Then put up your hand using the class rule.

You are a mobile student. When the students are working, get up out of your seat. Go back. Get up again. If the teacher redirects you, initially argue and then back down and resume your seat.

You are a task-refuser. You decide not to do the work. You argue *slightly* with the teacher, then comply.

You call out during class time. Do it twice (you'll probably be ignored). Give up and put your hand up to wait.

You are a task-refuser. The teacher says, 'Okay, let's get to work' or some other similar phrase. You sit and do nothing. When the teacher redirects you, start complaining, then give in sulkily and settle down within a minute or two.

You are a pain in the neck. As an attention-seeker you click your fingers and call out several times. If the teacher corrects you, you will shut up but you'll sulk and give a few grunts turning away to sulk mode.

Rights

Children's rights

1 To be able to learn in a friendly, encouraging, secure, supportive, and positive school environment.

Responsibilities

Children:
- to be cooperative and considerate
- to do their work on time

Parents:
- to be supportive in developing these responsibilities

Teachers:
- to work towards providing this environment by being encouraging, positive and disciplining fairly.

2 To have appropriate access to the school's facilities.

Responsibilities

Children:
- to share equipment
- to care for equipment

Teachers and school:
- to allocate use of facilities appropriately and fairly

3 To have appropriate access to the teacher's time.

Responsibilities

Children:
- not to demand attention all the time
- to try to be receptive and cooperative

Teachers:
- to allocate time fairly

4 To have a safe environment.

Responsibilities

Children:

❙ to act in a safe and responsible manner for themselves and others

Teachers:

❙ to try to ensure that the environment is safe and that children act safely

Education system:

❙ to provide a safe environment

5 To be heard and be able to express opinions.

Responsibilities

Children:

❙ to speak out but also to listen

❙ not to put others down

❙ not to dominate

Teachers:

❙ to encourage children to speak

❙ to listen

❙ to guide group discussions

❙ to teach non-assertive students appropriate assertive behaviour

6 To know what is acceptable behaviour and the consequences of unacceptable behaviour.

Responsibilities

Children, parents and teachers:

❙ to discuss this with students and make the issue clear through fair classroom rules and consequences

❙ to support students in changing inappropriate ways of behaving

Parents' rights

To be able to participate in their children's education by having two-way communication with the school as follows:

1 To have information on school processes and curriculum.

Responsibilities

Parents:

❙ to ask for information if they are unsure or want to know more

Teachers and school:

❙ to disseminate information

2 To be able to participate in school programs and decision-making processes.

Responsibilities

Parents:

❙ to make the time to be involved
❙ to make the effort

3 To receive and offer information about their children's education and behaviour.

Responsibilities

Parents and teachers:

❙ to be open and encouraging and willing to listen
❙ to develop workable solutions to problems

4 To expect consistent approaches to codes of behaviour used by teachers throughout the school.

Responsibilities

Parents:

❙ to be involved in planning school policy
❙ to let the school know of concerns about discipline

Teachers:

❙ to communicate with parents and reach agreement on discipline protocols and practice

5 To expect that there will be no cultural, sexual or physical discrimination against parents or children.

Responsibilities
Children, parents, teachers and school:
❙ not to discriminate or to accept others doing it

Teachers' rights

1 To work in a pleasant and safe environment and to be able to achieve job satisfaction.

Responsibilities
Children:
❙ to be considerate and provide support
Parents:
❙ to be considerate and provide support
Teachers:
❙ to play a part in the running of the school
❙ to prepare lessons thoughtfully
❙ to watch for unsafe things and practices
Education system:
❙ to provide a pleasant and safe environment (watch those worn-out desks and old portable classrooms)

2 To have support from within the education system, including other members of staff if required.

Responsibilities
Teachers:
❙ to provide that support both informally and formally (see Chapters 6 and 7).

3 To be involved in a collaborative decision-making model within the school (curriculum and organisation).

Responsibilities
Parents:
❙ to consult with teachers and reach agreement
Teachers:
❙ to consult with each other and reach agreement
❙ to make an effort to be involved

4 To be treated with courtesy by all.

Responsibilities

Children, parents and teachers:
I to treat others with courtesy

5 To be able to create time-out situations for children when they are disrupting other people's rights to safe movement, learning/teaching or communication.

Responsibilities

Parents:
I to support this as a feature of positive discipline (see Chapter 3).

Teachers:
I not to abuse this or use it to put down or ridicule children
I to follow up time-out with conferencing and contracting procedures (see Chapter 5).

6 To contact, and have back-up and cooperation from, parents and to be informed of family situations and home problems where they may affect behaviour and attitudes at school.

Responsibilities

Parents:
I to let the teacher know about relevant problems
I to provide support for the teacher

Teachers:
I to contact the parents if there is a problem
I to be approachable, to listen, to make the time, to act on information

7 To be seen as an individual by children and parents and be able to express a point of view without 'indoctrinating' children on social issues.

Responsibilities

Teachers:
I not to inflict unasked-for opinions on children

Based on the discipline/welfare policy of
Moonee Ponds West Primary School, Victoria.

Behaviour management survey

One way of developing a whole-school approach to discipline is to use a survey. Teachers are asked to observe their practice for a week or two. The answers can be used to help formulate discipline policy in the school. A similar survey process can be used to ascertain behaviour patterns in the playground.

Sample survey questions

1 What types of disruptive behaviours are presently occurring in the school?
   ▮ Can you rank them from most to least pressing?
   ▮ Can you note how regular such behaviours are?
2 What disciplinary procedures are you presently using to cope with these identifiable behaviours?
3 Which disciplinary procedures do you think are helpful and effective? Why?

Disruptive behaviour can, of course, range from tapping on the desk to the antics of the class 'strangler'. In one way or another it will be behaviour that disrupts another's right to work, safety, movement, security and so on. The data you collect will, therefore seek to:

▮ describe the disruptive incidents accurately
▮ note their frequency
▮ note the specific action taken
▮ note year level, sex, curriculum area, time of day and location
▮ rate the incidents in terms of frequency, intrusiveness or seriousness.

In developing a whole-school approach to more positive discipline, it is helpful to survey current practice to ascertain what teachers are currently doing regarding behaviour management.

Such a survey requires plenty of discussion before it is conducted and an assurance that the data will be used to improve discipline across the school.

1 Effect a systematic appraisal of what teachers perceive as 'disruptive behaviour'.

2 Determine what actions and procedures teachers are using which they find effective and ineffective when dealing with such disruptive behaviours.

3 Identify which teachers note undue strain from disruptive behaviours and what support is being offered, in a positive way, to address their concerns.

4 Note year levels or particular classes that seem to be overly disruptive.

5 Note particular students who appear to be causing problems and in what lessons.

6 Note any relationship between curriculum areas or time, and disruptive incidents.

7 Use the data collected over a four-week period as the basis for a discipline and welfare policy review.

Success criteria for school assemblies

Students and teacher collaborate on the theme 'what we have assemblies for' so that students can see the value and purpose of assemblies. Students brainstorm around the theme of assemblies: why we have them; what sorts of things we can do during assembly times; how we need to consider space, noise, consideration of the presenters, etc.; and the need for some behaviour expectations.

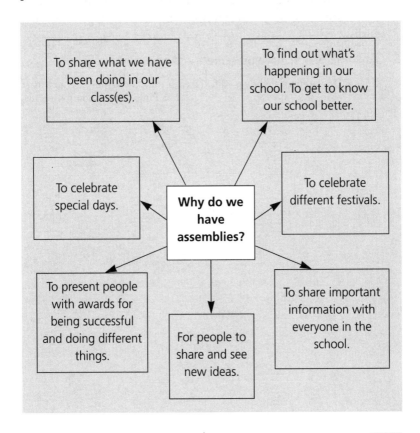

Students discuss basic behavioural needs during assembly times and come up with grade contributions to behaviour expectations, for example:

1 Leave your hats and toys in your own classroom.

2 Sit flat on your bottom and face the front.

3 Give eye contact to the speaker(s) and performers and listen to the person who is talking.

4 Listen when people are speaking, or giving a presentation up-front:
   ▮ Do not talk between acts.
   ▮ Join in with the songs (if you know the words).

5 Move to the front quickly and quietly when it's your turn to practise, or speak, or act on stage. Move on and off stage safely and sensibly.

6 Clap after people have presented—clap appropriately.

This has been slightly modified from a student collaboration activity at The Pines School, South Australia.

Playground questionnaire

The following questionnaire can be used with staff and students as a basis for both discussion and written comment on playground issues and playground behaviour.

1 What's working well in our playground (environment, seating, play, recreation etc.) and why?

2 What's not working well in our playground and why? (anything upsetting, concerning you—what, and why?)

3 Some things we need (want) to change? Why? How?

4 Let's discuss together a plan for action:
  I things we can start soon
  I things that'll take a bit longer
  I how we'll go about doing 'it'.

Thanks for your cooperation. We will give you feedback soon.

Establishing a class

REMEMBER

Before you leave your working area:

1 Put all materials away (lids on textas, pencils in containers, work away …)

2 Tidy your own work space; help others out too.

3 Chairs under table (ON table at end of day).

4 Litter in bin. Check.

THANKS! (teacher's name here)

Noise meters

A noise meter is a simple, visual training device for establishing workable noise levels in a classroom (see pp. 207–10).

When used with an upper primary class the first picture (top left) would show children sitting at desks or tables:

p.v. = partner voices   g.t.l. = getting too loud   s.r. = stop, reflect

At lower primary level the first picture would show children sitting on the mat:

APPENDIX XII

Visual rules

Bibliography

Axelrod, S. 1977, *Behaviour Modification for the Classroom Teacher*, McGraw-Hill, New York.

Ayers, H., Clarke, D. & Ross, A. (1996), *Assessing Individual Needs: A Practical Approach*, 2nd edn, David Fulton, London.

Barnes, D. & Daniels, R. 1996, unpublished ms.

Barrish, H.H., Saunders, M. & Wolf, M.M. 1969, 'Good behaviour game: Effects of individual contingencies for group consequences on disruptive behaviour in the classroom', *Journal of Applied Behaviour Analysis*, vol. 2, pp. 119–24.

Bedford, S. 1977, 'Instant replay: A method of counselling and talking to little (and other) people', in Wolfe, J. & Brand, E. *20 Years of Rational Therapy*, Institute for Rational Living.

Bernard, M.E. & Joyce, M.R. 1984, *Rational Emotive Therapy with Children and Adolescents: Theory, Treatment Strategies, Preventative Methods*, Wiley, New York.

Biggs, J. & Telfer, R. 1981, *The Process of Learning*, Prentice-Hall, Sydney.

Boer, B. & Gleeson, V. 1982, *The Law of Education*, Butterworths, Sydney.

Borba, M., & Borba C. 1980, 1982, *Self-Esteem: A Classroom Affair*, vols 1 & 2, Winston Press, Minneapolis.

Breheney, C., Mackrill, V. and Grady, N. 1996, *Making Peace at Mayfield: A Whole School Approach to Behaviour Management*, Eleanor Curtain, Armadale, Victoria.

Brown, D., Reschly, D. & Sabers, D. 1974, 'Using group contingencies with punishment and positive reinforcement to modify aggressive behaviours in a "Head Start" classroom', *Psychological Record*, vol. 24, pp. 291–496.

Bryant, B.K. 1977, 'The effects of the interpersonal context of self- and other-enhancement behaviour', *Child Development*, vol. 48, pp. 885–92.

Caffyn, R.E. 1989, 'Attitudes of British secondary school teachers and pupils to rewards and punishments', *Educational Research*, vol. 13, no. 3, Nov., pp. 210–20.

Charles, C.M. 1985, *Building Classroom Discipline: From Models to Practice*, 2nd edn, Longman, New York.

Clarke, R., *The Last of the Summer Wine*, BBC (video).

Coopersmith, S. 1967, *The Antecedents of Self-Esteem*, Freeman, San Francisco.

Cowin M. *et al.* 1985, *Positive School Discipline: A Practical Guide to Developing Policy*, Parents and Friends of Monnington Publications.

Cranfield, J. & Wells, H.C. 1976, *100 Ways to Enhance Self-Concept in the Classroom*, Prentice-Hall, New Jersey.

Dalton, J. 1985, *Adventures in Thinking: Creative Thinking and Co-operative Talk in Small Groups*, Nelson, Melbourne.

De Bono, E. 1986, *Conflicts: A Better Way to Resolve Them*, Penguin, Harmondsworth.

Dempster, M. & Raff, D. 1992, *Class Discussions: A Powerful Classroom Strategy*, (K–12), Hawker Brownlow Education, Cheltenham, Victoria.

Discipline in Schools: Report of the Committee of Enquiry 1989, Her Majesty's Stationery Office, London (The Elton Report).

Dodge, K.A. 1981, Social competence and aggressive behaviour in children, Paper presented to the Midwestern Psychological Association, Detroit.

Donaldson, M. 1978, *Children's Minds*, Fontana, London.

Doyle, W. 1986, 'Classroom organization and management', in Whitrock, M.C. (ed.), *Handbook of Research on Teaching*, Macmillan, New York.

Dreikurs, R. 1968, *Psychology in the Classroom: A Manual for Teachers*, 2nd edn, Harper & Row, New York.

Dreikurs, R., Grunwald, B. & Pepper, F. 1982, *Maintaining Sanity in the Classroom*, 2nd edn, Harper & Row, New York.

Erikson, E. 1960, 'Youth, fidelity and diversity', in *The Challenge of Youth*, E. Erikson (ed.), Anchor Books, New York.

Erikson, E. 1968, *Identity: Youth and Crisis*, Norton Press, London.

Fannin, L. & Clinard, M. 1965, 'Differences in conception of self as a male among lower and middle class delinquents', *Social Problems*, vol. 13, pp. 205–14.

Frankl, V.E. 1963, *Man's Search for Meaning*, Simon Schuster, Boston, Mass.

Froyen, L.A. 1988, *Classroom Management: Empowering Teacher-Leaders*, Merrill Publishing Co., Columbus, Ohio.

Ginott, H. 1972, *Teacher and Child*, Macmillan, New York.

Glasser, W. 1965, *Reality Therapy*, Harper & Row, New York.

Glasser, W. 1969, *Schools Without Failure*, Harper & Row, New York.

Glasser, W. 1985, *Control Theory*, Harper & Row, New York.

Glasser, W. 1986, *Control Theory in the Classroom*, Harper & Row, New York.

Gordon, T. 1974, *Teacher Effectiveness Training*, P.H. Wyden, New York.

Green, C. & Chee, K. 1996, *Understanding ADD*, Doubleday, Sydney.

Harris, S.J. 1973, *Winners and Losers*, Argus Communications, Illinois.

Hill, S. & Hill, T. 1990, *The Collaborative Classroom*, Eleanor Curtain, Armadale, Victoria.

Hill, S. 1992, *Games That Work: Co-operative Games and Activities for the Primary School Classroom*, Eleanor Curtain, Armadale, Victoria.

Hook, C. 1985, *Studying Classrooms*, Deakin University Press, Victoria.

Johnson, D.W. & Johnson, B.T. (eds) 1989, *Leading the Co-operative School*, Interaction Books, Minnesota.

Jones, P. 1996, *Talking to Learn*, PETA, Newtown, NSW.

Jones, P. & Tucker. E. (eds) 1990, *Mixed Ability Teaching—Classroom Experiences in English, ESC Mathematics and Science*, St Claire Press, Rozelle, NSW.

Kounin, J. 1977, *Discipline and Group Management in Classrooms*, Holt, Rinehart & Winston, New York.

Kounin, J. & Obradovic, S. 1968, 'Managing emotionally disturbed children in regular classrooms: A replication and extension', *Journal of Special Education*, vol. 2, no. 2, pp. 129–39.

Kyriacou, C. 1981, 'Social support and occupational stress among school teachers', *Educational Studies*, vol. 7, pp. 55–60.

Kyriacou, C. 1986, *Effective Teaching in Schools*, Basil Blackwell, Oxford.

Kyriacou, C. 1991, *Essential Teaching Skills*, Basil Blackwell, Oxford.

Lewin, G.W. (ed.) 1948, *Kurt Lewin: Resolving Social Conflicts, Selected Papers on Group Dynamics*, Harper & Row, New York.

Lewin, K. 1935, *A Dynamic Theory of Personality: Selected Papers of Kurt Lewin*, McGraw Hill, New York.

Lewin, K., Lippitt, R. & White, R.K. 1939, 'Patterns of aggressive behaviour in experimentally created "social climates"', *Journal of Social Psychology*, vol. 10, pp. 271–99.

Lewis, C.S. 1978, *The Abolition of Man*, Collins/Fount, Glasgow.

Lewis, R. & Lovegrove, M.N. 1985, 'Students' preferences for discipline practices in schools', *Teaching and Teacher Education*, vol. 1, pp. 325–33.

Lovegrove, M.N. & Lewis, R. 1985, 'Students' views of discipline in the classroom', *Educational Magazine*, vol. 42, no. 1, pp. 29–31.

Maccoby, E.E. & Jacklin, C.N. 1974, *The Psychology of Sex Differences*, Stanford University Press, California.

Maccoby, E.E. & Jacklin, C.N. 1980, 'Sex differences in aggression: A rejoinder and reprise', *Child Development*, vol. 51, pp. 964–80.

McCarthy, P., Freeman, L., Rothwell, C. & Arnheim, B. 1983, 'Is there life after 8D?: Group reinforcement at the post primary level', *Interview*, no. 11, Ministry of Education, Victoria.

McGrath, H. & Francey, S. 1993, *Friendly Kids, Friendly Classrooms*, Longman, Melbourne.

Merrett, F. & Tang, W.M., 1994, 'The attitudes of British primary school pupils to praise, rewards, punishments and reprimands', *British Journal of Educational Psychology*, vol. 64, pp. 91–103.

Milgram, S. & Shotland, R.L. 1973, *Television and Antisocial Behavior: Field Experiments*, Academic Press, New York.

Miller, S.E., Leinhardt, G. & Zigmond, N. 1991, *Accommodating At Risk Students*, ACER, Set 1, Item 8.

Morgan, D.P. & Jenson, W.R. 1988, *Teaching Behaviourally Disordered Students: Preferred Practices*, Merrill Publishing Co., Toronto.

Neill, A.S. 1960, *Summerhill*, Hart, New York.

Papalia, D.S. & Wendkos Olds, S. (eds) 1982, *A Child's World: Infancy Through Adolescence*, 3rd edn, McGraw-Hill, New York.

Pearce, H. 1995, Groupwork in Classrooms, Cambridge (unpublished).

Piaget, J. 1932, *The Moral Judgement of the Child*, Routledge & Kegan Paul, London.

Poteet, J.A. 1973, *Behaviour Modification: A Practical Guide for Teachers*, University of London Press, London.

Powell, J. 1976, *Fully Human, Fully Alive*, Argus Communications, Illinois.

Reading, H.F. 1977, *A Dictionary of the Social Sciences*, Routledge & Kegan Paul, London.

Rex, J. 1981, *Social Conflict: A Conceptual and Theoretical Analysis*, Longman, London.

Roberts, R. 1988, 'School yard menace: school bullying', *Psychology Today*, February, pp. 53–6.

Robertson, J. 1996, *Effective Classroom Control: Understanding Teacher–Pupil Relationships*, 3rd edn, Hodder & Stoughton, London.

Rogers, B. 1985, Conflict resolution among pre-adolescents, MEd thesis, University of Melbourne.

Rogers B. 1989, *Making a Discipline Plan*, Nelson, Melbourne.

Rogers, B. 1992, *Supporting Teachers in the Workplace*, Jacaranda, Milton, Queensland.

Rogers, B. 1994, *Behaviour Recovery: A Whole-school Program for Mainstream Schools*, ACER, Camberwell, Victoria.

Rogers, B. 1995, *Behaviour Management: A Whole-school Approach*, Scholastic Books, Gosford, NSW.

Rogers, B. 1997, *Cracking the Hard Class: Strategies for Managing the Harder Than Average Class*, Scholastic, Books, Gosford, NSW.

Rosenthal, R. & Fode, K. 1963, 'The effect of experimental bias on the performance of the albino rat', *Behavioural Science*, vol. 8, pp. 183–9.

Rutter, M. 1981, *Maternal Deprivation Reassessed*, Penguin, Middlesex, U.K.

Rutter, M. *et al.* 1979, *Fifteen Thousand Hours: Secondary Schools and Their Effects on Children*, Open Books, London.

Safran, S.P., Safran, J.S., & Barcikowski, R.S. 1985, 'Differences in teacher tolerance: An illusory phenomenon?', *Behaviour Disorders*, pp. 211–15.

Scott Peck, M. 1978, *The Road Less Travelled*, Arrow Books, London.

Serfontein, G. 1990, *The Hidden Handicap: How to Handle Children Who Suffer from Dyslexia, Hyperactivity and Learning Difficulties*, Simon and Schuster, Sydney.

Slee, R. (ed.) 1988, *Discipline and Schools: A Curriculum Perspective*, Macmillan, Melbourne.

Smith, M.J. 1981, *When I Say No, I Feel Guilty*, Bantam Books, Toronto.

Stanford, G. 1980, *Developing Effective Classroom Groups*, Hart Publishing Co., New York.

Tauber, R.T. 1990, *Classroom Management Theory and Practice*, 2nd edn, Harcourt Brace, Orlando, Florida.

Tavris, C. 1982, 'Anger Defused', *Psychology Today*, Nov.

Topping, K. 1987, *Educational Systems for Disruptive Adolescents*, Croom Helm, London.

Vernon, M.D. 1969, *Human Motivation*, Cambridge University Press, London.

Wheldhall, K. (ed.) 1992, *Discipline in Schools: Psychological Perspectives on the Elton Report*, Routledge, London.

Wilkes, R. 1981, 'Fly me to the moon: A classroom behaviour management program to enhance learning', *Interview*, no. 3, Ministry of Education, Victoria.

Williams, J., Bennet, S. & Best, D. 1982, 'Awareness and expression of sex stereotypes in young children', in Papalia, D.S. & Wendkos Olds, S. (eds), *A Child's World: Infancy through Adolescence*, 3rd edn, McGraw-Hill, New York.

Wolfgang, C. & Glickman, C. 1986, *Solving Classroom Discipline Problems*, 2nd edn, Allyn & Bacon, Boston.

Wragg, J. 1989, *Talk Sense to Yourself: A Program for Children and Adolescents*, ACER, Hawthorn, Victoria.

Resources

Rogers, B. 1989, *Decisive Discipline: Every Move You Make, Every Step You Take*, The SART Conference and Training Centre, Geelong, Victoria, (071) 522 825 (a video learning package: two videos and a workbook).

Rogers, B. 1995, *Managing Behaviour Series*, available from Quartus Productions, P.O. Box 2069, Bundaberg, Queensland, 4670 (a video series—four videos on prevention, positive correction, consequences, repairing and rebuilding).

Index